MISSION INTERRUPTED

QUEEN WILHELMINA

MISSION INTERRUPTED

THE DUTCH IN THE EAST INDIES AND THEIR WORK
IN THE XXTH CENTURY

A SYMPOSIUM EDITED BY

Dr W. H. VAN HELSDINGEN

FORMER CHAIRMAN OF THE EAST-INDIAN PEOPLE'S COUNCIL

AND

Dr H. HOOGENBERK

EAST-INDIAN CIVIL SERVICE

ELSEVIER 1945

AMSTERDAM - BRUSSELS - LONDON - NEW YORK

ABRIDGED ENGLISH VERSION BY

Dr J. J. L. DUYVENDAK

PROFESSOR AT LEYDEN UNIVERSITY

*"Behold and consider what a good courage may accomplish!...
Great things can be done in the Indies".*

Jan Pietersz. Coen

CONTENTS

PREFACE

Mercantile considerations prompted the Dutch, three and a half centuries ago, to follow in the wake of the Portuguese and seek the sea route to the Indies.

Mercantile considerations again decided the form of the risky enterprise: local trading companies at first, soon to be replaced by the one United East Indian Company, enjoying a monopolistic charter granted by the States General of the United Provinces, in the same way as had been done by the Portuguese and British for their companies.

Mercantile considerations once more decided the attitude of the East Indian Company toward the indigenous population of the archipelago: it seemed sufficient to establish safe trading factories, and for the rest the less contact with the population the better. But sure enough, the nation that showed itself sufficiently powerful with armed force to oust other white competitors, repeatedly was sued for help in the mutual quarrels of the native Princes, and so gradually it established its authority, at first chiefly on Java, later also on the Outer Islands.

The charter granted to the East Indian Company secured for it the monopoly of trade. That monopoly made it strong, but it also was the cause of its decline and fall. By the end of the 18th century the State had no choice but to take over the entire concern with all its goods and chattels. From that time on interference with the internal affairs of the Indian peoples went ever further, though the principle of leaving the native population as much as possible under its own chiefs was always respected. The mutual relationship was dominated by the conception that colonies existed for the benefit of the home-country. There was one purse and whatever was saved out there was spent at home. Small wonder then that the temptation was strong to save as much as possible out there. For centuries this point of view was quite frankly admitted everywhere in the world. Only very slowly did another conception arise. The western powers began to seek a moral justification for the possession of colonies. They averred that it consisted in holding themselves responsible for the development of the peoples living under their rule.

With this changed view the relationship between the Indies and the Netherlands also has been completely altered. At the turn of the century this moral vocation toward the population as a new guiding principle in colonial policy was recognised officially in a Speech from the Throne by Her Majesty the Queen. At first the accomplishment of that task was sought in action for the benefit of the population, but gradually it was realised that this method could not yield good results. Then came the slogans: "Cooperation with the population", "Education for self-activity", "Opening up for the world market of all treasures that modern technique can wrest from the Indian soil with the cooperation of all the forces of all the population groups."

Meanwhile the unparallelled worldwide depression made international tendencies felt, while on the other hand common interests linked the different social groups in the Indies closer together.

What point in this development had been reached when the fury of war was unleashed on this land of peace and quiet is told in this book. It is not written in the spirit of self-glorification. On the contrary, no attempt is made to gloss over the fact that errors have been committed and our policy often was no more than a groping in the dark. But, in fulfillment of the prophetic words written by the Governor-General Jan Pietersz. Coen in 1628: "Great things can be done in the Indies", the authors of this book believe that "great things", indeed, have been done. They admit at the same time that in many respects Coen's words still retain their value as a stimulant and that in some cases a beginning toward their realisation has scarcely been made.

As indicated by the subtitle the full accent lies on the Dutch East Indies in the 20th century, that is to say on the work of the present generation. In view of the limited scope no attempt was made to be complete. A choice had to be made from a multitude of subjects and each of these could only be treated cursorily so as to give some understanding of the problems current in the richly varied life of the Dutch East Indies. A further abridgment was necessary in this English edition, some chapters being omitted altogether.

The story which this book tells closes on May 10th 1940, the fatal date on which the enemy, without even a declaration of war, attacked Holland with overwhelming force. At that moment contact with the Indies was interrupted. Nevertheless the book expresses the confidence that in future more "great things" will be done in the Indies and that they will be done by the Dutch. May the Mission Interrupted become a Mission Fulfilled!

W. H. van Helsdingen

NOTE BY THE ENGLISH EDITOR

In preparing this English version of a book about the Dutch East Indies originally written for the Dutch public, a severe abridgment was necessary. Of the 38 original authors, each of whom was fully competent in his own field, the contributions of only 26 could be selected for translation. Moreover, the first chapter was specially written for this edition by a new contributor and the 14th was entirely recast by one of the two original authors.

Though faithfully rendering the meaning, this translation nowhere slavishly followed the text, but freely condensed or revised wherever it seemed desirable. Since conditions did not permit to secure the authors' approval for these alterations, I alone am responsible for the English text of their contributions. I should add that all through the work of translation, — undertaken under the strange circumstances of wartime when my normal scholastic activities were suspended, — I was greatly assisted by my wife, without whose aid, indeed, it could never have been accomplished. Any barbarisms that remain are my own.

J. J. L. DUYVENDAK

LIST OF CONTRIBUTORS

The names of the contributors to this edition, in the order in which their articles appear, are the following:

Dr W. Ph. Coolhaas

Dr F. W. Stapel

Professor F. C. Gerretson

J. A. M. Bruineman

Professor H. Th. Fischer

Professor J. Gonda

Dr Th. P. Galestin

Professor W. J. A. Kernkamp

Professor H. Kraemer

Dr L. van Ryckevorsel S.J.

Dr J. C. Westermann

S. A. Reitsma

Hans Martin

A. van Dooren

Professor H. C. P. de Vos

Professor G. A. P. Weyer

P. Hövig

Professor A. te Wechel

Professor J. H. Boeke

Dr G. J. Vink

Miss Cecile Rothe

Professor C. D. de Langen

Professor J. H. Bavinck

Dr W. H. van Helsdingen

J. de Waard

Professor J. Tinbergen and

Dr J. B. D. Derksen

(the last two in collaboration)

The following authors also contributed to the Dutch edition:

J. C. Mollema

Leonhard Huizinga

Professor L. van Vuuren

Professor V. E. Korn

D. de Jongh

Professor F. D. K. Bosch

Professor G. Brom

Dr Th. A. Fruin

J. Tideman

Professor H. A. Idema

E. Gobee

R. K. A. Bertsch

CHAPTER 1

Land and people

"... The magnificent empire of Insulinde encircling the equator like a girdle of emeralds", thus runs the immortal phrase of a Dutch poet, as true as it is beautiful. What a girdle indeed! If one could lift it and fit it in the same shape across the face of Europe, the most western tip pinned down on the westcoast of Ireland, the eastern border of Dutch New-Guinea would be located east of the Crimea, the most northern point somewhere in the Baltic between Germany and Sweden, the most southern point in Albania. In other words: the East Indian Archipelago covers one sixth part of the circumference of the globe and the Netherlands form the largest equatorial power in the world!

To be sure, the major part of this section of the globe consists of water, but nevertheless the islands, composing the "girdle", cover considerable areas. There are five major ones: Sumatra, as large as Germany (in 1937), Java, somewhat smaller than England, somewhat larger than Greece and a good deal larger than Cuba, Borneo, the Dutch part of which nearly equals France, Celebes, about one and a half times the size of Java, and New-Guinea, the Dutch western half of which is just as big as the Republic of Paraguay, much larger therefore than Poland or Finland, Norway or Italy. Then come a dozen islands varying in size between one seventh to one half of the area of the Netherlands. Among them are important ones such as the tin-islands Banka and Billiton and beautiful Bali, "the last paradise on earth". Lesser islands may be counted by the score, small ones by the hundred and the number of minute islands, reefs and rocks runs into tens or hundreds of thousands.

The lay-out of this region is most curious. If the islands form a bridge between Asia and Australia, the seas and straits open up numerous passages

Mission 1

49985

between the Pacific and the Indian Ocean. The elongated southern peninsula of Further India enters like a wedge into the archipelago with which in
former geological periods it no doubt was joined. The depth of the seas
between this peninsula, Cochin-China, Sumatra, Java and Borneo, that is
to say the South-China Sea, the Java Sea and the Straits of Malacca in only
a few places is a little more than 100 meters. This gigantic "Sunda plateau"
is as it were a partial subterranean continuation of Asia. New-Guinea and
the Aru Islands with Australia are situated on a similar plateau; the seas
of this "Sahul plateau", the Arafura Sea and the Gulf of Carpentaria also
reach a depth of more than 100 m. at a few places only. The situation is
quite different in the relatively narrow region between these two plateaux.
There, around grotestesquely shaped islands one finds very deep water: the
Straits of Makassar between Borneo and Celebes reaches a depth of 3000 m.,
the Sea of Celebes to the north of that island reaches 5500 m., the Sea of
Flores in the south 5140 m. The small Sea of Sawu in the Archipelago of
Timor has depths above 3000 m., the Sea of the Moluccas between Celebes
and Halmahera of 4800 m., the small Sea of Seran (Ceram), south of that
island, reaches 5750 m., and the Sea of Banda reaches the greatest depth
in the Archipelago, viz. 7440 m. South-west of Sumatra and south of Java
the borders of the Sunda plateau are also soon reached. The islands parallel
to Sumatra are separated from the main island by depths of 600 to 2000 m.

In many respects the archipelago is the transition zone between Asia and
Australia, the influence of the former continent reaching in general further
than that of the latter, as is shown especially by the fauna and flora. To
mention only the former, on the large islands in the west, though no longer
everywhere, one finds numerous mammals also known on the neighbouring
continent: tigers, elephants, rhinocerosses, many species of monkeys, deer,
wild cattle, wild goats. New-Guinea and the other islands in the east on the
other hand have far fewer and quite different mammals, lacking entirely
in the west, but characteristic for Australia, such as opossums and duckbills.
Common to both groups are only pigs, and some species of rodents and bats.
The interjacent islands form a typical transition zone: tigers, elephants and
rhinocerosses are lacking, more and more western mammals disappear as
one goes further east, while forms of the Australian fauna begin to occur.
On these islands one finds in the centre a remarkable number of mammals

not found elsewhere, as on Celebes such curious animals as the hogdeer (Babirussa Alfurus) and the dwarf buffalo (Anoa depressicornis). For other animals than mammals similar phenomena occur.

A glance at a map of South-eastern Asia and Australia shows at once the importance of the Archipelago with relation to traffic. Very old centres of civilisation such as India proper and China being separated on land by extremely difficult belts of mountains or deserts, traffic naturally chose the waterway leading through the Straits of Malacca round the southern tip of the Malay Peninsula, that is to say by or through the Archipelago. Centuries or milleniums before the beginning of this extremely important movement of navigation and commerce with all that it entailed for the cultural and social development, migrations took place in a direction vertical to this traffic. In one wave after another the ancestors of the present Indonesian population poured into the Archipelago. Not everywhere did they expel entirely the older inhabitants. On the large islands between the sleek-headed, lightbrown Indonesians are found remnants of other races, among which, as one goes east, more and more fuzzy-haired people appear who, on New-Guinea, as Papuans form the main stock of the population. With the exception of these numerically unimportant groups the entire population is descended from people whose land of origin lay near the point where China, Thibet, Nearer and Further India meet. From there they descended the large rivers of Further India in order to reach the islands of the Archipelago by sea. In anthropological respect therefore this also forms a transition zone, though the Asiatic element conquered here the Australian one to an even greater extent than in other fields: here the former was the giver, the latter the recipient.

The most important waves of newcomers were that of the people of the Stonecutters, Proto-Malays or Proto-Indonesians that must have arrived between 1500—1000 B.C. and that of the Coastal Malays, coming later. To the first belong chiefly the tribes now living in the mountains; the latter are settled at present in the lowlands near the coast. Many of them still are excellent sailors; the descendants of the Proto-Malays however generally hate the sea and everything connected with it. This may be a result of the treatment they received on the part of the Coastal Malays.

If we turn our thoughts to later periods, centuries after the beginning of traffic through the Straits of Malacca between China and India proper, we find navigation carrying the valuable products of the Archipelago, chiefly spice, to the West and bringing fertilising cultural influences in return.

The first mention of the Archipelago in European writings is probably in the Periplous tès Erythras Thalassès, a Greek treatise of the first century A.D. In any case it is certain that the famous geographer Ptolemy in the second half of the second century A.D. mentions products of Sumatra with the region of origin. Navigation also carried to these islands Hinduism and Buddhism and later Islam.

All these religions were introduced by inhabitants of India, coming as traders but, because of their higher level of civilisation, also gaining great influence as priests and even establishing dynasties. Hindu states were founded especially on Java and Sumatra and even today in the Javanese aristocracy their descent from Aryan ancestors is noticeable. Islam was introduced from the fourteenth century on by people from North-west India, the Gujerats, also arriving in the Archipelago as traders. The Arabs proper came much later. Though no Gujerat dynasties have been founded some Arab ones have. The further expansion of Islam however was due to the Indonesians themselves. The fact that the acceptance of a world religion made him who professed it, instead of a "despised heathen" the equal of millions of co-religionists, was a powerful factor in the spread of Islam that gradually replaced Hinduism nearly everywhere and pushed heathenism back to remote corners. Against all these gifts from Asia, Australia had nothing to offer. It was the Light from the West that dominated.

At the beginning of the 16th century the Europeans appeared, whose arrival meant a revolution for the Southern-Asiatic world. First it was the Portuguese who began to sail the old route through the Straits of Malacca, then people from North-western Europe, chiefly the Dutch, who transferred the traffic to the Sunda Straits between Java and Sumatra. They kept to this even after Sir Stamford Raffles had founded the great emporium of Singapore, until the opening of the Suez Canal gave the victory to the Straits of Malacca. In the 19th century ships in ever greater numbers pressed through those straits on their way to Eastern Asia. But in that same century traffic with other regions also developed; not only the communications between the islands became more frequent, but those with Australia began, where in the last century and a half a white population had settled. If one sails from Australia to Eastern Asia there is the necessity, if one goes to Southern Asia at least, the possibility of passing through the Archipelago. On the north-eastern side, towards the Pacific, it is very open. The islands lying there are however too unimportant to attract much navigation. There was a certain amount of traffic with the westcoast of America that will doubtless increase considerably in the future. Finally the twenties of this century developed air-traffic in which the Archipelago soon became an important junction, especially for the lines from the west and the north to Australia.

Girdle of emeralds, the poet said. Emerald green is indeed the dominating colour of all the islands, for the Archipelago has an equatorial climate, knowing neither the aridity nor the scorching heat nor the cold nights of deserts. The climate is very even; the maximum temperature of 35° registered at Batavia is only one degree higher than the highest temperature registered in Holland. This is low as compared to temperatures of 52° occurring in the Sahara, the Persian desert or in Australia. The minimum temperature at Batavia was 18°. The average annual temperature there is very constant, being 26,2° and neither the average of the warmest nor that of the coolest month varies more than one degree from this temperature. The difference of temperature between day and night is also slight. Yet this temperature, though actually not very high, is hard to bear because of the high degree of humidity, not less than 83 % at Batavia. It is a real hothouse atmosphere. For this reason and also on account of the regularity of the climate the skin is extremely sensitive to small differences of temperature. Especially in the rainy season, just before the showers pour down in the afternoon, on days when there is no refreshing sea-breeze, one has the impression of an intense heat. In the absence of the rain, the hothouse atmosphere at night is very disagreeable. No wonder therefore that Europeans in a position to do so like to spend their weekends in the hills in order to "get a cold nose". For there it is not only much cooler but the variations between day and night temperatures are also much greater. This outweighs the disadvantage that the degree of humidity is even greater than in the plains.

As regular as the temperature are the winds. There are two winds which, more than the difference in temperature, divide the year into seasons, viz. the west and east monsoon, both not strong but very constant winds. The average velocity is very small; at Batavia for instance it is less than one meter per second, while in Western Europe it is 5,5 m. The nights are nearly always perfectly calm. The quietness of the tropical night, only disturbed by the whirr of innumerable insects, always deeply impresses the European. Tropical night storms are rare, occurring almost without exception only locally in the hills. The difference between the two monsoon winds is, that the west monsoon, blowing from the Asiatic mountains across wide seas, brings rain, in contrast with the east monsoon originating in arid Australia. The former therefore, prevailing from the end of November to May, causes the rainy season, the latter the dry season. The turn of the monsoons between these two periods is characterised by very oppressive heat and violent thunderstorms which indeed are not rare throughout the year. There are considerable local variations in the rainfall. In the hills it increases rapidly: Buitenzorg, at an altitude of 250 m. and only 60 km. from Batavia, shows an annual average of 4614 mm. against Batavia 1999 mm. The rainfall decreases the further one goes south-east. Though in the west it is possible to distinguish between a wet and dry season, this does not mean that in the latter there is no rainfall at all. This is different in East-Java and the Lesser Sunda Islands. The nearer one approaches Australia, the more one feels the influence of the dry east monsoon. In the furthest south-east for months there may be no rainfall at all. At Kupang on Timor for example in the dry season from May to November there was only 50 mm. downfall, against 772 mm. at Batavia and 1934 at Buitenzorg.

In a tropical downpour the volume of water is enormous; at Buitenzorg 2,5 cm. per minute were measured. Such a shower however never lasts long; even in the rainy season there are many hours of sunshine.

The region dominated by Asiatic climatic influences is also much greater than that where Australian influences prevail. In this respect the Spice-islands and New-Guinea agree with the west; it is only the south-east that suffers from the heat and dryness of Australia.

In far and away the largest part of the Archipelago the rainfall is so abundant that in the landscape unchanged by the hand of man endless tropical forests are predominant. Traversing the plains of East Sumatra, Borneo or New-Guinea in an aeroplane, for hours on end one passes over limitless green masses, from the air looking for all the world not so much like emeralds but, less poetically, like kale. The monotony of this landscape is only broken by the rivers. Naturally they are not very long, but owing to the abundant tropical rainfall they carry large quantities of water in spite of the rapid evaporation. They are therefore very wide and clearly discernible from the air, also because their banks with their fields and villages clearly betray the traces of human labour.

On approaching an untouched territory like East-Sumatra from the sea, one first beholds the very remarkable zone of coastal forests, the home of mangroves and rhizophores, whose strange appearance is caused by the air-roots clinging to the muddy soil. Such a region of swampy mud is not passable; the most one can do is to penetrate into the numerous creeks on flatbottomed barges. On shore one enters into the tropical virginal forest, dank and dark, not, as tenderfoots may think, full of palmtrees, but filled with a very great variety of evergreen foliage trees. The forest is far less homogeneous than the European forest. It is dominated by gigantic trees such as the various species of ficus, of which on Java alone 60 to 70 species are known, reaching a height of 60 m., under which a multitude of smaller trees are found, in their turn rising above almost impenetrable undergrowth, the whole being covered and entwined by various kinds of ratan, parasites etc. A sojourn in this dark domain where the sunlight practically never enters is far from agreeable. A protracted stay brings on a melancholy mood. Rarely is the eye struck by flowers, but if at all, it may be by a gigantic tree whose crown has become one flaming red bouquet or by gorgeous orchids. Of the animal world, apart from innumerable insects, one is chiefly aware of the bloodsucker whose presence is detestable indeed. From time to time one hears the cry of monkeys among whom there are orang-utans and gibbons, or the croaking of the hornbill or other birds. The enchanting warble of our singing birds is entirely absent. Numerous tracks only betray the presence of far more mammals than one suspects at first.

In the forest mountains tree ferns and numerous epiphytes, especially foliaceous mosses and lichens are characteristic. Here and there, chiefly in the south-east of the Archipelago, in the mountains there are fairly homogeneous forests of casuary trees resembling fir trees; the soil underneath these trees is not covered by undergrowth. On Java there are teak forests carefully kept in good shape because of the valuable timber; in the dry

season they lose their foliage. A Westerner's attention is also particularly
arrested by fairly homogeneous forests of bamboos, a gigantic grass species.

Only in the extreme south-east of the Archipelago it is no longer forests
that are predominant in the natural landscape, but savannahs with graceful
acacia trees or even small grass steppes. Yet even here it is not dry enough
to prevent green being the dominant colour during the larger part of the
year. In the middle of the Australian winter the south-east wind passing
over the mountains of the Lesser Sunda Islands is so dry that in certain
regions on the northern slopes the cactus seems to be the principal vegetation. But no sooner do the rains come with the west monsoon than the green
carpet of vegetation recovers and the wealth of flowers is more striking here
than elsewhere. It is then seen that the island of Flores is rightly so named.

An examination of the structure of the islands shows everywhere a skele-
ton of mountain chains, on Java largely dating from the Tertiary Period.
Elsewhere there is also much old slate and limestone. As is the case everywhere else in the world the limestone formations are very freakish and fantastic, now projecting in sharp corners, now rounded off in soft curves with
caves and rivers disappearing underground, and sometimes with globe-
shaped hills to which a mountainous region in southern central Java owes
the name of Gunung Sèwu "The Thousand Mountains". Most limestone
mountains are raised coral reefs. Living coral-reefs near the coasts also occur
in several places especially as shoal-reefs and beach-reefs. In the bays of the
Spice-islands the latter form particularly fine "sea-gardens", marvellous in
their wealth of colours and fauna.

A strong contrast to these "Neptunic" forms is presented by the volcanic
rock. Volcanoes are very numerous. They occur in many forms, from pure
cones to completely shattered mountain-wrecks. Some craters have a diameter of only a few dozen meters; others, as for example that of the Tengger
in East Java with a diameter of 17 km, are large enough to contain entire
plantations. Their degree of activity also varies greatly; some of them have
not been known to be active in historical times, others have violent eruptions
at long intervals, others again are always active, their top being crowned
by a corona of smoke; some, finally, are in the solfatar or fumarol stage. In
general the volcanoes are situated in long rows, beginning in western Further
India and running via the Andaman and Nicobar Islands through the longitu-

dinal axis of Sumatra, Java and the Northern Lesser Sunda Islands. Shorter
semi-circles of volcanoes border the sea-basins of the Spice Islands. The
lowlands of Sumatra, the whole of Borneo, Celebes with the exception of
its northern point and practically all Dutch New-Guinea are outside the
volcanic zone. The mountains are surrounded by alluvial plains, particularly wide where the coast is washed by shallow seas, as in southern New-
Guinea, South Borneo and East Sumatra.

Earthquakes are far from rare; their centres are in the volcanic zones,
but those of very heavy earthquakes are generally in the seas south-west of
Sumatra, south of Java and between Celebes and New-Guinea. There very
great deviations of gravitation have been registered.

For a long time it was held that the Smeru on Java with its altitude of 3676 m
was the highest mountain of the Archipelago. On Sumatra, Java, Bali, Lombok, Celebes and Seran isolated peaks reached more than 3000 m but entire
plateaux above that altitude had not been found. None of the other islands
reached such an altitude. Not until our century has it been discovered that the
Dutch skipper who, two centuries ago skirting the south coast of New-Guinea,
descried there snow mountains, had observed well. A large part of the
mountains of New-Guinea turned out to be above 3000 m, and there are in that
region peaks of much greater altitude, several of which are snowcapped. The
highest peaks of the Nassau mountains, the Carstensz peaks, are 5000 m high.

In many respects Java occupies a very special place among the islands of
the Dutch East Indies. This is already manifest in the distinction made by
the official administration and by usage between Java and the Outer Islands.
The difference is evinced most eloquently by the population figures. On
Java occupying less than one fourteenth of the total area of the Dutch East
Indies there live two thirds of all inhabitants of the Archipelago. In 1940
the total population was estimated at around 70 million, of whom 48 million
lived on Java. The figures of the careful census held in 1930 give many details.
At that time Java comprised nearly 42 million inhabitants; the density of the
population was about 350 per km², that is to say, it was greater than that of
Bengal, the Netherlands, Great Britain and the most densely populated provinces of China. In the Outer Islands on the other hand there were only 19
million people and the density of the population was not more than 11 per km².

Naturally this influenced very greatly the entire condition of the island.

Primeval forests have become rare; they only occur here and there in remote districts chiefly in the mountains of the extreme south-west. Flying above Java one is struck by the succession of cultivated plots among which numerous villages are scattered, easily recognisable by the dark green of the fruit trees and cocotrees hiding the wooden or bamboo houses from view. An extensive network of motor roads and railways also strikes the eye. Though the other islands possess excellent motor roads they are not so numerous and as yet only Sumatra has railways. A trip by air made in the beginning of the rainy season, when the irrigated ricefields are under cultivation, presents a beautiful view of the island. In the west, south of the rather narrow flat coastal belt there is a coherent system of mountains, the Prijangan; further east the volcanoes rise up from the plain one by one or in small clusters, bordered on either side by narrow chains of low limestone hills.

The cultivation of rice on Java is so intensive that the densely populated island does not only provide for its own need of this staple food, but even exports it. More than 34.000 km², that is to say nearly one fourth of the island, is planted with it. Partly on the sawahs after the harvest, partly on non-irrigated fields, forming in the aggregate an even larger area also occasionally producing rice, other alimentary crops are planted. In the first place, chiefly in the dryer east, maize, then tuberous plants, such as cassave (inanihot utilissima) and batatas (Ipomoea batatas); also peanuts (arachis) and soya beans (Glycine soja). Furthermore there are the products of the western plantations. In so far as the soil is tilled by the natives it cannot be alienated. Sale of native soil to non-natives is forbidden. The latter, for their cultivation of superannual crops, may obtain untilled land in long lease for 75 years; for other crops such as sugar and tobacco they may hire land from the population for short periods and under strict supervision of the government authorities. The total area of the land cultivated by western enterprize is less than one third of that of the sawahs. Until 1930 sugar was by far the most important export product of Java; it received a grave setback by the economic depression then beginning. In 1938 the export value still was 45 million florins but other agricultural products such as tea, tobacco, coffee and fibres were then nearly equally important. Quinine and kapok, yielding respectively 90 and 64 % of the world-production are also important export products, kapok being produced by native enterprise.

Three nations live on Java, each speaking their own language and differing in several characteristics. By far the most numerous are the true Javanese, numbering nearly 27 million souls. Starting in the west their habitat begins where Java narrows down for the first time and continues to where this happens again. The Javanese is a very docile and formalistic person, a farmer attached to his traditions and closely connected with his village. Especially in those parts of the island where oriental despotism was long dominant, he has become somewhat servile and sombre, witness the dark colours of his clothing. Yet it does not prevent him enjoying immensely the music of his gamelan orchestra, dancing and the national shadow-play, the wajang. It is chiefly the centres of the true Javanese region that are extremely densely populated. The heart of Java is formed by the so-called Principalities, where the Javanese princes, the Susuhunan or "Emperor" of Surakarta and the Sultan of Jocjakarta have been maintained in authority under supervision of the Dutch Government. The rural towns with about 150.000 inhabitants in which they reside are very remarkable in cultural respect. Much of the old Javanese culture, as it was formed in the Middle Ages under Hindu influence, has persisted in the very extensive kratons or palacecomplexes of the princes and grandees. The levelling process, brought about in the 19th century by the opening up of Java to the world, did not do much harm here.

Here one finds also the most important remains of old Hindu architecture, such as the magnificent Shivaitic funeral temple of Prambanan and the Buddhistic sanctuary of Kalasan. The best known of all these architectural monuments, the world-famous Borobudur, also Buddhistic in character, lies a little more to the west.

This region with the surrounding government's territory has a density of population of not less than 679,3; the plain south of Surabaya as well as that along the north coast of the narrow part of central Java are also very densely populated. Surabaya, a town of 350.000 inhabitants, is the largest port for export on Java and also the converging centre of all shipping from the east of the Archipelago and Australia. At the eastern extremity of the northern plain lies the second town of Java proper, Semarang, also a port for export, with 220.000 inhabitants. The relatively small number of inhabitants of the four largest towns of such a densely populated country proves that Javanese society, like that of the rest of the Dutch East Indies, has a strongly agrarian character. Any Javanese or Indonesian one may meet has a three to one chance of being a small farmer. On Java he is generally a man who with unremitting zeal tills his irrigated field to raise a rice-crop for his own family; on the Outer Islands the native generally works for the world-market in more extensive agricultural enterprises.

The Western neighbours of the Javanese are the Sundanese, a much gayer people, fond of frolic and colourful clothing and far less formalistic. They are about 8½ million strong. In their mountains, the Prijangan, they are often teaplanters. Their chief city is the beautiful and gay city of Bandung (± 165.000 souls), an important garrison town and one of the few places where retired Europeans settle down. Some Government departments have been established at Bandung; there is also the Technical College (ranking as a University). From a cultural point of view the Sundanese are less interesting than the Javanese. On the north coast of their territory lies Batavia, the largest city of all the Dutch East Indies (533.000 souls). Batavia, founded by the Dutch in 1619, always remained the seat of the Government. Nowhere does one find so many Europeans (37.000, that is more than one sixth of the total number), nor so many Chinese (80.000) and other foreign orientals like Arabs and Indians. Batavia is not merely the governmental centre, but it also is an important port of export; there also the head-offices of most commercial, agricultural and industrial companies are established; it is the most important meeting-point for shipping and is also the centre of western science represented by the faculties of medicine, of law and of letters and philosophy. The town does not have a specially Sundanese character; its native population is a mixture from all parts of the Archipelago; it speaks Malay, here as elsewhere, the lingua franca in the intercourse between the various races. The highest representative of the Dutch sovereignty, the Governor-General, does not reside in the city but in nearby Buitenzorg. In Buitenzorg there is also an agricultural college.

Javanese are also found in the southern half of the second narrow part of Java, but there they are mixed with Madurese. The home of these Madurese is the island of Madura, forming a unit with Java in administrative and social respect, but they have also largely settled in the northern half of this narrow part of Java. They number 4,3 million; their character lacks both the gayety of the Sundanese and the docility of the Javanese. They are more energetic and more short-tempered than their neighbours. The smaller productivity of their island compels them to emigrate, so they are less sedentary and more used to regular manual labour. From among them sailors for European shipping are recruited.

They are maize-growers and maize-eaters and they also raise cattle; many of them are fishermen too. The largest place in the eastern narrow part of Java, the attractive mountain-town of Malang has more a Javanese than Madurese character; it is like another Bandung on a smaller scale.

East of Java lies the small island of Bali, parts of which are as densely populated as Java. The culture of the Balinese, numbering 1.100.000, shows great resemblance to that of the Javanese. Its remarkable feature is that Islam did not penetrate to their island, so that they remained in the cultural stage where Java was before A.D. 1500. At the princely courts there is a relatively pure Hinduistic culture; among the peasants this is largely interspersed with very old Indonesian elements still entirely predominant in remote mountain villages. Of small importance for the world market in economic respect, Bali is unique as a cultural centre. The entire life is pervaded by the service of the gods. The population worships its gods with song, dance and offerings of fruit and flowers in sanctuaries that are testimonies of the superb development of Balinese sculpture, woodcarving and silverwork. Simple villagers turn out to be great artists as craftsmen or as dancers or musicans and all that from a purely creative urge in honour of the gods. The island moreover is greatly favoured with natural beauty and the Balinese are a beautifully built, graceful people.

The neighbouring island of Lombok is also very densely populated in the central plain. The native Sasaks, numbering 650.000, profess a form of Islam strongly mixed with animistic elements. Until fifty years ago, when the Dutch Government put an end to it, they had to suffer from a scandalous misrule of a small group of Balinese, here displaying less attractive features of their character. In the western part one finds large Balinese villages where extensive pleasure-grounds still convey an idea of the magnificence achieved there by the ruling class at the expense of the Sasaks. Lombok is now a rich rice-producing and rice-exporting country.

These two islands occupy a special position among the Outer Islands. Leaving them let us look at Sumatra with its more than 8 million inhabitants.

East of the longitudinal mountain chain there is a wide, heavily wooded, alluvial plain, washed by very wide rivers along whose banks are scattered settlements of Malays. Around these the forest has been cleared to make room for extensive hevea plantations. Djambi on the Batang Hari and Palembang on the Musi, are centres for the export of this rubber. Palembang, largely built on rafts, with its 110.000 inhabitants is the largest town in the Outer Islands. It is also a centre for the petroleum industry, for which another centre is Pangkalan Brandan, far to the north, in the region generally called Deli, one of the most important districts for European large-scale agriculture. In the sixties of last century the cultivation of tobacco was introduced there, supplying the covering-leaf of good cigars all over the world. The tobacco plantations now alternate with rubber, fibre, palmoil and tea plantations. Deli developed rapidly owing to the enterprize of European planters, turning in a very short time the "rimbu" (primeval forest) into an important productive area with the aid of Chinese and Javanese labour. The native Malay population, being of an indolent character, only profits from this development by the large incomes drawn by the princes from the agricultural concessions. Medan, though not a very large city, has had a development not unlike an Australian town. It had recently become the residence of the governor of Sumatra.

The rest of the island may be of less interest to the world market, in other respects the mountains are more interesting than the plains. They are more populous and the people are of better calibre than the Malays. In the north live the Atchinese, more than 800.000 strong, strict Mohammedans. During the last thirty years of the 19th century they, or rather, certain unruly elements among them who profited from disorder and piracy, kept a war going against Dutch rule. Since that time all this has completely changed; they now live quietly in small states under their numerous chiefs. They are a proud race of great personal courage. Neither they nor the other inhabitants of the Outer Islands possess the formalism so characteristic of the Javanese.

Follow the Bataks (1.2 million) the only one of the Sumatran peoples not entirely islamised. Formerly they had to suffer a great deal from their Mohammedan neighbours who compelled the Southern Bataks to accept Islam. In the north Christianity, already strong, is gaining, but there, on the banks of the wide and beautiful Toba Lake, heathens are still numerous.

Each of the three religious groups is about equally strong. The Bataks have ill husbanded the soil of their mountain country; as a result, large stretches of primeval forest have now become bare hills and valleys covered with grasses. The Bataks do not impress strangers favourably because of a certain gruffness, excusable perhaps in a people that has had nothing but evil experiences with its neighbours. On closer acquaintance one certainly comes to appreciate this people, distinguished by its intelligence and energy, as shown by the fact that the Bataks, like their southern neighbours, succeeded in keeping in their own hands the retail trade nearly everywhere controlled by the Chinese. In ever growing measure the Bataks in the western part of the Archipelago get hold of the numerous minor posts in Government service, such as clerks, schoolteachers etc. Their society has a patrilineal organisation, in sharp contrast to that of their southern neighbours, the Menangkabaus (2 million) where one finds a matriarchate. This means that one belongs to the mother's family and that a man's possessions are not inherited by his childern but by those of his sisters. This is entirely in conflict with the law of Islam professed by the people. Hence a continual struggle between the conservative group of the adat chiefs, the representatives of tradition desirous to maintain old national institutions, and that of the orthodox Mohammedans. Latterly a third group appeared, that of the younger generation, neither very respectful of the law of adat nor that of Islam but, under the influence of the progressing western development, sympathetic to modern ideas. The Menangkabaus have a gayer character than the other Sumatrans; in their youth they like to swarm out so that one finds them all over Sumatra and the Malay Peninsula. Padang is the port of export, chiefly shipping coffee and copra (the dried pulp of the coconut), both native-grown products. Fort de Kock in the beautiful mountains shows much more pronounced Menangkabau features with its colourful long-stretched houses with fine roofs in which numerous related families live together.

Further south still one finds in the mountains the same Palembangese or allied peoples as live in the plains. They also belong to the groups with the best economic sense of the entire Archipelago. Quite in the south are the Lampong districts; their principal export product is pepper of which the Dutch East Indies supply 85 % of the worldexport. The pepper is only cultivated by the population itself. More and more numerous, alongside of the native Lampongese, are the Javanese, emigrating from too densely populated parts of their island and, under the auspices of the Government, settling here with increasing success. It is striking how rapidly they here reach prosperity once they are in possession of larger fields than they had on Java.

Of the islands west of Sumatra may be mentioned Nias whose population has a curious megalithic culture and Mentawei inhabited by a very primitive people. East of Sumatra is the Riau Archipelago, the centre of the Malay world proper, though many Chinese live here too. Economically it is strongly influenced by the great worldport Singapore. Further to the South follow the tin islands Banka and Billiton where Chinese labour extracts this metal under Dutch direction. Its export value amounted in 1939 to 54½ florins? The Chinese constitute one half of the population.

Then follows the gigantic island of Borneo, except for certain cultivated parts still one huge primeval forest. The most inhabited parts are the riverbanks; the rivers Kapuas, the Barito and the Makaham flow from the mountains in the centre west, east and south. In the Dutch part live only two million people. In the centre live the heathen Dayaks, true forest people, some of whom do not even have fixed dwelling places. They find in the forests all kinds of forest products, forming a large part of the export of the island. In the west where Pontianak is the port, apart from Dayaks there are Malays and Chinese, the latter here being farmers which they rarely are elsewhere in the Archipelago. Apart from forest products Pontianak exports copra and rubber. The latter are even more important products in the south where live the Banjarese, strongly influenced by Java and belonging, from an economic point of view, to the better developed peoples. Their principal town is Banjermasin, the residence of the governor of Borneo. The east coast, though not very important for agriculture, is the more so for the treasures of the earth which it yields. Balik Papan and Tarakan are the centres of the important oil industry. The export value of the petroleum products extracted here and elsewhere in the Dutch East Indies, amounted in 1938 to 164 million florins; the next export figure was that of rubber with 135 million florins; the third on the list was tea with 56 million. In 1939 rubber was first with a value of 195 million against 155 million for petroleum products.

Celebes, like all the other islands east and south, is in economic respect chiefly important for copra and forest products, especially resins. The

Kraton servants with bare upper bod

grotesquely shaped island has exactly twice as many inhabitants as Borneo (4,2 million). Most of these live on the southwestern peninsula and on the extreme end of the northern peninsula. In the south there are 1 ½ million Buginese and 650.000 Makassarese, Mohammedans all. They are seafaring peoples whose aristocracy affects baronial airs, though until recently chiefly robber-baronial airs. Not only in South-Celebes but also on the Eastcoast of Borneo and in some other parts of the Archipelago they constitute the governing class. In their country lies Makassar, residence of the governor of the "Great East", that is all the islands east of Java and Borneo. The town is an important shipping centre. In the extreme north, in Minahassa, live 250.000 Christian Menadonese, of all the peoples of Indonesia the one most assimilated to the Dutch. Their chiefs who in daily life also speak Dutch, like to call their country the twelfth province of the Netherlands. Fairly numerous are also the Butonnese, living partly on the south-eastern peninsula and for the major part on the nearby lesser islands. The rest of Celebes, like the islands still to be mentioned, is inhabited by numerous small, mostly primitive, heathen tribes, numbering generally only some tens of thousands, sometimes much less, and very rarely more than a couple of hundred thousand people. The Mohammedan inhabitants of the coast usually call the heathen by contemptuous collective names, meaning highlanders, yokels, such as Torajas on Celebes, Alfurs on the Spice Islands. The Torajas live in the very wild mountains in small groups in constant feud with each other: headhunting and slave-raids were of daily occurrence. The tribes of the Torajas are differentiated according to the words used in their several languages for the negative, e.g. Bareë-Torajas, Taë-Torajas etc. This state of warfare has now been stopped; the Government established law and order and Christianity is strongly expanding among them. This is also the case with the inhabitants of the Sangir and Talaud Islands, the northern neighbours of the Menadonese.

It is out of the question to enumerate here all the names of the most important remaining islands. For centuries the islands east of Celebes were known as the Spice Islands, because in the north the Lesser Moluccas, in the centre Seran and Amboina furnished cloves, and the even smaller Banda group furnished nutmeg and mace to the entire world. Since the second half of the 18th century however, these products also being cultivated

Mission 2

elsewhere, their cultivation on these islands strongly decreased. The once famed Moluccas, — a name sometimes used not very correctly for all the Spice Islands collectively, — that in the past lured Indians, Chinese and Europeans to the Archipelago, now belong to the least important parts of the Dutch East Indies. They are moreover sparsely inhabited. The popular food here is not rice, as on all the islands further west, but sago, the marrow of a palmtree (metroxylon sagu). On many islands this palmtree grows wild in large numbers and the preparation of sago is so easy that the inhabitants are not stimulated to any further labour, with the result that they remain on a very low level of culture. From an ethnographical point of view however they are interesting and a trip through these island groups belongs to the finest anywhere in the world. The Ambonnese, more than half of whom are Christians, and who for the rest are Mohammedans, form the most important group of inhabitants. Their sons, with those of the Menadonese, constitute an important element of the Dutch army in the Indies. For these people who, further east, take the place of the Bataks in the west, the military calling is the highest.

Somewhat more important, because they are more populated, are the Lesser Sunda Islands of which the following were not yet mentioned: Sumbawa, largely islamised and strongly under Makassarese influence, Flores, where Roman Catholicism is rapidly gaining ground, Sumba and Timor. Only the south-western half of the latter island belongs to the Dutch East Indies, the rest being Portuguese These islands are known for their excellent breed of horses. The exquisite woven fabrics of the population are highly valued by Europeans. Along with rice maize forms an important element of the people's diet.

In order to give some idea of these islands, a few notes on Flores may suffice. It is a beautiful, mountainous island with volcanoes up to 2300 m. For the anthropologist and the ethnologist it is a true paradise with its numerous tribes, varying from completely Malay in the west (sleek-headed and lightbrown) to almost pure Papuan in the east (fuzzy-haired and black). The social institutions of these tribes are equally rich in variety. For export the island only produces some coffee, copra and beeswax, but it is quite able to provide the foodstuffs for its population.

The density of the population of New-Guinea is extremely small. In this enormous territory live only 300.000 Papuans. In the plains their degree of civilisation is very low. Sago is here the people's diet. In the mountains are primitive tribes, partly not yet acquainted with the use of metal, with pottery and weaving, in other respects however not without a measure of development, for fortunately the sago palmtree, making all exertion super-fluous, does not occur here. The pigmy tribes there are very remarkable, the more so since the Papuans otherwise are much taller and more strongly built than the Indonesians generally. In economic respect the island is not yet out of the exploration stage; in the last fifteen years this had been pro-ceeding very energetically.

The Chinese have been mentioned several times. They are found practi-cally all over the Archipelago as retail traders and artizans, forming an indispensable part of the Dutch East Indian society. Their number amounted to 1,2 million. Far less numerous are the other foreign Asiatics, together only about 100.000 people. Among them the Arabs are by far the most numerous; because of their religion and kinship with the prophet they have great influence among the Mohammedans, that is the major part of the population. Then follow the Indians. There were scarely more than 3000 Japanese.

More important than all these foreigners are the 225.000 Europeans, among whom the Dutch (210.000) are by far the largest group. They not only direct the economic life, but it is also owing to them that the indispens-able foundations for it, that is to say peace, order and safety, are nowhere lacking. This is very noticeable in the Outer Islands, where until 1900 large territories were left to their own fate. There was then a condition of anarchy making development and progress of any kind impossible. By establishing the Pax Neerlandica everywhere this intolerable situation was ended for-ever. The difference in density of population with Java is, among other reasons, due to the fact that there, more than a century ago, orderly condi-tions were created by the Government. In 1900 everywhere in the Dutch East Indies a purposeful social and economic policy was initiated, attaining great results in many domains, such as roadbuilding, popular education, hygiene etc. In recent years from out of the population an increasing number of young peo-ple were coming to the fore, and were able to shoulder part of this heavy task.

These few pages merely intend to set the stage and present the *dramatis personae* about to appear in due order in the various chapters of this book.

CHAPTER 2

How the Indies Became the Dutch East Indies

The Prelude

Why did the Dutch go to the Indies? They certainly did not dream of founding colonies or permanent plantations, when, toward the end of the 16th and the beginning of the 17th centuries, they ventured out on their hazardous voyages. They merely desired to secure the profits of a direct trade with the fabulous spice-producing lands. In the past the products of the Orient had been obtained second-hand, mainly from the Portuguese, and the Dutch merchants had been content with a fair profit made by carrying the goods from Portugal on all over Europe. But in the last quarter of the 16th century they began to realise that the enormous gains, reaped by the Portuguese in the East-Indian trade, might be theirs, could they succeed in eliminating the Portuguese as go-betweens and buying the goods directly in the land of origin. Moreover, in 1580 Portugal was conquered by the Spanish, our hereditary enemies, with whom we were still carrying on the war of independence, and signs were not wanting that traffic with Lisbon would soon become a risky business for the Dutch. This circumstance was a powerful incentive for some enterprising men to consider seriously the possibilities of an independent traffic with the Indies which, certainly, would not be without risks, but once established, would yield far greater profits.

It happened that, in the nineties of the 16th century, some men returned to Holland, who had served under the Portuguese in the Indies and who, therefore, were familiar with the route. One of these, Jan Huygen van Linschoten, had been many years at Goa, and had collected a wealth of information of the greatest usefulness. He published an excellent Itinerary, giving detailed sailing-directions to mariners and, some years later, a book, describing the countries and people of India and the Far East, their manners and customs, and their products. Another, Dirck Gerritsz Pomp, nicknamed Dirck China, had made two voyages to China with the Portuguese and he published a brief but enthusiastic description of what he had seen. These and other accounts did much to stimulate the popular interest and furnished important data to those who were considering the possiblities of this bold enterprize.

The route of the Portuguese to the Indies went by the Cape of Good Hope. Before they saw a way to follow in their wake the Dutch had made three attempts to discover a route to the Indies along the Northcoast of Europe and Asia. They failed, as fail they must, but especially the third of these frustrated expeditions, which spent an ice-bound winter on the island of Nova-Zembla, left a glorious record of human courage and endurance. Meanwhile some important merchants at Amsterdam, not more than three at first, were preparing an expedition round the Cape. Cornelis de Houtman, a relative of one of this little group, was sent to Lisbon as commercial agent, with orders secretly to collect some information about the Indian trade that was still wanting. When he returned in 1596, the original triumvirate had interested six more citizens of Amsterdam in their scheme and together they had founded a trading company, called the "Compagnie van Verre", which fitted out four ships. On April 2nd 1595 this small fleet weighed anchor in the roadstead of Tessel and started out on its perilous voyage. It had 249 souls on board. Cornelis de Houtman was in charge of all commercial affairs.

It was a much depleted crew that returned nearly two and a half years later on August 14th 1597. One half of the men had reached the Indies, but when they got home, not more than 89 were still alive, and of these 7 promptly died of the rich home food after the meagre ship's fare. Not less than 120 men had died of scurvy, that dread disease; 12 had been killed in a brawl with natives. One of the ships had had to be abandoned and set on fire, because of the lack of hands. Outward bound the cruising speed had been 2.17 miles p.h. in 324 days; homeward bound 3.64 miles p.h. in 169 days.

In spite of the heavy losses in men and material, the long duration of the voyage, and the almost unsurmountable difficulties with which this first expedition had to cope, the results showed a gross profit of 80.000 florins on the invested capital of 290.000 florins. No doubt this was disappointing to some whose imagination had pictured a treble or quadruple profit, and de Houtman came in for severe censure for his conduct of affairs. Nevertheless, his trip had proved that direct commerce with the Indies was not a chimera, and his experience showed that the power of the Portuguese in those far-off regions was far less securely founded than had previously been surmized. As a result, immediately after the return of de Houtman new fleets were equipped in different ports of Holland and Zeeland. An expedition under Jacob van Neck sailed in May 1598 and became a complete success from a business point of view, making no less than 400 % profit. Now other fleets followed head over heels and before the end of 1601 fourteen fleets, totalling sixty-five ships, had started for the Indies. These were the years of the so-called Wild Navigation. They gave proof of an abundant spirit of enterprise, but before long grave drawbacks became apparent in this happy-go-lucky development of the East-Indian commerce. Far-seeing men understood that things should not be allowed to drift in this haphazard fashion, for a sharp competition arose that would in the long run kill all trade. Each separate company was only interested in its own momentary profit; its agents bid against competitors from sister-towns and tried to get hold of the most valuable cargoes. As compared with these unorganised, individual business methods the Portuguese enjoyed the great advantage of having a centralised colonial trade that was the crown's monopoly, since the colonies were all crown-colonies. The Portuguese were therefore in a much stronger position both from a commercial and from a military point of view.

To John van Oldenbarnevelt, the statesman who chiefly conducted the affairs of the Dutch Republic in these years, the credit is due for having clearly perceived the dangers arising out of this situation for the East-Indian commerce as well as for the Republic itself. For it was only from the trade-profits that the ever mounting costs of the war with Spain could be defrayed. Oldenbarnevelt therefore prepared to avert the threatening danger. Overcoming endless difficulties, caused by the local and provincial jealousies so characteristic of Dutch society at the time, he succeeded in bringing about a fusion between all existing companies. This happened in 1602 and from that time on the United East-Indian Company, called for short V.O.C., had the monopoly of all Indian trade. By charter of March 20th 1602 the States-General delegated to the United Company several of its sovereign rights as pertaining to the Indies. It was authorised to appoint officials, officers and judges, to raise troops, to declare war on, make peace and conclude alliances with native princes, to build forts, to conquer territory and to mint coins. The charter forbade all citizens of the Republic, except servants of the United Company, to navigate and to traffic "round the Cape of Good Hope and through the Straits of Magellan". Hence the V.O.C. received the monopoly for all the seas, bound, on the one side, by the Eastcoast of Africa, and, on the other, by the Westcoast of America.

The first years of this new, highly privileged organisation were difficult. It had to fight against Portuguese and Spanish competitors, and also against the British who, as early as 1600, had founded an East India Company. At first the fleets of the V.O.C. were more equipped for war than for commerce, and it was 1610 before the shareholders received their first dividends. But then those dividends were not less than $132\frac{1}{2}$ %!

The Company soon perceived that, for the sake of an untroubled trade, it was necessary to establish a number of fortified settlements. The necessary sites were obtained by contract, purchase or conquest. Its first property was Ambon, seized in 1605 from the Portuguese. Thus more or less compelled by necessity, the Company, from a purely commercial body, developed into one exercising sovereign rights, although it is true that the Directors of the Company continued to regard it in the first place as a commercial organisation. When, for example, toward the end of the 17th century, Ryckloff van Goens proposed to establish Dutch sovereignty all over Ceylon, the Court of Directors declined this proposal on the ground that "this would be the work of a great and ambitious king and not one of merchants, who only look for profit". The occupation of territory was always a means to an end, and never an end in itself, albeit the Dutch East-Indian empire is the result. The true founder of this empire in the beginning of the 17th century was Jan Pietersz. Coen; at the close of the 19th century van Heutsz was to round it off and to complete it.

The Men

After three centuries Coen's personality is as fascinating to us as it was impressive to his contemporaries. Devout, stalward and gruff, these three words sum up his character. Born and educated in the difficult years of the end of the 16th century he had, at an early age, become familar with the serious side of life. His early youth he spent in a simple home with his parents, who were strict Calvinists, in the small provincial town of Hoorn, on the Zuyderzee, which was then taking a lively part in the overseas trade. At thirteen he was sent to a Flemish commercial house in Rome where he stayed for six years. What went on in him there during those years? How did he feel among people who were strangers to him, differing in appearance, in language, in customs, and who were hostile to what he had learnt to prize as the highest good? We do not know: Coen, in his after life, never referred to those years. We know however that, when he was nineteen, he returned home to Hoorn as an experienced merchant, who understood Italian bookkeeping and knew several foreign languages. We also know that he had remained faithful to his Calvinistic faith. This faith put its stamp on all Coen's further life and, looking at his portrait, one may well ask if a sunny laugh ever illuminated that face.

After a first voyage to the Indies, lasting three years, upon returning to Amsterdam, he was noticed by the Directors of the Company and not long afterwards, barely 25 years old, he was again sent to the Indies, as commander of two valuable ships. When he arrived there, Pieter Both, the first Governor-General, was in serious trouble. His presence was urgently needed in the eastern regions, where the spice-islands were, the principal interest of the Company, that carried on a hard struggle there against enemies and competitors. The Spanish and the Portuguese in the Indies did not observe the Twelve-years' Truce .hat in 1609 had been concluded with them by the Republic, and moreover the British competitors tried with all their might to obtain a strong foothold in the Moluccas. Strong and constant action against all these was necessary. But at the same time the Governor-General's presence was required at Bantam on the western tip of Java, a long way off from the Moluccas. Bantam was the first place in the Indies where the ships from Holland used to come to anchor and from where they also undertook the voyage home; consequently it had so far been the principal factory of the Company. The natives at Bantam were difficult, fully conscious of their power in a situation where Dutch, British and French all tried to get hold of the Bantam pepper and did not scruple to stoop to intrigues in undercutting each other. The Company therefore also needed a strong man at Bantam. Unfortunately many of its employees so far, setting to naught all expectations built on them, had grievously injured Dutch prestige by their scandalous conduct. Both, becoming acquainted with Coen during a journey of inspection in the Moluccas, saw in him the solution of his difficulties. He appointed the young man, 26 years old, bookkeeper-general and director of the factories at Bantam and Jacatra. In communicating this important appointment to the authorities at home Both described him as "an honest and devout young man, very modest in his conduct, sober and of a good character, no drunkard, not arrogant, very capable in council, and well versed in commerce and bookkeeping".

At Bantam Coen's historic part began. From the first his attitude was equally firm towards his dissolute subordinates, the intrigues of the native regent of Bantam and the European competitors. Of the latter he particularly disliked the British, who fully reciprocated his sentiments. When the tension became too great and the Europeans moreover died like rats, owing to the miserable climatic and hygienic conditions, he looked for another centre. The most suitable place seemed to be the neighbouring Jacatra where the Compagny for some years had owned a small factory and a storehouse. When he began to build there a large and strong factory, he offended the ruler of that town, a vassal of the Sultan of Bantam. The British also interfered and before long all were united against the Dutch. Since the British happened to have a fleet on the spot, twice as large as that of the Dutch, the position of Coen and his men seemed hopeless. He succeeded in beating off a first attack, but he lacked ammunition for a second fight, and was obliged to sail all the way to the Moluccas in order to get reinforcements. Nearly five months later, back before Jacatra, he landed his troops and took the city on May 30th 1619. On its ruins he built the new Dutch "rendez-vous", which shortly afterwards was named Batavia.

In his report to the Directors of the Company Coen wrote with pardonable satisfaction: "The foundation of the rendez-vous, so long desired, has now been laid. A large part of the most fertile land and the most prolific seas of the Indies is now yours ... Behold and consider what a good courage may accomplish and how the Almighty has fought for us and blessed your Honours."

Even before Jacatra had fallen into his hands, Coen had received word of his appointment as Governor-General. He was then 31 years old. The appointment did not surprise him; nor did he display any enthusiasm over it. He pledged himself however to do his utmost not to disappoint the confidence put in him and to send rich returns home, provided the Directors would not stint him in men, money and ships. "Let us plough and sow; the Lord will give the growth." As long as he was in a position of authority Coen battled against stinginess and the exaggerated prudence of the Governors of the Company who lacked the large vision of their youthful Governor-General. The more admirable is it that he achieved so much, since the means at his disposal were always strictly limited.

By the foundation of Batavia one of the wishes of the Directors had been fulfilled. But there was another point, still dearer to their hearts. That was to obtain the monopoly of the precious spices, chiefly cloves, nutmeg and mace. Contracts with the sultans and chiefs of the various islands of the Moluccas and Ambon secured an almost complete monopoly of cloves, but this method did not succeed so well with regard to the nutmeg of the Banda-islands. Repeatedly the Bandanese made solemn pledges — especially whenever the forces of the Company were in the vicinity. — that they would sell their entire harvest exclusively to the Dutch at contract prices, but as soon as they saw a chance of getting better prices elsewhere, they would forget their promises. The fact that British skippers incited the Bandanese to such behaviour was particularly galling to Coen and it led him to forget all moderation. In 1621 he subdued the Banda-islands with ruthless severity: the large majority of the original native population perished or fled and about one thousand men were deported to Batavia as colonists. The nutmeg groves were divided into a number of lots which were given in cultivation to former employees of the Company. In this way an absolute monopoly was obtained of nutmeg and mace which were only grown on the Banda islands.

When in 1623 Coen repatriated, he presented to the Directors of the Company far-reaching proposals of reform. He wished to allow free trade to European citizens between the various Indian ports under supervision of the Company; he also proposed to establish at various suitable places settlements of Europeans. These ideas of Coen's were too far ahead of the time, and although the Directors were at first not unwilling to act upon them, later the fear prevailed that private navigation and commerce would seriously threaten their monopoly of spice and they withheld their approval of Coen's reforms.

Once more, in 1627, Coen returned to the Indies as Governor-General. For two more years he struggled hard to prevent the downfall of Batavia. Twice it was besieged by the Sultan of Mataram. He died during the second siege, on September 21st 1629. By his firm attitude towards native rulers and European competitors alike he unquestionably laid the foundations of the Dutch East Indies.

Anthony van Diemen built a strong superstructure on the foundations laid by Coen. Van Diemen, son of the burgomaster of the small town of Culemborg, received a good education. Going into business he was unfortunate and went bankrupt. In a desperate mood he signed up as common soldier for the Indies. By a lucky chance the refined and intelligent youth was noticed by Coen; he was released from military service and was given a clerk's post in Coen's office. He rose rapidly in the service. On the eve of Coen's repatriation in 1623 van Diemen was appointed First Merchant. Two years later he became member of the Council and, when Coen returned to Batavia in 1627, van Diemen was made Director-General. After a short stay in Europe in 1633 he returned to the Indies and three years later was appointed Governor-General. He held this office for nearly nine years and accomplished a very great deal. He made Batavia into a "modern" city. He built European houses, two churches, canals with bridges. He protected the Chinese settlement and the sugar industry in which the Chinese were engaged. In 1642 he promulgated the Company's Code, the so-called Batavian Statutes and he also established a statute for the church. He considerably improved the relations with the two great native states on Java, Bantam and Mataram, restored peace in the Moluccas and concluded a treaty with Makassar. Under his government the Company's influence on Ceylon began to overshadow that of the Portuguese. In January 1641 the important town of Malacca, which since 1511 had been in the hands of the Portuguese, was conquered by the Company.

Remarkable also is his initiative in the "discovery of the remaining un-known parts of the globe". He sent expeditions to the seas East and North of Japan. Twice he equipped a small fleet under Abel Janszoon Tasman who circumnavigated Australia, discovered Tasmania, New-Zealand and a number of lesser islands and gave Dutch names to many places of the fifth continent. Under van Diemen the Company's influence became so great that it began to be reckoned with among the great powers. Van Diemen died at Batavia on April 19th 1645, just when he was getting ready to sail for home.

The third great empire-builder among the Governors-General is Joan Maetsuycker. In the nearly 25 years during which he held that high office (1653—1678) he was assisted by a number of able advisers, of whom Ryck-loff van Goens and Cornelis Speelman were the most important.

Under van Diemen, Maetsuycker, who had studied law, was juridical adviser to the government and he it was who chiefly composed the Batavian Statutes. For four years he was governor of Ceylon (1646—1650), and he also headed an embassy to Goa, the capital of the Portuguese colonial em-pire. The rest of his career was spent at Batavia: first for many years as member of the Council and from 1653 till his death in 1678 as Governor-General. Under his rule van Goens established the Dutch dominion over the cinnamon-producing coastal regions of Ceylon, the coast of Malabar and part of the coast of Coromandel. Speelman during these years definitely subdued Makassar and extended the influence of the Company in Mataram and Bantam. Both van Goens and Speelman were distinguished by an unu-sual interest in native culture. Though both ended their careers as Governor-General, their greatest glory was achieved under Maetsuycker.

When Speelman died in January 1684 the Company's empire was establi-shed along definite lines. While during the rest of the 17th and a large part of the 18th century the Dutch influence on Java steadily was extended, it gradually decreased in the regions outside the Archipelago. The days of the great expansion were over, and the Company enjoyed the fruit of the labour of its pioneers. It did not desire any more territory and even complained of having "too much land". It aimed at exploiting the territories which it owned as intensively and as cheaply as possible. To this end it encouraged the growing of products for which there was a demand in Europe. Governor-General Joan van Hoorn (1704—1709) began to plant coffee on Java and after an initial failure this became a great success. Some other experiments, such as the planting of dyewood and the introduction of sericultuie failed, in spite of the great pains taken by Hendrick Zwaardecroon (Governor-General 1718—1725). There are many reasons why, commercially speaking, the 18th century was not equal to the 17th. In India powerful British and French colonial empires developed, which ousted the Dutch Company from the leading place. The desire for private profit also tempted many servants of the Company to neglect the interests of the Company for their own.

Two men should be mentioned in the 18th century, who seriously attempted to mend these abuses: Gustaaf Willem baron van Imhoff and Jacob Mossel. The former, after having cleansed the Augean stables as governor of Ceylon, became Governor-General (1743—1750). He was a man full of good intentions and many original ideas which, as regards the development of European settlements and the opening of a limited free navigation, show a striking resemblance to those of Coen. Van Imhoff's error was that he attempted too much all at once, undertook all sorts of things and completed next to nothing. He was no match either for the prevailing indolence and selfishness and in the end his period of office proved a disappointment to himself as well as to the Directors of the Company.

Mossel, who had started life before the mast, was Governor-General from 1750—1761. He tried hard to "keep the Company's ark afloat". Like van Imhoff he succeeded in bringing about some partial reforms but in the main his efforts failed. After his death the Company went from bad to worse, until finally, December 31st 1799, it was dissolved. All its possessions and its debts passed into the hands of the Batavian Republic which had succeeded the old United Netherlands.

The East Indies now became a state colony. For eleven years they dragged on an uncertain existence in a time full of international difficulties, until they finally fell into the hands of the British. During these eleven years however once more a great figure took the helm. This was Herman Willem Daendels, Governor-General from 1808—1811. In spite of striking faults he was a man possessed of exceptional gifts and power and he was entirely free from the bondage of precedent, so powerful in the East Indies. He was exceptional not only by the fact that he had never before been in the Indies. Like a whirlwind he passed over the remnants of the old Company system, was neither impressed by family ties, nor influential relations, nor oriental state and splendour. Without regard for anybody or anything he abolished century-old titles and dignities and replaced the old by the new. "Tuan besar njang guntur", "The Great Lord who is like the thunder", he was called by the simple villagers years after his death. Deprived of all contact with the Netherlands he organised, largely with native forces, an army and coast-defences, improved government and jurisdiction, built the great post road and replaced the old residential town of Batavia, ill-famed for its high death rate, by the more healthy Weltevreden. All this brought him into conflict with the clique of old residents and it was partly owing to their accusations that Napoleon, in 1811, recalled Daendels. Had he remained, it is likely that the Dutch East Indies would never have known the interlude, generally called the British Interregnum.

With this interregnum however is connected the name of one very remarkable man: Thomas Stamford Raffles. His system of landrent was a great improvement for the Javanese on the old system of compulsory sale of products. But he did not succeed in making Java into a profitable possession for the East India Company and his annual deficits were not pleasing to the British company.

In 1816 Holland received its colonies back, with the exception of the Cape of Good Hope and Ceylon. The mother-country, sorely impoverished during the Napoleonic rule, hoped and expected that "the days of the Company" would return and that once more, as in the golden century, the Indies would shower their treasures over Holland. This soon proved to be a complete miscalculation. The first Governor-General of the resuscitated Indies, G. A. G. P. baron van der Capellen, animated by the best intentions, especially towards the native population, was not even able to defray the expenditure of his Indian government itself and, between 1816 and 1822, he created an Indian debt amounting to more than twenty million florins. In the beginning of 1826 he was replaced by Viscount L. P. J. du Bus de Gisignies, whose orders were by drastic economy to balance the budget and, if possible, to remit a surplus to the mother country. In this respect he did not succeed; shortly before his arrival a rebellion broke out in Central Java, led by Dipo Negoro, the so-called Java-war. Although, after a severe struggle, the rebellion was quelled, and in the end the sovereignty of the government over Java was considerably strengthened, the war cost such enormous sums that both the Indies and the motherland were threatened by state bankruptcy.

In this state of affairs there intervened a man who, by an ingenious scheme, saved the situation, though, as events proved, the Javanese people had to foot the bill.

This man was Johannes van den Bosch. After a distinguished military career, partly in the Dutch East Indies, he had devoted himself to the fight against unemployment among the impoverished population of the great cities, and, at the king's request, in 1827 he went to the West Indies in order to introduce certain reforms there. When, in the following year, he returned to Holland, the king discussed with him the critical financial situation of the East Indies, groaning under a debt of thirty seven millions. Being appointed Governor-General in the same year, he did not sail until a year later, because, most conscientiously, he insisted on making a thorough study of the Indian situation and particularly of Du Bus' proposals to establish large European agricultural enterprises on Java. He finally arrived at the conclusion that only by exercising compulsion on the population of Java, as in the days of the Company, the production of profitable crops could be made sufficient to defray all Indian expenditure and provide an annual surplus for the home country as well. The king and the Minister of Colonies, C. Th. Elout, were opposed to a return to the compulsory system, but, not seeing another way out, the king finally gave his consent. His minister however resigned.

In the years 1830—1834 van den Bosch, first as Governor-General and, from 1832 on, vested with full dictatorial powers, introduced the "culture-system" on Java. It compelled the population to reserve one fifth of its land for growing such products for the state as were in great demand on the European market. The Javanese therefore was no longer free to decide himself what to grow on his sawahs, but on part of his fields he had to raise those crops which the officials dictated to him: sugar, coffee, indigo, tea, tobacco, cinnamon etc. Worse was that many abuses crept into the execution of this scheme, mainly because the officials shared in a certain percentage of the yield and were therefore personally interested in its volume. It cannot be denied that the culture-system greatly impoverished the Javanese people and in some places led to famine. It was not long before in the Indies and in Holland opposition arose against this system. Though at that time the Government could not carry on without the annual Indian surplus, by degrees the system was mitigated and all but abandoned until finally, in 1917, the last remmant of it, the compulsory coffee-culture, was abolished.

From a purely financial point of view van den Bosch's system fully came up to the most sanguine expectations. Thanks to it the Indian budget could be balanced, the Indian debt be paid off, and annually an important surplus be placed at the disposal of the motherland, amounting in the best years to as much as twenty million florins.

As long as the home budget was dependent on this annual surplus the Government's attention was almost exclusively centred on Java. In the other islands of the Archipelago the authority of the Government was in many places fictitious and the introduction of such a compulsory system of agriculture was out of the question there. These "Outer Possessions", in fact, cost more than they brought in and the Government therefore had but scanty interest in them. The danger of such a policy became apparent when in 1841 a British adventurer, James Brooke, occupied part of North Borneo and had himself proclaimed Raja of Serawak. His success encouraged some other American and British adventurers to try and do the same. These events made the Government realise that it was necessary to establish at least a nominal authority over the Outer Islands. Governor-General J. J. Rochussen (1845—1851), supported by the Minister of Colonies J. Ch. Baud, initiated a policy which his successors followed for many years. They asserted the authority of the Dutch government in the entire Archipelago. Whenever this authority was ignored or flouted by native chiefs or princes a punitive expedition was sent, which returned to its garrisons on Java as soon as the refractory leaders had surrendered. Such punitive expeditions naturally had no lasting effect. Full and unchallenged sovereignty could only exist when the Government's authority had become a permanent and established fact throughout the entire Archipelago.

Kraton ,,Regents" from the Principali

This result was achieved by van Heutsz. The Atchinese in North Sumatra had for many years caused a great deal of trouble. Van Heutsz, a
capable military officer, brought a long drawn-out war against them to a
successful close. Then, as Governor-General (1904—1909) he pursued the
same forceful policy in other distant parts, and since his days Dutch sovereignty has been recognised everywhere throughout the East Indies.

The Commerce

The Company regarded itself as a mercantile body first and foremost.
More than once its Directors defined its purpose as: exclusion of competitors, buying cheap, selling dear. Their main interest was spice and their servants were under instructions to secure the monopoly of spice "by treaty or
by force". The conquest of the Banda Islands in 1621 gave them that monopoly for nutmeg and mace. With regard to cloves they followed a different
policy: on Ternate, Tidore, Halmaheira and neighbouring islands, which
were the lands of origin of this product, the Company completely exterminated the plantations, aided and abetted (against payment!) by the local
princes, and it concentrated the cultivation of cloves on Ambon which, since
1605, had stood under her dominion. The monopoly, thus obtained, was
energetically defended against competitors who, by offering better prices than
the Company, tried to get hold of part of the harvest. The Company always
maintained a small fleet of cruisers to prevent smuggling. Though this
entailed heavy expenditure, its chief profit was nevertheless made on spice.
The world-consumption of cloves for example amounted in the 17th and
18th centuries to an average of 300 or 400.000 pounds per annum, furnished
entirely by the Dutch Company. This paid the natives threepence a pound;
with costs of storage and transportation the cost price at Amsterdam may
be reckoned at sixpence a pound. The selling-price was more or less constantly maintained at six shillings and threepence per pound, so that the
profit was at least one million florins per annum. However, apart from the
300 or 400.000 pounds for Europe, the Company also sold large quantities
to India (Hindostan and Surattee), Persia, Arabia, China and Japan, with
a profit of 900 or 1000 %, so that the entire annual profit of this article alone
may be put on at least one and a half million florins.

Not until the end of the 18th century did competitors succeed in growing the spice of the Moluccas elsewhere. At present about three quarters of the world consumption of cloves is produced by Zanzibar on the east coast of Africa.

Thus although, in the course of the 19th century, the old Moluccan trade was sadly on the wane, for a long time the Government maintained its monopoly there by forbidding free sale and by maintaining compulsory cultivation. In 1860 slavery was abolished, which measure brought about grave difficulties for the cultivation of nutmeg and mace on Banda, since it was largely dependent on the employment of slave labour. In 1863 the cultivation and trade of the Moluccan spice became free.

For cinnamon the situation was different. Cinnamon was produced in different places in India, especially in Malabar. This however was an inferior kind, called by the Portuguese "canella da matta", i.e. wild or forest cinnamon. The fine whole cinnamon was indigenous on Ceylon and was long a monopoly of the Portuguese, who in the middle of the 16th century had conquered the coastal regions of Ceylon. In the course of the 17th century the Dutch Company seized this territory from the Portuguese, conquering, after heavy fighting, the capital Colombo in 1656, and consequently the Dutch obtained the monopoly of the Ceylon cinnamon. They lost it when in 1795 and 1796 the British in their turn took Ceylon from the Dutch.

Pepper was grown extensively in widely separated areas: Malabar, Sumatra, South Borneo and Bantam. The Company never had an absolute monopoly of this product, but, through treaties with the native princes, it obtained the lion's share of the annual harvest. Annually from 5 to 6 million pounds of brown (i.e. black) and 100.000 pounds of white pepper were shipped home, and a great deal was also exported to China. At present the annual export of pepper from the Dutch East Indies is about 80—100 million pounds.

Coffee and tea were always very important articles of our Indian trade. Coffee was not indigenous in the Indies. Its home is Arabia. Pieter van den Broecke, who in 1614 with his yacht Nassau as the first Hollander entered the Red Sea and visited Arabia, described in his journal coffee as "a species of beans, of which they make black water which they drink hot". It was some time before this beverage was known and appreciated in Europe. Not until 1663 did the Company carry the first "cauwa de Mocha"

(Mocca-coffee) to Amsterdam. Then very soon the taste became general; "cafés" sprang up everywhere and in many households coffee became a favourite beverage. In 1700 the Company's turnover of coffee was more than 350.000 pounds. The well-known burgomaster of Amsterdam, Nicolas Witsen, had, at his request, some coffeeplants sent to him. These he presented to the botanical gardens of Amsterdam, where they were cultivated with the utmost care. A few of these tender shoots were, by way of experiment, sent to the West and became the progenitors of the enormous Brazilian coffeeculture.

Since trade with the Arabs was very difficult and vexatious the Company experimented in different places with the cultivation of coffee. In Malabar, Ceylon, and the Moluccas it failed, but in Java, after many disappointments, the culture became a success. In 1712 the first sample of Java coffee, 899 pounds, was shipped to Amsterdam. Fair prices were paid by the Company, as much as 15 dollars per picol of 125 pounds, and the native chiefs, who received their share of the output, were glad to cooperate. Thus gradually and without objection the cultivation of coffee was made compulsory in certain districts of Java. In 1724 the harvest was as much as two million pounds! Then in 1726 it was decided to decrease the price paid: 9 dollars for the current year and in future 5 dollars. The exasperated population began to destroy the coffee trees, so that strong measures were necessary. Coffee remained an important source of profit for the Company but the natives found only a meagre living in its cultivation.

Daendels extended the cultivation of coffee to East Java; he raised the number of coffee trees on the island from 27 to 72 million. Raffles who so strongly opposed the compulsory cultivation of other products did not interfere in that of coffee. When van den Bosch introduced his culture system, compulsory cultivation of coffee was introduced in the Minahassa (i.e. the northern part of Celebes) and on the west coast of Sumatra. In 1917 the last remnants of compulsion were abolished. The output had then much decreased owing to the havoc wrought by the coffeeleaf disease.

At present the production of coffee in the Dutch East Indies, although considerable, forms only a small percentage of world-production, and the planters have to face a very fierce competition especially from Brasil.

The first tea was shipped to Europe by the Dutch Company, curiously, not from China, but from Japan. In 1654 it ordered there, by way of experiment, 150 to 200 pounds of the best quality. The beverage was well received. Its medicinal properties were praised as highly beneficial by a certain doctor Bontekoe, who, in 1684, at the request of the Company, wrote a pamphlet on tea. When the demand increased the Company tried to get the tea in China itself. The direct China trade however was so uncertain that most of the tea was bought from the Chinese junks who came to Batavia. The normal price paid was 60 dollars per picol of 125 pounds. An attempt, made in 1717 to reduce the price to 40 dollars, had as only result that the Chinese junks stayed away, much to the chagrin of the Company's Directors at Amsterdam who never forgot their device of "buying cheap". Later a factory was established at Canton. There was however never any question of a monopoly, for the British, the French and the Americans also had factories at Canton.

The Company never seems to have tried the cultivation itself. A German scholar, Dr Ph. F. von Siebold, who served under the Dutch on the small settlement of Deshima in Japan, in 1826 sent some tea plants and tea seeds to Java, where they were cultivated in the Botanical Gardens at Buitenzorg. A specialist was sent to China to study the cultivation and preparation of tea. With the aid of some Chinese tea-growers this expert, on his return in 1833, started the first tea plantations on Java, thirteen in number. At first the cultivation was for Government's account, but from 1842 on the plantations were leased out. Especially after 1870 the cultivation of tea greatly increased and had to meet a steadily growing demand in Europe. Since 1914 there are also tea plantations on the island of Sumatra. In the best years of the 20th century the total export of tea from the Dutch East Indies totalled 100 million pounds.

Rice was in Java always a truly native crop. The Company was only moderately interested in it. Rice was bought to victual the ships and factories, but in the statistics of the V.O.C. it never figures as an export article. In the 17th and 18th centuries the Dutch in the Indies did not yet appreciate the famous "rysttafel". Rice was considered a somewhat inferior food, fit for natives. Only Europeans of lower social position would take rice for breakfast, cooked dry, with some herbs, or they would have an after-dinner desert, called "grobbejak", a kind of porridge, consisting of rice, sugar, arak, tamarind and various spices. As late as 1844 a young officer wrote home that the eating of rice did not seem to be "bon ton". Since then the white people, in the Indies as well as elsewhere, have learned to appreciate rice. The export of rice from the Dutch East Indies however has remained insignificant, since practically the whole of the enormous production is wanted for home consumption.

In sugar however the Company was always interested. Between 1630 and 1662 it received large quantities from Formosa, which was then a Dutch possession, but after this was lost the flow of sugar ceased.

Although of old the natives in Java cultivated and prepared sugar in a somewhat primitive way, the Chinese immigrants introduced the real cane sugar industry. Shortly after the foundation of Batavia sugarmills were established in the environs by Chinese who knew the business. They pressed the cane between millstones, put in motion by oxen or by waterpower. In 1652 the "Captain-Chinese" Jancon could already sell 12.000 picols of sugar to the Company. Gradually the number of mills in the vicinity of Batavia increased, so that in 1710 they numbered 130. Then followed a slump, caused by exhaustion of the soil, scarcity of labour, the pillaging raids of the Bantamese and finally the revolt of the Chinese in 1740. In Daendel's time only 30 mills remained. All sugar had to be delivered to the Company.

In the lowlands of central Java sugarcane was also cultivated. Except for what was needed for local consumption this sugar also could only be sold to the Company. For the establishing of a new mill a licence was needed. Part of this sugar was shipped to Europe, but large quantities were sold to India and Persia.

Upon the introduction of van den Bosch' culture-system sugar was one of the most important compulsory products. Steampower gradually took the place of the old mills. After 1870 the cultivation of sugar was no longer compulsory, but the possibility was opened for private enterprise to lease from the Javanese the land necessary for sugar cultivation. Since then the Javanese sugar-industry took an almost fantastic flight. At its peak the export totalled about 2 million tons!

Among the forest products which the Company exported we find benzoin, camphor, lacquer, gum, resin, wax and ratan, also vegetable dyes such as indigo, kasumba, kunjit or Indian saffron, sapanwood and moreover from India proper various dye-roots, mostly red ones, such as foa, mandosti, saya and galigo. Not inconsiderable also was the export of fine fragrant wood, like sapanwood, from the Lesser Sunda islands, and aguilwood (from the aloë), which were in great demand both in Europe and China. Of the various kinds of hardwood should be mentioned djatiwood, ironwood and ebony.

An important article of the Company's return-trade was opium. Originally it procured the opium in Bengal; toward the end of the 18th century it received part of it in the Near East; this was a cheaper and inferior kind. Whenever the Company concluded a treaty with some native ruler, it always tried to secure the export-monopoly of the special product of the country concerned and the import-monopoly for Coromandel linens and opium. This policy often succeeded and these monopolies were among the richest sources of its revenue. Opium dens were leased out by the Government under Daendels.

The trade in minerals was far less important in the 17th and 18th centuries than that in vegetable products. In Borneo a small trade in diamonds was carried on; in places outside the Archipelago, such as India, Surattee, Golconda, Gingi, Pegu, Birma, Tanjore and Ceylon this trade however was much more considerable. Tin and gold were the two most important metals. Tin was much in demand and the Company sought relations with the tin-producing countries. One of these was Siam; also Perak and Quedah on the Malay Peninsula. In 1650 the Company obtained from the Sultana of Atchin, who then reigned over Perak, the monopoly of tin in that region. Similar treaties were concluded with Quedah and other places. Nevertheless there were many complaints that the tin trade of the Company was undercut by "Moors", that is Mohammedans from India.

Banka and Billiton then belonged to the Sultan of Palembang. Probably as early as the first half of the 17th century he got tin from Banka which he sold to Chinese, but fearing the obtrusive interest of Europeans he kept this a secret. In the long run the secret however transpired and in 1722 the Company concluded a treaty with him, by which he undertook to sell all Banka tin to the Company at 10 dollars per picol of 125 pounds. Although this contract was several times renewed with certain changes as to the price and the quantity to be delivered, it is but natural that, with the waning power of the Company in the second half of the 18th century, the feeling of independence of the Sultan waxed proportionally, and in spite of existing obligations he sold a large part of his tin to others.

During the British interregnum the Sultan of Palembang was forced to cede Banka and Billiton to the British. In 1814 by the Convention of London the Dutch received Banka from the British in exchange for Cochin on the coast of Malabar. Billiton was returned to the Dutch by the treaty of London in 1824. Shortly before it had been discovered that this island also contained tin, but, as it then seemed, not in exploitable quantity. When however further satisfactory tests had been made, in 1852 the Billiton Company was founded. The exploitation on Banka always was a government concern; that on Billiton was a private enterprise, in which the Government has an important share. This is also the case with the Singkep Tin Company in the Riau Archipelago.

Gold always interested the Company, but it was never very successful in its efforts to mine gold in the Indies. On the west coast of Sumatra, in North Celebes, in various districts of Java, where gold was found, the results of mining were disappointing. Chinese immigrants on the west coast of Borneo had better luck. They arrived in large numbers in the middle of the 18th century to wash gold and established a great many prosperous communities. The Company always imported a good deal of gold, chiefly from Japan and Coromandel. From Japan also came large quantities of silver and copper.

Coal and petroleum, which are both plentiful in the Indies, were not exploited in the days of the Company. The coal needed for the Company's smithies was imported from Europe!

In modern times textiles are probably the first import article for southern and eastern Asia. In the days of the Company it was just the other way: textiles travelled from East to West. The centre of the textile industry was Bengal for muslins and gauzes, Coromandel for fine calico and chintzes. The Company established agencies in Mazulipatnam and Petapuli as early as 1605 and 1606, in order to buy these articles wholesale. It kept many "painters" in its various "lodges" to apply the patterns which had won the approval of the customers at home or in the Asiatic ports in which they were sold. The variety in the patterns was endless. Especially popular in Holland and England were the common checks and the chintzes. The many-coloured cloths covering part of the back and chest in most provincial costumes in Holland often are even today real Indian chintzes, handed down for generations from mother to daughter.

The textiles from India have been superseded by the products of Manchester and Twente (Holland). The once famous places have disappeared or have dwindled into miserable villages. Java alone still saved the art of batik, which is a development of the art of the chintz-painters. The patterns and colours of the imported cottons which the natives now mostly wear are still reminiscent of the original chintzes.

A valuable export article was silk. It was obtained from Persia, Bengal, Tonkin and China, both in raw and spun state, or as silk goods. The principal markets for the Company were Japan and Europe. Japan used enormous quantities of silk for the clothing of men and women, but did not know the silk industry. Part of the silk which the Dutch and the Chinese imported into Japan, was exported in the form of kimonos or wide gowns to India or Europe. This silk trade of the Company was exceedingly profitable; in the top years of the 17th century it carried sometimes more than one million florins worth of raw silk to Japan on which 100 % profit was made.

The fact that in the lands of origin of silk, Persia, Bengal and China the Company never had any territorial possessions and was merely tolerated, induced it to experiment within its own dominions in the establishment of a silk industry. Neither in Ceylon nor in Java however did these experiments have any permanent results. At present here and there in West-Java and in Sumatra small quantities of silk are produced by natives and Chinese.

Wool was exported from Holland to the Indies, China and Japan. It was used by our ancestors on Java not only for covering walls and upholstering chairs in reception rooms, but, in genteel disregard of the tropical temperature, even for clothing! Woollen cloth was much esteemed too as presents for native princes. Some fine woollens from Persia were also shipped to Holland.

There were of course many other articles in the Company's Indian commerce. Among the sundries may be mentioned: elephants from Ceylon, Arabian and Persian horses, Bengal salpeter which was a lucrative cargo whenever there was war in Europe. Furthermore there was a trade in wine from Shiraz in Persia, pearls from Ceylon, amber, rosewater, civet, kulit lawang, medicines, cowri-shells from the Maladives, lacquer from Japan, teasets and other porcelain from China, coral and tortoiseshell from the Archipelago and various ethnographical curiosa from different countries. On the other hand, on scanning the cargo lists, one looks in vain for many things which now come immediately to mind when we speak of the Indian trade: petroleum, coal, bauxite and other minerals, quinine, various fibres, rubber etc. Thus commerce and industry reflect the development of the world's civilisation.

The Territory

As has been said before, the East Indian Company was first and foremost a commercial organisation and it only aimed at the occupation of territory, when the necessities of an undisturbed trade made this imperative or desirable. Trade was often carried on in countries where the Company had not the least territorial rights. On the other hand it would never occupy any territory that, either by its geographical position or by its products, was not important for its trade. With regard to the fabulous Southland (Australia or New-Holland) which was discovered by its mariners, it did not claim the jus primi occupantis, because from a commercial point of view it seemed valueless. At the same time it carried on an important trade in Arabia, Persia, Surattee, Bengal, Siam, Cambodia, Tonkin, China and Japan without ever possessing any sovereign rights. It only enjoyed certain mercantile privileges such as exterritoriality and monopoly in so far and so long as it pleased the lawful sovereign. It is only circumstances that compelled the Company in widely scattered regions in and outside the Archipelago, in Coromandel, Malabar, Ceylon, the Cape, Mauritius, and Malacca to obtain territory by right of conquest or by amicable settlement. Such is the origin of the Dutch East Indies. It is worth while to trace the growth of this empire.

Let us begin with the Moluccas.

At the request of the Ambonese Admiral Steven van der Haghen sailed in 1605 from Bantam to Ambon in order to deliver them from the dominion of the Portuguese. On February 23rd of that year he took the Portuguese fort, renamed it Victoria and left there a Dutch garrison. Thereupon he concluded treaties with the principal Ambonese chiefs, who put themselves under the protection of the States-General and Prince Maurice of Nassau, called themselves vassals of the Dutch and promised to sell them all their cloves. This treaty is the foundation of the first territorial possession of the Dutch in the Archipelago. Gradually their dominion in the 17th century was extended to the Ambonese possessions on the neighbouring islands.

The story of the conquest of the Banda islands has been told before: Coen conquered and largely depopulated them in 1621, replacing the original population by Dutch colonists.

The third and most powerful part of the Eastern Archipelago, the Moluccas proper (Ternate, Tidore, Batjan and dependencies) were not so easily conquered. The Company, hankering after the monopoly of spice, at first concluded agreements with the sultans, by which these rulers, against payment of heavy annuities, undertook to exterminate all their cloves, so as to prevent these from falling into the hands of competitors. Ambon's output was enough for the needs of the Company. In spite of this the rulers of Halmaheira, Buru and Ceram frequently grew clandestine cloves and sold them to others. Open opposition against the demands of the Dutch was encouraged by the Spanish and Portuguese. In a process of gradual penetration conventions were forced on the native rulers, ending in a treaty of 1683, by which the Dutch Company was recognised as the lawful owner of these lands. The sultans from then on only reigned as vassals by the grace of the Company.

The most powerful state of Celebes was Makassar. Supported by the British and the Portuguese, it long withstood Dutch influence. It was again the clandestine cloves, sold to others than the Company, which compelled it to take a strong hand with this country. After a three years' war the Company in 1667 obtained the monopoly of trade and the sultan allied himself with the Dutch in eternal friendship. This treaty was later extended to Sumbawa which was a dependency of Makassar, as well as to several other neighbouring countries. All efforts of the Makassar people to rescind the treaty imposed on them failed.

The Spanish from their base on the Philippines tried to establish their influence on the northern part of Celebes. Some native ruler came to ask the Governor of the Moluccas to protect him against them, and, seizing this as an excuse, the Governor in 1677 concluded a treaty, whereby certain rajah's in these parts, recognising the Company as overlord, were reinstated as vassals. The treaty contained one curious provision, which was directly aimed at the Spanish propaganda of Roman-Catholicism, viz. that no other religion would be tolerated in these lands than the Reformed (Calvinistic) religion. A few years later the remaining states of North Celebes, including the Minahassa, accepted the Dutch overlordship and they have remained loyal vassals until this day.

In the large island of Borneo there were, early in the 17th century, some settlements on the coast. The most important one was Banjermasin which produced pepper. The output had however to be shared with the British, Portuguese and Chinese. After many vicissitudes and disappointments Daendels in 1809 withdrew definitely from Banjermasin, merely retaining the nominal sovereignty. On the west coast an Arabian pirate had, in 1772, established himself with his followers on Pontianak, then a deserted island in the Kapuas river. He called himself Sultan and began to extend his influence. The Sultan of Bantam on Java, who was the overlord of one of the small states adjoining Pontianak, feeling his territory there threatened, asked the Company to interfere. An expedition was sent out, and the result was that the Company decided to recognise the former pirate if he would acknowledge Dutch sovereignty. This he did and his threatened neighbour did likewise. The Company now established an agency at Pontianak and expected great things. When these expectations were not realised, it withdrew altogether in 1791. Thus, at the beginning of the 19th century, all relations of the Dutch with Borneo had ceased.

More important were the relations with Sumatra. In the 17th century the Company had factories in Atchin, along the west coast, at Palembang, Djambi and Indragiri. The relations with Atchin were often strained, sometimes because of the tin in Malacca, sometimes because of the trade on Sumatra's west coast, over which Atchin claimed sovereignty. After 1659 all relations with Atchin itself ceased and a long struggle began on the west coast. One after another the local rulers had to accept treaties imposed

upon them by the Company whom they recognised as their lord and pro-
tector against the Atchinese.

On the east coast, in Palembang, Djambi and Indragiri the Company
in the course of the 17th century succeeded in obtaining monopolies. It
never acquired any territory there.

Malacca, which geographically speaking belongs to the Asiatic Continent, was regarded as part of the Archipelago. It had been conquered by
the Portuguese in 1511. Malacca then held the place that was to be taken
later by Singapore. It was the principal station on the route from Southern
to Eastern Asia and it was one of the most powerful bases of the Portuguese
colonial empire. In 1633 the Company began to cruise in the Straits of
Malacca during the favorable season in order to harass the enemy's shipping. This blockade was intensified from year to year and in 1640 a regular
siege was undertaken. Through the heroic resistance of the Portuguese and
the great mortality from disease, both of besiegers and besieged, this action
cost many thousand lives. In January 1641 the city fell to the Dutch, who
from then on exercised the authority there, as well as over the dependencies
Rembau and Naning.

After the Moluccas Java was regarded as the most important of the Company's dominions. Its oldest territory there was Batavia and vicinity. When
Coen, on May 30th 1619, had conquered the city of Jacatra, and began to
organise administration and jurisdiction, he quite arbitrarily fixed the boundaries of the conquered territory as: west, the sultanate of Bantam; north,
the islands in the bay; east, the sultanate of Cheribon; and south, the Indian
Ocean. After two attacks on the new city of Batavia by the Susuhunan of
Mataram, calling himself "emperor" of Java, had been repulsed in 1628
and 1629, this territory came under undisputed Dutch sovereignty.

The land west of Batavia belonged to the Sultan of Bantam; east, including Cheribon, recognised the overlordship of Mataram. The gradual extension of Dutch sovereignty on Java was therefore at the expense of these
two countries. In spite of peace treaties in 1645 and 1646 it was inevitable
that there should be trouble. The Bantamese secretly aided the Company's
enemies in the Moluccas and Celebes or raided the environs of Batavia. By
clever manœuvres, making use of civil war or dynastic quarrels the Com-

pany step by step increased its influence in Bantam, maintained strong garrisons in certain forts, obtained trade monopolies, and had more and more land ceded to it. Finally, in 1752, the Sultan of Bantam became a mere vassal of the Company. Under Daendel's government there was a sharp conflict on account of his demands for the defence of Java. The Dutch garrison and Dutch officials were massacred. Daendels attacked and seized the fortified "kraton" and further limitations of power were enforced upon the reigning house. In 1813 Raffles concluded a final agreement whereby the Sultan ceded all his rights to the government against payment of an annuity.

The peace concluded with Mataram in 1646 was maintained for many years, thanks to the tactful behaviour of the Government at Batavia and its ambassadors who, on their annual journey to the court, succeeded in "caressing" the cruel Sunan Ageng. In a rebellion against his misrule in 1676 his dynasty was saved by the Company's interference, for which it obtained the following important privileges:

Extension of its Batavian territory to the river Pamanukan; cession of the town and land of Semarang and Kaligawe; a general monopoly of trade and freedom of customs duties; indemnity of all expenditure incurred in the course of its action, as security for which the Company obtained control over all the seaports and their revenues.

Further wars of succession gave the Company more privileges in 1705, including certain lands on the island of Madura. The hand of the Company began to weigh very heavily over the court at Kartasura. When in 1740 the Chinese rose and the war spread to central Java, the Sunan seized this opportunity and supported the rebels. After some hard fighting he was defeated and sued for peace. The peace treaty of 1743 further restricted his power and the entire island of Madura, the eastern corner of Java, the districts of Surabaja, Rembang and Japara, as well as a narrow belt of land along the entire seacoast were ceded. The end of Mataram's independence was at hand. The dying Sunan in 1749 bequeathed his entire country to the Company "in order to keep it safe out of all confusion and governed properly". The legacy was accepted, but transferred to the Sunan's eldest son who undertook to observe all existing treaties. In spite of this a new war of succession broke out, which thoroughly devastated central Java and plunged the population into abject poverty. In 1755 the Company succeeded in reconciling the two principal pretenders to the crown, by splitting up the empire into two halves, called Surakarta and Jocjakarta. A few years later a third pretender surrendered and received a few districts of Surakarta, called the Mangkunegaran. A fourth division, called Pakualaman, was added in 1812. So the once powerful empire of Mararam was divided into "Principalities" which stood in a position of vassalage to the Company.

By the middle of the 18th century the best days of the Company were over. Its weakness, long known to insiders, became painfully apparent to the world in the fourth war with England, 1780—1784. The Cape Colony was saved only with the help of French allies but the west coast of Sumatra was surrendered without even a fight. Negapatnam, reputed to be the strongest fortress in Eastern Asia, capitulated in the same year, 1781. The other settlements on the coast of Coromandel were, like those in Bengal, too weak to offer any resistance. Only in Ceylon the enemy was beaten off. Although at the peace of Paris all conquered places were restored, with the sole exception of Negapatnam, the British had to be granted free navigation in the Archipelago. This was the first great blow at the Company's system of monopoly. Another blow was the great expenditure which the war had necessitated: more than 30 million florins. It made the Company gasp for breath and it was clear that it could not long survive such disasters.

In 1795 the Republic of the United Netherlands expired. In its place came the Batavian Republic, allied with France. War with England was the result. With brief interruptions this state of war lasted till 1813. One by one all the possessions of the old Company fell into British hands or were surrendered to them by the officials in "safe keeping" for the Prince of Orange who resided in England. Last of all, in 1811, Java was conquered.

The peace treaties after the Napoleonic wars restored the former possessions of the Company to the newly established Kingdom of the Netherlands, that was to serve as a strong bulwark against French expansion. Ceylon, already ceded in 1802, and the Cape Colony, were alone excepted. August 13th 1814, the Convention of London, meant the resurrection of the Dutch colonial empire.

When the decisions of the Convention had to be carried into effect, they showed a sad lack of precision. The Dutch demanded the evacuation by the

British of Singapore which Raffles occupied in 1819. On the other hand the British claimed that the Dutch had no rights on Billiton. These points were settled at the Treaty of London, March 1824, which was an exchange on a large scale. England obtained all Dutch possessions on the Asiatic continent, including Malacca and Singapore. The Netherlands obtained all British possessions on the islands: Benkulen, Nias and Billiton. Each of the contracting parties was to abstain from relations with native rulers within the other's territories. This proviso compelled England to dissolve its contract of monopoly with the Sultan of Atchin, concluded in 1819. In return it demanded a pledge from the Dutch government that it would never violate the independence of Atchin.

How slow the Dutch were in asserting their regained sovereignty in the Outer Islands, but how, once they woke up to the danger of losing it altogether, they pursued a more forceful policy of military expeditions, has already been narrated. With regard to Atchin they found themselves in a quandary. Even though the Atchinese made themselves obnoxious as pirates or slavetraders, the treaty of 1824 forbade the Dutch to undertake anything against them. The Atchinese, fully aware of this, were on every occasion quick with their complaints to England. In the long run the British recognised that this created an impossible situation and by the Sumatra Treaty of November 2nd 1871 the British crown relinquished all rights of interference with the extension of Dutch sovereignty anywhere in Sumatra. This opened the possibility of proceeding against Atchin. War broke out in 1873. It proved the heaviest struggle which the Dutch ever had to carry on in the colonies, but after many disappointments and reverses van Heutsz subdued Atchin. He it was who also had Dutch sovereignty recognised everywhere in the Outer Islands. With the exception of Northwest Borneo and Portuguese Timor the entire Archipelago is now an integral part of the Netherlands' empire.

CHAPTER 3

The Place of the Indies in Asia

The significance of the Dutch East Indies in Asia is dependent on their location in the southeast corner of the Asiatic continent. The Indian Archipelago, to which, in this connection, the Malay peninsula should also be reckoned, separates the Indian Ocean from the Pacific. But it also links them. Its sea passages are the arteries for the traffic between the coasts west and north of the southern point of the Peninsula. Australia and Oceania never influenced its development. The Indies therefore by their very nature form a transition zone and a traffic belt. Their importance as such always was commercial and economic. Until the last war, in a political and strategic sense they scarcely played a part in the world's history. Only once before, in the Napoleonic era, the Indies for a short time were of some use as a military base against the power that controlled the searoute from India to China. Since the restoration of Dutch rule however, until our own time, they have known no more war than their growing importance to world-traffic and world-production made inevitable for forging them into a governable unity under Dutch leadership.

This chapter then is to deal with the place of the Indies in Asiatic commerce and production. It may appear that such a subject falls outside the scope of this book, which chiefly deals with the aspect of the Indies as part of the Netherlands' empire. This however is only an appearance, because, from early times, and particularly since the arrival of the commercial nations from the West, the place of the Indies in Asia was dependent on the relationship of the Indies to Europe. Therefore, though we may attempt to view the Indies in Asia as a distinct unity, we can not separate them from the Dutch Empire of which they form part.

Objections are sometimes raised against the use of the word Dutch in the

„Prajurits", soldiers of the Sultan of Jocjaka

appellation "Dutch East Indies", because this disregards the fact, that the East Indies "existed and lived long before the first Dutchman had made his appearance in the tropics". A worse disavowal of reality however is it, to call the present Indies by names borrowed from race, language or geographical location, and thus ignore the fact, that the Indies owe their position as a political-economic unity *exclusively* to the operation of Dutch rule and Dutch energy.

The Indies, then, form by their very nature a traffic belt and their original significance was dependent on the character of this traffic. Freedom of traffic on the seas formerly no more existed than freedom of traffic on the rivers. Seatrade was exclusively coastwise trade, and just as people living by a river usually monopolise all trade passing along its banks, the inhabitants of a coast try to control all traffic in their coastal waters. A strict application of this principle however would have prevented all expansion of commerce. The seagoing merchants therefore procured themselves an entrance to the neighbouring coasts by establishing port-settlements, which served as bases for the seasonal trade dependent on wind and current.

In this way the strongest commercial nations in each period obtained the hegemony and almost the monopoly in large parts of the oriental seas. Before the arrival of the Europeans no nation had succeeded in controlling the traffic both on the southern and the eastern coasts of the Asiatic continent. It is true that in very early times Indian merchants ventured into the Gulf of Siam and the South-China Sea and Chinese junks were found in the Gulf of Pegu and the Andaman Sea, but this did not lead to permanent settlements. There was always a strong rivalry and before the arrival of the Westerners, as far as we know, there never was a time in which the Indians or Arabs controlled the traffic in the South-China Sea or, vice-versa, the Chinese that in the Gulf of Bengal, except, as regards the latter, for a brief period in the early part of the fifteenth century. The Indies therefore, while being a thoroughfare, generally also acted as a barrier. The ports of the Archipelago provided a convenient rendez-vous for merchants from the Middle and the Far East; in this fact lay their importance. It was a passive part that the Indies played in this process. Their inhabitants, immigrants from Further India, were as yet not very numerous and still in a primitive stage of civilisation. They were not able to act themselves as go-betweens in these trade relations. Navigators from the north and the west were obliged to sail to the Indies and establish settlements. Whether trade led to colonisation or colonisation to trade is an insoluble question!

The Chinese came from the north. People from South-China formed connections with native chieftains on the coast and founded semi-independent colonies. The Chinese Court entertained certain relations with these colonies. In the early 15th century there was a marked tendency on the part of the Chinese to establish their suzerainty in the Archipelago.

Westward, in the Indian Ocean, the traffic on the east and on the west coasts of India was not interdependent. Trade in the Arabian sea with its entrance into the Persian Gulf and into the Red Sea and the Near East as hinterland was developed earlier than that in the Gulf of Bengal, and to bring about contact between these two worlds around Cape Comorin was somewhat hazardous. Small wonder, therefore, that the first arrivals in the Archipelago from India hailed from the east coast, the estuary of the Kistna, that is, the river which borders the later Coromandel to the north. These people were Brahmins. After them followed Buddhist emigrants from the west coast, from Gujarat, the commercial centre round the Gulf of Cambay. The Buddhists chased the Brahmins from Java; these went further eastward where they founded new states. Their influence was at its height towards the end of the 14th century. The contact between Chinese and Hindu influences was only incidental and no sort of permanent political unity or coherent commercial entity with a place of its own between the eastern and western fronts of the Asiatic continent was established.

Meanwhile the inhabitants of the East Indies themselves began to play their part in commerce. The Malays spread all over the Archipelago and controlled the trade on the inland seas especially in the western half. By settling on the island of Singapore in 1160 they established themselves on the principal channel, where they also controlled the passage and thus the outward trade of the Archipelago. This was intolerable for the greatest territorial power in the East Indies, the empire of Singasari in East Java, which aspired toward extending its authority over Sumatra. In 1252 it conquered Singapore, and the Malays thereupon founded a new emporium, Malacca. Here they came into contact with the Arabs. These, bearers and propagators of the Islamic faith, were founding colonies everywhere along the Indian coasts. Pushing ever further to the east they finally archieved commercial hegemony in the entire Indian Ocean and tried to penetrate into the South China Sea. Malacca now became the centre of radiation of Islam through the Archipelago. By the end of the 15th century all coastal places on Sumatra and Java had become Mohammedan, and Hindu influence was moribund.

The commercial power of the Malays was based on their control of the East Indian products wanted by the Arabs: pepper and the two monopoly products from the east of the Archipelago, cloves and nutmeg. These spices had, long before, procured the Indies a place, not only in Asiatic, but in world commerce, for as early as 200 A.D. they had reached Rome, the capital of Europe, by way of Alexandria. This Indo-European trade was carried on in stages. Now the Arabs succeeded in getting the entire trade from Malacca to Alexandria into their hands.

Next in turn came the Portuguese, who, sailing around the Cape of Good Hope, and conquering Ormuz, Goa and Malacca, seized the control of the entire trade route from the Moluccas to the staple market in Lisbon. The antagonism both of interest and religion made the Portuguese and the "Moors" implacable enemies. Chinese merchants, meeting the Portuguese at Malacca, and seeing in them desirable allies against the Arabs who were pushing into the South China Sea, showed them the way to Canton, the metropolis of South China, and the Portuguese obtained a foothold at Macao, not far from Canton. Thus the direct navigation between India and China began to be in the hands of one commercial power and the Archipelago threatened to become a mere hinterland and appendix to Malacca.

It was made a centre by the arrival of the Dutch. These, coming from the Cape and, avoiding the Arabic and Indian ports, sailing straight northeastward, entered the Archipelago through the Straits of Sunda. They established themselves at Bantam, in the back of the Portuguese position on Malacca. They drove the Portuguese from the Moluccas, where they soon occupied the principal spice islands. At first they had to share the trade with the British, but, after these too had been driven out, they exercised sole control. Consequently their East Indian Company, before long, became the first great European territorial power in the East, with Batavia as emporium.

The view, here presented, may seem strange, if one takes into consideration how extremely small were the territories under the actual rule of the Company: nothing more, in fact, than the Moluccas and the hinterland of Batavia. The larger islands, however, were valueless from an economic point of view. The Company's rule in the island world of the East Indies was, pre-eminently, a rule over a sea-dominion; one only gets a true picture of its extent by regarding its area on land and sea as one. The unity thus created, it is true, was a negative one, for the Company used all its military power and political prestige to create and maintain the seclusion of the Indies from all other mercantile nations. Though it never completely controlled the East Indian internal trade, it played at once an increasingly great part as mediator and regulator in matters of domestic policy in the countries of the Archipelago, the more so, since almost from the beginning, the government was conducted from the citadel at Batavia as a centre. The Indies therefore only won a permanent place of their own after they had been paled off by the Company as its own preserve for commerce and production. For the Company controlled their outward trade; all their products were sold abroad from one hand. The place which the Indies thus obtained in the world was an important one; though the producing centre, the spice islands, were small in size, the commercial value of its products for many years exceeded the value of the entire remaining oriental trade.

All this chiefly regards the place of the Indies on the world market. What did the Company contribute towards creating a place for the Indies in Asia?

The Company was in origin an import concern; its ships sailed to the East in order to purchase certain goods, especially spice. Preferably these were bought in the producing countries, where, unless there was too much competition, they would naturally be cheapest; they might however be bought wherever they were obtainable at a fair price. All cargoes taken on from Mocca to Deshima in Japan were forwarded to Batavia from where, in so far as the goods had been ordered at home, they were shipped on fixed dates by the return fleet. Only so much was ordered as, with a view to demand and stock on hand at home, seemed to promise a possibility of selling at a reasonable profit. The prices were maintained at the level necessary to pay annually, and as regularly as possible, high dividends on the relatively modest capital invested. This trade restriction, based on monopoly of transportation, was severely criticised especially towards the end of the 18th century, when the idea of free trade began to be popular, and even today colonial historians voice that criticism. Says one of these: "The figures do not give the impression that in the long run monopoly was more profitable for the Company than competition would have been". Such criticism forgets that practically all colonial wares which the Company sold in Europe were articles of luxury with a market which, by its very nature, was limited and which, for some of the wares that were in greatest demand, such as spice, diminished considerably in the course of years. An irregular import in unlimited quantities would immediately have changed profit into loss. Even a slightly larger supply would at once have affected the prices so unfavourably, that a larger turnover would not have made good the smaller margin of profit. From the point of view of sales policy at home the maintenance of the trade restriction was therefore strictly necessary. However, if the Company's activity had been limited to export from the Indies to Holland, this restriction would have circumscribed too much the scope and profit-earning capacity of the Company's trade. Moreover there were other disadvantages in an exclusively European trade. This meant carrying goods away from the East without being able to sell anything in return needed by the Indian producers. It had therefore to be paid for in ready cash. The producers however preferred to do business with merchants who were able, like their Asiatic customers, to supply them with other goods, such as cloth, in return, rather than take money. Since these articles were not available at home, they had to be fetched in the same places where the Asiatic competitors obtained them. Thus, apart from the trade on Europe, a trade movement developed between the Archipelago where the Company was supreme through its monopolistic position, and the most distant Asiatic markets. Although this commerce certainly intended to facilitate purchase in the East Indies and thereby to feed the export to Europe, its large possibilities of profit soon justified its existence for its own sake. Batavia therefore played a dual part: it was the centre of a limited export to Europe, and it was the centre of a general Asiatic trade movement that could be illimitably expanded. After the establishment of the Company in the Archipelago this Asiatic trade developed with astonishing rapidity, but it did not prosper everywhere for long. Some factories, more especially those furthest west, had soon to be abandoned. Others, like Deshima furthest north, although they still yielded profit, had a more and more limited turnover. The factories in India proper on the other hand prospered greatly, in so far as the expenditure for defence did not swallow up the gross profit. Least of all was this the case in Bengal, where the Company did not own a fort.

The essential condition for the prosperity of this kind of commerce was the existence of a large measure of freedom to trade in the Asiatic commercial spheres outside the Archipelago. As soon as a more or less important monopoly zone developed there in imitation of that of the Dutch Company inside the Archipelago, it was all over with the exceptionally favourable position of the Company, based as it was on a happy combination of monopoly and free trade.

This is precisely what happened in the Ganges valley in the second half of the 18th century. The European trading companies had settled in India in the first place in the two old commercial centres from where the Hindoo colonists had started for the East Indies. From the unhealthy Kistna estuary on the coast the British moved in 1639 to fort St. George near Madras and from Surattee, on the Gulf of Cambay, where the French and Dutch also had a factory, the British in 1687 transferred their centre to Bombay, which they had obtained as a wedding gift at the marriage of Charles II to Catharine of Braganza. As a result of the sharp competition of the neighbouring foreign factories neither Madras nor Bombay could prosper. The British realised very well the advantage which their monopoly position in the Archipelago gave the Dutch, but the position of the London Company was too weak and that of the Indian princes, especially that of the Great-Mogol Aurangzeb, too strong, for them to think of following the Dutch example. A change came about when in 1707—1708 the various competing English companies were united into one United British Company, and when, on the other hand, after Aurangzeb's death in 1707, the empire of the Great-Mogol began to break up. Further fundamental changes were the result of the Seven Years' War, in the course of which the British gained the military and naval hegemony in Bengal. After 1771 the British Company was the *de facto* ruler of a large territory in the Ganges valley, which became the basis of the British Indian Empire. The British Company now used its territorial powers in Bengal to the same purpose as the Dutch had done in the Archipelago. It secured for itself a monopoly of all products. This meant that, since all opium had to be delivered to the British, the Dutch factories in Bengal, for which the opium trade had been the mainstay, were severely hit. They merely received a couple of hundred chests annually by way of transition. A small part of the Indian opium used to be sold at Batavia for shipment to Holland for medicinal purposes; of the major part that remained about two fifths were imported into the Archipelago and sold at monopoly pricess while three fifths were resold to the Chinese at Batavia who brought tea and took the opium as return cargo to China. Now the delicate connection of the Company's most lucrative branch of outer trade in India with the inner trade of the Archipelago and the re-export from there to China and Holland was severed. The Dutch Company in India never recovered from that blow. Even the prosperity of trade at Ceylon, requiring as it did expensive military protection, could not make up for this loss.

The Dutch monopoly in the Archipelago survived the establishment of the British monopoly in India only a few years. By the Peace of Paris of 1784 the Company was forced to grant the British free navigation in the Archipelago. This was merely the logical conclusion of a development that could no longer be arrested. Since through the decay of its seapower the Dutch Company was no longer able to maintain its monopoly, there had been for many years a British smuggling trade on the tin and spice islands, which sometimes even ventured to the very roadstead of Batavia. This trade was not without grave risks, because the sea passages in the Archipelago had been kept secret and were therefore insufficiently known to the British, though a semi-official English Seaman's Guide of that time contained sailing directions for those waters! This smuggling trade, which was not carried on by ships of the British Company but by so-called country-ships, belonging to free British or British-Indian traders, received a new stimulus, when the import of opium at Canton was forbidden by the Imperial Government. The British Company which officially could not compromise itself by smuggling, now sold its opium at public auction, and it was then shipped to Canton by the free traders in country ships. This led to a combination of the free British trade on South China with the smuggling trade on the Archipelago. The light and fast country-ships, chiefly laden with opium, would sail ahead of the heavy Company ships, the "East India men", destined for Canton, and, on the way, in the various ports of the western Archipelago they would pick up some secondary cargo in demand at Canton, — such things as tin on Banka, gold on Borneo, pepper in Palembang, ratan, betel and beeswax almost everywhere. This they would resell, against drafts on Canton, to the Company ships that in the meantime would turn up. The small craft would then undertake the voyage back to India, but the larger ones, laden to the hatches with opium, would accompany the fleet of the British Company to Canton. The meetingplace of these free traders and the Company ships was at first Banka, but after 1786 it became the present Penang in the Straits of Malacca, then called Prince of Wales Land. This served to protect the British China trade, but also to lure the remaining navigation away from Malacca, which was still Dutch. In this it succeeded only too well. Its situation was very favourable as a maritime base for further enterprises against Batavia; for that purpose it was fortified by (the later) Lord Wellington in 1797. His secretary was Raffles, who then acquired his views of the importance of the Straits of Malacca. By this development of the British India-China trade Batavia was gradually isolated, the more so because the British ships, homebound from China, that, in order to lose no time in the tea trade, did not touch any Indian ports en route, more and more began to avoid the Sunda Straits and to lay their course through the Straits of Bali, or, further eastward, by way of the "Eastern Passage" through the Moluccas. Long before the fall of the Company its fate as a commercial concern was decided, especially by the decline of its outer trade in India. Batavia, once the centre of its island empire and the emporium of an Asia-wide activity, was a deserted roadstead before it became a moribund city.

The hard lesson which the "Batavian Indies" drew from the downfall of the Company was this, that a colonial commerce, not based on production in the homeland, is in the long run an impossibility. It cannot be denied that the Company at times had realised this truth. At one time it obtained much sugar from Formosa; after the loss of that island it began to give its attention to the sugar industry in the vicinity of Batavia. The metal which it had to import, it also tried to mine within its own territory. Nearly all its efforts in that direction however failed. There is but one glorious exception: when the supply of coffee from Mocca met with obstacles, some shoots were successfully transplanted to Java. The cultivation of coffee was a resounding success and became one of the chief sources of profit to the Company, which was of the greater value, since the cultivation of cloves, which had also been transplanted to other regions, showed diminishing returns.

Though Batavia seemed moribund, it was not dead. In those years when all communication between the town and the homeland was cut off, the colony was kept alive by the revenue from coffee. It rose steadily in price because its most important producing centre in the West Indies, the island of San Domingo, had dropped out of the market, and ships of all flags came to fetch it from the once more teeming roadstead of Batavia.

After the restoration of Dutch sovereignty and the resumption of communication with the home country, this lesson was not forgotten by those who had witnessed this period of compulsory autarchy. The Governors-General, delegated by the Sovereign King to reorganise the government and the agrarian system, also learnt this lesson, though somewhat reluctantly. At a time when free trade and free industry, in imitation of England, was applauded nearly everywhere, in the Indies, after some experiments and failures with the then fashionable systems, van den Bosch, supported by a strong king, returned to the system of compulsory coffee cultivation, tried and improved by experience, and not found wanting in difficult years. The commercial colony which the Indies had been in the days of the Company, was now, under Dutch Government control, purposely reformed into an agricultural colony. The output of cheap staple products, ensured by the culture system, found a regular customer in the colonial staple market at Amsterdam. By this means the Indies were able to shift for themselves when, in 1829, the States-General were unwilling to vote the moneys for interest and discharge of loans concluded on behalf of the Indies for which they had stood security. By this means also the Indies, lately still necessitous, were able to come to the rescue when the homeland, as a result of the Belgian revolution, fell on evil days. It was not the fault of this much maligned system that the creditbalance was not employed for the benefit of the colony after the hour of danger at home was passed. In spite however of its spoliation of the colonial surplus Java prospered. The rapid and steady increase of its population is an index, entitling one to regard momentary want and local falling off of the population as merely incidental. The Moluccas had dropped out as a production area. Java for the time being was the real colony, for which the scarcely protected Outer Territories served as a glacis. Not until 1870 enough capital became free in the long impoverished homeland to develop these, beginning with the east coast of Sumatra.

The products grown in Java under the culture system were mostly shipped to Holland in Dutch ships and were *more majorum* publicly sold at Amsterdam by the Netherlands' Trading Society, founded for this purpose on the King's initiative. The output of the agricultural enterprises which, from 1870 on, developed on the Outer Islands, for the most part also reached the Amsterdam staple market, though mostly carried by ships under foreign flags. In so far did the Indies in the 19th century again become a Dutch colony and did the home country, apart from the important direct profit, regain the even more important indirect profit which the colonial staple market at Amsterdam and the activity of the Company's sales had given the Republic. Nevertheless the advantageous position of the days of the Company could not be entirely restored after 1816. The direct trade from Europe and India through the Malacca Straits increased and was regularised after Raffles had refounded Singapore. The unprecedented and rapid prosperity of this new trading centre was no doubt partly due to its being a free port, as was generally recognized at the time, partly also to its location on the shortest route from the Indian Ocean to the South-China Sea. Though for sailing-vessels this shortest route was not always the best, because of the irregularity of the monsoon winds in the Malacca Straits, for which reason the longer route through Sunda Straits sometimes was preferred, the advent of the steamship gave Singapore definitely the advantage of the shortest route.

However hard King William the First strove to make the relationship between Holland and its colonies closer, it was impossible to undo the influence of the founding of Singapore and the preponderance which British commercial houses had gained during the British occupation of Java. The inner trade of the Archipelago, never entirely controlled by the Company, carried on an independent existence. The native products especially of the Outer Islands continued to find their way to Singapore and all the more easily, because the regular shipping connections, subsidised by the Government, were operated by a British firm. This evil was ended by the founding of the Dutch "Packet" Steamship Company.

In the 19th century then the interdependence of the export to Holland and the outer trade of the Indies never became as close as it had been in the days of the Company's prosperity. As before, however, the place of the Indies as a production area remained more important for the world market than for Asia. The value of the Indian products, exported either directly or via Singapore to Holland and other European countries, exceeds many times that of the export to Asiatic customers.

This fact far from prejudiced the development of a place of their own for the Indies in Asia. On the contrary. The exploitation of the Outer Islands by European capital for the European market compelled the Government to more intensive political interference. From 1898 onward the Outer Islands in the entire Archipelago were, one after the other, rapidly brought under direct governmental control.

The results of this development in many domains of life are described in the following chapters. They may be summed up in a few words. United, under the Company, as a commercial zone, reared, under the Crown, as an agricultural colony, the Indies realised, under the Law, their political unity and so, in principle, their national individuality. There is some reason to stress this point. An unrealistic dogmatism, to the detriment of both Holland and the Indies, has attempted to create an irreconcilable antagonism between Holland's leadership and Indian independence. An historical view shows the opposite! For the great paradox, governing the development of the Indies into a unity is this: the foreign domination did not alienate the Indies from their own character but revealed this to them; Dutch leadership did not rob the Indies of their place in Asia but, on the contrary, gave them their place.

CHAPTER 4

The Chinese

A mere generation ago the importance of the Japanese for the Dutch East Indies was all but negligible. The Chinese was everything. There was no commercial centre that did not teem with all kinds of Chinese, while the Japanese, with the exception of a certain kind of women, were almost entirely absent. In the course of years this altered. The Chinese remained still far more numerous, but their importance decreased and the Japanese, though not very strong numerically, gained a position in commercial life analogous to, and yet differing from, that of the Europeans. It differed chiefly in that he aimed at being sufficient unto himself and did not desire any middleman between himself and the native consumer and producer, while the European formed a kind of duality with the Chinese: the former as importer or exporter, the latter as middleman. Though some Chinese traded without European connection, yet the part of middleman was characteristic for the large majority of those engaged in commerce.

Long before the Dutch arrived in the Archipelago, the Chinese were there, not only as traders, but also as adventurers who founded shortlived states. The "Son of Heaven" regarded himself as the suzerain of all surrounding barbarians and he saw to it that he received fitting tribute at regular intervals.

During these centuries there were no Japanese. Perhaps an occasional Japanese navigator may have drifted south into tropical waters, but as a people they were unknown. One of the causes certainly was the prohibition under pain of death to leave the country. But this does not explain everything. The Japanese do not seem to have felt the urge to go south of the Southern Chinese, who, like the Dutch and other peoples from Western Europe were irresistibly driven over the seven seas in quest of profit and booty. The emigration of the Japanese had to await impulses from above. When the

Emperor had been restored and imperial Japan began to dream dreams of world dominion, the Japanese were also sent south as bearers and servants of this imperial idea. From the first therefore there was in this case an organised movement, whereas the Chinese left their country in a disorderly stream that poured out over the land, where they hoped to find a better livelihood than in their own poverty-stricken country. No edicts against emigration which, during the Manchu dynasty, were no less severe than the prohibitions existing in Japan under the Shogunate, could dam that stream.

At an early date the Dutch perceived that they could best get along with the Chinese by leaving them to their own devices, and by not interfering with their private relationships, their family life, or anything which did not directly concern the Government. Considering the Chinese tendency to live, with as many relatives as possible, close together within as narrow a space as possible, the so-called "Chinese camps" soon developed, that is, special quarters of the town, where, at first entirely of their own free will, lived only Chinese. Further a kind of Chinese self-government was organised, in charge of all internal affairs within that "camp", consisting of a "major", assisted by "captains" and "lieutenants", — who, in spite of their military titles, had nothing martial about them, — and the Chinese were left in the enjoyment of their own manners and customs.

For several centuries the mutual relations were on the whole excellent, the one sad exception being the massacre of the Chinese at Batavia in 1740. Chinese society did not change much, and about 1900 it was, to a large extent, still the same as in Coen's day.

Their relations with the Dutch were chiefly commercial, but with the natives they were infinitely varied. In Borneo for example the Chinese washed gold, for which they had to pay tribute to the Sultans. Differences about the amount repeatedly led to armed conflicts and so, in order to protect themselves, the Chinese formed organised communities, little republics in fact, known as "kongsies". When the Dutch asserted their authority in West-Borneo, they clashed with these kongsies and abolished them, much to the chagrin of the Chinese. This more or less put a stop to the goldwashing business and the Chinese transformed themselves into the farmers which they are by nature and tradition. West-Borneo has in this way become one of the most intensely Chinese parts of the Archipelago.

Elsewhere the Chinese did not mine gold, but tin. Long before the Dutch they worked the tinmines on Banka in their own way and alternately they quarelled and made peace with the Sultan of Palembang who claimed his tribute of tin.

A place that has become entirely Chinese is Bagan Si Api Api, one of the largest fishing ports in the world, which produces "trassi". The smell in that place defies that of any centre of herring fisheries at the height of the season!

Though there has been no census since 1930 and consequently exact figures are not available, it is known that the total Chinese population of the Archipelago amounts to about one and a half million. Approximately half of these, called "peranakans", are born in the Indies and live on Java and the eastern islands. The other half are new immigrants, "sinkehs", who with the sweat of their labour have fertilised the later developed islands.

It is a truism to say that without the Chinese, though they are certainly no saints, the Indies would never have reached their economic prosperity.

The Japanese only arrived in appreciable numbers in the twentieth century. Many of these were no doubt people with secret missions, though it would be an exaggeration to say that they were all spies. It may be supposed that among them were the first pioneers of what turned out to be a considerable economic effort. It is well known that as a rule the Japanese are no match for the Chinese in matters of economy and trade, but, supported by the Japanese government and with a planned economy, things were different. The Japanese thus not only became serious competitors of the Europeans and the Chinese in the Dutch East Indies, but the entire European economic life and the Chinese commission-business were threatened in their very existence.

The Japanese had legal parity with the Europeans. In their hearts they felt far superior, but in reality they were a foreign element which the East-Indian society was not able to absorb and which remained strange to that society.

Since the beginning of this century Japan, in competition with Europe and America, gained a very important place as importer. But even before this she had also become one of the large exporters of the staple products of the Indian Archipelago. Hence the Chinese who in former centuries dominated the economic life, — for there were also Chinese wholesale houses, — were to a large extent ousted from their place by the Japanese, because, in spite of their greater natural commercial ability and the fact that in retail business they are easily superior to the Japanese, their particularism prevented them from looking beyond their own families and building up world organisations like the Japanese Mitsui and Mitsubishi.

The political statute of the Dutch East Indies makes a distinction between, on the one side, Europeans and those placed on a parity with them, and on the other, natives and those placed on a parity with them. Chinese and Japanese used to belong to the latter category. As soon however as Japan had emancipated itself and felt strong enough, after the Russo-Japanese war, it demanded and obtained for its subjects parity with Europeans. This measure offended the Chinese and was one of the contributing causes of the so-called Chinese movement.

It was however not only a question of parity. The Chinese were under a special regime of their own. The Company of old, not wishing to interfere in the internal affairs of its subjects, had left them in full enjoyment of their own institutions and customs. This entailed certain consequences that became the more pressing after the Dutch Commercial Code had been made applicable to the Chinese, especially those in Java. This had severely shaken the old Chinese business morals. It had also erroneously been held that Chinese husbands and wives were not married "in community of goods", so that Chinese family law including heredity law had been destroyed. For according to the old Chinese patriarchal law, far from having property, woman herself is her husband's property. As a result of this interference in the old Chinese customary law, a so-called Indo-Chinese customary law was developed, which varied from place to place, or rather was interpreted differently by successive law courts according to the lights of the various "experts" consulted.

In spite of these unquestionable blunders of the East-Indian legislature for a long time all seemed well with the Chinese. They prospered greatly and a powerful group was interested in the continuation of the existing state of affairs. Though there were some malcontents, the authorities believed they could leave the conditions unchanged. These included such regulations as sequestration within a certain quarter of the towns for all Chinese not specially exempted, the obligation of a travelling-permit even for short journeys, a different system of jurisdiction, a difference in fiscal obligations, etc. Once the Chinese "movement", originating from other causes, had been launched, these and other grievances were taken up.

These grievances only concerned those Chinese who were born in the Dutch East Indies and had their interests there. The others were politically interested in China itself.

Waking up to the necessity of reforms, the Government, from about 1908 on, inaugurated a series of measures designed to end the exceptional position of the Chinese. The Indo-Chinese customary law was abolished, and the entire Dutch civil code made applicable to Chinese with some minor exceptions in respect to marriage law. The Chinese were also granted the right of adoption, which, in the Chinese view, is of the greatest importance for ensuring the continuation of the familyline. A Chinese wife now married "in community of goods" and, moreover, polygamy was not allowed. Daughters, who, according to the old conceptions, only received a dowry but did not inherit, now had the same share in the inheritance as sons. The Chinese were now subject to the Dutch penal code with the exception of penal proceedings. This last exception was still felt as a grievance but its removal was dependent on a general reform of the East Indian judiciary system. Many other grievances also disappeared: there were no longer any compulsory sequestration or travelling-permits; the taxation system was unified; various governmental positions were opened to the Chinese; the institution of Chinese "officers" which had become an anachronism, was vanishing. It may be said therefore that there were no longer any grievances specifically Chinese.

In spite of this there was a small but turbulent group that remained very critical of Dutch East Indian governmental policy. Their aim was: back to China. They wished to be Chinese subjects and enjoy a kind of exterritoriality in the East Indies. Pretending to regard the Dutch as a passing phenomenon, they affiliated themselves with some extremists among the Indonesian nationalists. Others, however, while wishing to remain Chinese,

Morning effect in a Javanese villag

desired a loyal cooperation with the Government. Compared to the total mass of Chinese, sinkehs as well as peranakans, the group of the Government's opponents, though vocally very importunate, was exceedlingly small.

Not many years ago conditions in China were so unsettled through civil war that large numbers sought escape from starvation by emigration to foreign lands. They threatened to become a real invasion which it would be impossible to absorb. Restrictions had to be placed on the admission of immigrants in order to stem that tide. At the same time the altered economic conditions considerably reduced the need of Chinese coolies. Banka and Billiton which, so long as tin mining was done by manual labour, employed each respectively forty and twenty thousand Chinese coolies, mechanised this industry. Large dredging-mills do the work of hundreds of Chinese, and where once tens of thousands were needed, a few thousand were sufficient. Deli also used different methods. In place of the Chinese labourers natives were employed, especially in the cultivation of tobacco. Though in the exploitation of oil Chinese were still employed in large numbers, the other concerns in the Outer Islands also became more and more mechanised. Consequently conditions for the Chinese there resembled more closely those on Java. There the Chinese, as a rule, was not directly employed by Europeans. He was either independent or employed by another Chinese who sold to Europeans the product of his hands or brains. On the Outer Islands the large armies of Chinese coolies who worked on a contract basis for a fixed number of years were rapidly becoming a thing of the past. The small number of Chinese immigrants arrived during the last years no longer threatened to overwhelm the peranakans by sheer weight of numbers. They were, on the contrary, gradually being absorbed by East Indian society.

It is, of course, absurd to suppose that every Chinese, arriving in nothing but a hat and a pair of pants, died a millionnaire. Yet not a few made their fortunes in the Dutch East Indies. Though the days of great wealth were over there still were very well-to-do Chinese citizens. The sugar industry remained partly Chinese even after its modernisation and the introduction of scientific methods. In places like Semarang and Surabaja there were large Chinese business houses; most of these however gradually disappeared. Even the intermediary trade was no longer exclusively in Chinese hands.

Mission 5

With their position in business no longer safe, a new orientation for the Chinese became necessary. It was the Government that gave them that opportunity.

One of the symptoms of the Chinese national movement as reflected in the Dutch East Indies was a craving for modern education. In the East Indies, stimulated by Chinese reformers, this took the form of a desire for Chinese education which was to strengthen the ties between the homeland and the colonists who had largely lost the knowledge of the Chinese language. A great number of schools on this basis were founded by private subscription. The danger that the peranakan Chinese would become estranged from their adopted country was not imaginary. The Government at Batavia which had never concerned itself much about the education of the Chinese, now designed for them a primary school system where the teaching was entirely in Dutch. These schools were a resounding success and many graduates continued their studies in secondary schools and at the colleges and universities in Java and Holland. Many Chinese qualified as doctors, lawyers or engineers, and in this way new careers were opened up for them. For Europeans who often earned a good income in the Dutch East Indies in these professions, Chinese competition stole some of the golden opportunities. On the other hand, with natives also more and more following the professions, the traditional barriers between the races were crumbling and prejudices vanishing. The cooperation of all will be needed for the common weal of the Dutch East Indies in the future.

CHAPTER 5

Heathenism and Popular Religion

Every culture is more than the aggegrate of its component elements. The notion of cultural elements only serves to differentiate, not to separate. No cultural element exists by itself; it cannot be understood without its relation to other elements. A piece of cloth, or a gong, or a kris may be objects of material culture, but it should be remembered that they are also of great importance in magico-religious respect; a dowry does not only have an economic function but also serves other purposes; the organisation of the community and the family has many different aspects; public and private law frequently coalesce; the same person often is at the same time the secular and the spiritual chief of the community, that is, he is judge, scribe, immolator and medicine-man.

This relationship of the parts to the whole is true of all cultures, but it is particularly striking in the less differentiated primitive cultures. While in western culture religion, science, technique, art, politics, etc. for many people are separate domains which they definitely wish to keep separate, this is not so in the primitive world. Religion there is not a thing apart, in which one may or may not be interested. For the Timorese, the Dayak, the simple desa-man of Java, the Balinese, etc. religion is something that is given with existence itself and is inseparable from life. Religion is found wherever man lives, wherever culture exists, as are social organisation, art, means of livelihood, marriage etc.

In writing about heathenism and popular religion in the East-Indies one is compelled to review the entire culture of these regions. If special attention is given to the religious aspect of a cultural element, it should be kept in mind that in this way distinctions are made that are not real for the bearers of that culture.

Let us, by way of example, examine the magico-religious aspect of agriculture. The culture of the East Indies has an agricultural character throughout. Cattle-breeding, hunting, fishing and industry are all of secondary importance compared to agriculture. In many communities everyone from high to low works on the wet and dry fields. Problems of land-tenure, methods of tilling the soil, of sowing and reaping all have great ethnographical interest.

Take the rice-knives. They are used by women for cutting the rice on Java, Sumatra, Borneo, Celebes, the Philippines and on some of the Lesser Sunda Islands and the Moluccas. The rice-knife is also known on Malacca and far away in the interior of French Indo-China. This curious instrument, called *ani-ani*, goes back to very early times. In the East Indies it is certainly pre-Hindu. On Java therefore, from pre-historic times till to-day, rice has been reaped with a tool no more fit for the purpose than a pair of nail-scissors. Only in North Sumatra has it been largely supplanted by the sickle.

How is such uneconomic tenacity to be explained? It can only be understood, when we know the magico-religious ideas connected with harvesting. Rice is supposed to have a "soul" or "life-force" and the harvester is anxious not only to garner the grain but also this *sumangat*, without which rice has neither nutritive nor germinative power. In the ritual of harvesting the reinforcing and preserving of this rice-soul is therefore of vital importance, and various taboos serve this purpose. It is forbidden to shout or make other loud noises on the rice-field because it might frighten the *sumangat*. For the same reason the small rice-knife, completely concealed in the hand, is preferable to the terrifying sickle that would certainly frighten the rice-soul away. One should not even drop the rice-knife. Even where a sickle is used, a rice-knife serves for the ritual cutting of the first stalks. A rice-knife that comes into such close contact with the rice-soul should never be taken home so long as the field has not been completely reaped, for fear that the rice-soul might leave the field with it. The rice-soul on the other hand may be reinforced by inserting strengthening herbs into the bamboo handle of the rice-knife.

The outer form of this little knife also shows that such an object of utility can only be understood in the light of religion and magic. The knives often have the shape of a bird or are decorated with something resembling wings,

or with a horse or horse's head. On the magical principle that like produces
like these decorations serve to make the rice-knife go faster. The same principle is at the bottom of certain prohibitions. During the work on the field
women should not wear their hair loose lest the grains might get loose and
drop out of the ears. In Atchin it is taboo to carry bamboo-sticks on the
rice-field, lest the stalks might become as straight as the bamboo and so
have empty ears.

Though every one, engaged in agricultural work, should observe various
prescriptions and prohibitions, intended to ensure a rich harvest, the agricultural priests, usually priestesses, should do so most strictly. They represent
the community and their knowledge of the agricultural ritual and their
strict observance of the ancient prescriptions, largely relieves the ordinary
man and woman from the burden of these indispensable magico-religious
obligations. Agriculture is only made possible by their action, not only in
the sense understood by the natives, but also by the fact that otherwise the
numerous taboos, the watching for favourable portents and the many
magico-religious rules of various kinds would prevent people from ever
settling down to the real business of agriculture.

This agricultural ritual is found in the heathen interior of Borneo as well
as among the Mohammedan Atchinese or Javanese and on Bali, with variations according to the different types of culture. On Bali the worship of the
spirits of the earth has developed into an elaborate ritual. Both there and
on Java there is a rice-goddess with a Hindu name and character (Dewi Sri)
who is the counterpart of the "rice-mother", worshipped elsewhere in the
Archipelago, the lifeforce or soul of the rice-field personified by one or more
sheaves of rice.

No more than the success of agriculture is dependent only on technical
skill in sowing, planting, weeding etc. but also on the knowledge of ritual
and taboos, does technical skill alone suffice for hunting, fishing, the building of a house or boat, the forging of a kris or gong. In all these enterprizes
rational and irrational notions are strangely mixed. Before the forging of a
kris of a gong, for example, the smith, by way of ritual preparation, retires
for some time from ordinary life. The work starts with a sacrifice. The smith
and his assistants bear names reminiscent of the mythical world. The entire
work has a definitely sacred character. A kris that will be just exactly

right takes a long time to forge. If all the rules are observed and the smith only works on the specially propitious days such a work may perhaps take a whole year.

In the building of a house the Indonesian will take many things into account which we ignore, and vice versa. In selecting a site for his building a western architect will be guided by economic or aesthetic considerations, but for the Oriental favourable or unfavourable portents decide his choice. In selecting the wood and other building materials other than practical motives play their part: one should never use timber from a tree felled by a storm, for that would shorten the life of the inhabitants of the house. If by chance the name of a certain kind of wood resembles the word for "to die", then it should not be used; on the other hand, if the name resembles words like "to grow rich", "to be strong", it is very auspicious. For moving into a new house portents should be favourable, a sacrifice should be performed and the house be consecrated by a ceremonial meal with the ancestors.

The hearth, as among many other peoples, is the dwelling-place of the spirits and everybody's house therefore, if not his castle, is his temple. The decoration reveals the magico-religious character of the house. Among the Toba- and Karo-Bataks of North Sumatra it is protected by wooden "lion-heads" in the façade and by horns placed on the roof-points. The rest of the Toba-Batak frontal decoration symbolises fecundity and the desire to bring this about for the benefit of the inhabitants.

It is but natural that decoration should give expression to popular religious conceptions. The woven patterns or those obtained by the technique of ikat or batik may also have a magical significance. The Timorese ikat-cloths, representing a woman in labour, have fecundity force; other cloths are supposed to bestow long life. The tattooing signs are also meant to have some religious-magical sense, but they are sometimes no longer understood and have degenerated into a traditional decoration.

The study of the Indonesian ornamentation may introduce us not only into the native religion, but also into the true religion of the people, which is not always the same. On Javanese batiks one finds motifs of a Hindu religious character, but the technique of batik is prehistoric, thus showing how the new is expressed in old forms. In Atchin and Minangkabau in the same way Koran texts are interwoven with an ornamentation of old Indonesian origin.

A more specially religious art is found on Bali. The rich ornamentation of the Balinese temples and of everything connected with the worship testifies to religious consciousness. Until recently all Balinese art was religious art. In modern times some secular art, both in painting and sculpture, is produced: a family scene, a ploughing buffalo, a figure, etc., etc.

In speaking of the religious aspect of agriculture, mention was made of the priestess or priest who represents the community in the work on the field. This is characteristic. In religious affairs a single man or woman may act as representative of a community, because such a community does not only have a local or economic or family character, but also a magico-religious one. A village for example represents more than a community of interests of a number of individuals dwelling together in a certain locality. The members of this community are joined together by the spiritual bond of blood-relationship, made a religious one by ancestor-worship. To be a member of the village entails taking part in the religious festivals, celebrated by the village in honour of the venerable founders. Even where foreign influences like Hinduism or Islam severed the family connection between the villagers and the celestial beings, similar obligations continue to exist. The gods are then regarded as the owners of the soil; the duty of the villagers, on Bali for instance, is to keep the village clean and to worship the gods.

It is obvious that in such a situation the secular head of the village also has a religious function. It is not possible to distinguish between the two. At the village festivals he acts as priest and performs the sacrifices on behalf of the villagers. The same holds true for rulers of larger communities. The word *datu*, meaning in Javanese "prince", "lord", has in Malay the meaning of "grandfather", "head of the family", and in Batak that of "priest". There are other words of this type, sometimes rendered by "chief", sometimes by "priest".

It can thus be proved that originally headship and priesthood were identical and that the chief was regarded as family-chief. Various circumstances brought about a differentiation. The family-priesthood in its purest form still exists whenever the members of the family sacrifice together. Then they are led by the elder.

The Bataks have a myth explaining the differentiation between *datu*-ship (priesthood) and *rajah*-ship (kingship): Si Rajah Batak, the mythical ancestor of all Bataks, had two sons. They wished to possess "what had never been seen or heard". Their father then offered a sacrifice to Debata Mulajadi Nabolon, the god-creator, and asked for his special blessing. The god then sent down two scrolls, one for each of the sons. The one contained: *datu*-wisdom, courage, the art of fencing and the art of leading people astray; the other: power to reign, agriculture, jurisdiction, commerce and wood-carving. — This myth evidently is intended to justify the existing state of affairs.

Apart from those who, on account of their special position as head of the family, or their special knowledge of agriculture, forging or architecture, take the lead in religious ceremonies, there are people who, by dint of special psychic gifts, are able to act as mediums. These are mostly women. They are consulted as seers or shamans in case of sickness, death or natural calamities. In their trance the seers ask the spirits or the gods the cause of the calamity and they fetch new life-force for the community from the other world. Through the mediation of the shaman the ordinary person enters into direct contact with the spirit, though the words, spoken through the shaman's mouth, may require further interpretation.

Prince, village-chief, priest, seer, shaman are all "special" people. They are the superiors who have power, they inspire respect and awe and as such they have a magico-religious aspect. Contact with them may bring blessings but also calamities to the ordinary person. They are bearers of *mana*, disposing of special powers that may be used either for people's benefit or detriment.

The medicine man may smear a sick man with his saliva and thus transfer some of his power to him. The *rajah* lays his hands on a new-born child and thus confers on him life-force. The bath-water of Javanese princes has medicinal force.

Man in general is a source of magical powers, but the "superiors" possess these in a special degree. The ordinary person however possesses similar powers with regard to those who are his inferiors. The relationship of superior and inferior has therefore more than a social significance. The superior should be treated with respect, not only because a different attitude might endanger one's social or economic position, but rather because one's own health and well-being, as well as the fortune of one's family are dependent on it.

Such statements naturally separate again what is inseparable in this oriental world. Yet the magico-religious character of these relationships colours them in a peculiar way. A single example may serve to illustrate this point.

In the West it is considered regrettable when the relationship between a young couple and the bride's parents is not all that could be desired. Much happiness may be spoiled and an estrangement may ensue between man and wife. From an economic point of view it may have definite disadvantages. All this is also true for the inhabitants of the East Indies, but there is more than this. Among the Bataks, Timorese, Ambonnese, Keiese, Tenimbarese and some other groups the young couple is in a curious position of dependence with regard to the wife's parents. The latter, the givers of the bride, are the superiors, while the young couple and the entire patrilineal family-group of the groom, the takers of the bride, are the inferiors. The givers of the bride are bearers of *mana* and in a proper relationship the takers of the bride will experience its favourable effect. Friction, on the other hand, will bring about evil results: the young couple will remain childless, or the children that are born die young, or the harvest not be prosperous, etc. Matters can only improve after husband and wife, in a ceremonial manner, have offered presents, confessed their guilt and begged forgiveness. Then the givers of the bride will likewise, in a ceremonial manner, give presents in return and speak fine words that will show their good will and confer their blessing on the young couple. For words spoken and presents given by bearers of *mana* are charged with beneficial force.

Such powerful words also play a part in jurisdiction. The oath taken by native witnesses and the accused even when Europeans are presiding still has, as a rule, the old heathen form of a conditional curse over oneself: "May I die if I do not speak the truth". Sometimes an act is performed to reinforce the power of these words. On Seran during the oath a man dips his weapon in a basin containing a mixture of powerful herbs. If one intends to swear a false oath one should protect oneself against the evil results of the curse invoked by wearing a special curse-averting charm.

In case the oath does not bring a solution, an "ordeal" may be resorted to in order to find out the truth. In a charge of witchcraft this is the only means of arriving at a verdict.

The penalties inflicted also have a peculiar function. A crime disturbs the cosmic equilibrium which can only be restored by an act of propitiation, that is, either by paying an expiatory fine or, in case of a murder, by a death. It is however not strictly necessary that the guilty person himself should die. It is sufficient that a slave be put to death in his place: the blood that is shed will redeem the crime.

In other cases such as witchcraft the guilty person may only be drowned or beaten to death because the blood of such a person should not stain the earth, lest it become arid forever.

Let us now turn for a moment to the magico-religious aspect of the social organisation. It has already been observed that the chiefs are bearers of *mana* and that superiors have magical powers which inferiors should always heed. In societies in which the class-system has been developed this is even more apparent. In the Buginese creation-myth the nobles are the direct descendants of the gods: the son of the god of the heavens married the daughter of the god of the netherworld and they became the ancestors of the higher classes; the descendants of the servants, male and female, forming their train, became the ordinary mortals Similarly in the myths of other peoples the princes trace their familytree back to some god or demi-god.

For the ordinary man or woman of the people the prince himself may be a kind of divine being, whose presence he cannot bear. If an ordinary Toraja should see the princess of Luwu, his body would swell up till he died. The great Singa Mangarajah of the Bataks who, in the beginning of this century, was killed in action against the Dutch, still lives in the minds of the Bataks as a kind of Barbarossa and they believe that some time he will lead them to greatness and independence.

It is however not the class organisation alone that has a religious foundation. The same is true of the classification in age-groups which is so characteristic of primitive societies. The transition from one age-group to another is always associated with or rather effected by a number of ceremonies, generally called "rites de passage". The ceremonies at or immediately

after the birth of a child, when it receives its name or when its hair is cut
for the first time, effect its admission into the community of father's and
mother's relatives. If a child dies before it has been received in this manner
little notice is taken of its demise and it is not buried with the usual care.

The passing from childhood into the marriageable age is of special importance. The rites of puberty such as filing of the teeth, circumcision and
tattooing can only be understood as "rites de passage". They owe their
significance partly to the fact that the age-group of marriageable and nubile
young men and women socially is of great importance. These young folk
are the *spes patriae;* among them are the great head-hunters and before
they are married these men, living together in their young-men's houses,
sometimes behave like little tyrants. They associate in a kind of youth-
leagues; for young women there are similar organisations. They form a
society of their own within that of the adults and their mutual relations are
sometimes very free.

On Bali, where these youth-leagues play a great part in village-life and
are subject to strict rules, they also have a special function in the religious
life. This is so on account of the fact that one can only remain a member of
the league so long as one has had no sexual intercourse. Such people are
"clean" and therefore very suitable for the intercourse with the gods.

On West-Seran and on New-Guinea the men form secret societies which
clearly show the magico-religious character of this kind of groups. Women
and children are the outsiders, the men-members the initiated. The ritual
life is largely bound up with these societies. The initiated know what is
necessary to dispose the spirits and gods favourably and thus to prosper the
harvest. At the ceremonies they are supposed to commune with the spirits of
the ancestors and they impersonate them in their masked dances.

Marriage introduces man into a new social group and the marriage ceremonies are to be regarded also as "rites de passage". The idea at the back
of the dowry can only be understood from a magical point of view. Originally the presents given as dowry were things possessing magical power like
elephant's teeth, old heirlooms that have acquired the *mana* of the venerable
ancestors, gongs, Company's cannon and such like. They were to ensure a
happy marriage blessed with many healthy children.

The last transition is that of death and the journey to the other world.

The ritual for the dead has retained the ideas of popular religion even whert Islam or Christianity are professed. The dead is supposed to remain at first near the grave where he should be taken care of and worshipped; later the soul departs for the other world where it joins the ancestors and almost completely severs the bonds with this world. Then is the time for the great festivals for the dead which, from an economic point of view, are ruinous. After that the mourning period is over and the many taboos, obligatory for the next-of-kin of the deceased, are lifted.

Thus from the cradle to beyond the grave man is supported by the repeated contact with the supernatural world and so one understands why the entire culture so clearly shows a religious aspect.

CHAPTER 6

The Diversity of Native Languages
and Literature

With regard to the languages spoken in the Dutch East Indies, their multiplicity and their extension, there are many confused and incomplete notions. What language do people speak in the Indies in so far as it is not Dutch? The first answer will be: Malay. Yes, but who speak Malay and where do they speak it? And is all Malay the same? And how about Java? Javanese of course. But this is not true for the entire island. In the western part people speak a language that certainly is similar to Javanese but nevertheless shows many peculiarities of its own: the vivacious and melodious Sundanese. In the eastern part are regions colonised by Madurese who speak their own language, and at Batavia the so-called Batavian Malay is current. All the same it is true that by far the larger part of the population of Java, that is about 30 million people, speak Javanese. There are however local differences; the standard-dialect is that of Solo because the principalities were long the political and longer still the cultural centre of the island.

The languages of the other islands also show a motley diversity. The larger ones are often conglomerations of dialects. On Sumatra one finds Atchinese, Gajo, a group of strongly varying Batak languages, Minangkabau on the west coast, the Lampong dialects in the south, and further some "Middle-Malay" idioms. The lesser islands like Nias, Enggano, Mentawei have each its own language, as well as the numerous islets in the eastern part of the Archipelago, not to mention the larger Celebes where about 35 different languages are spoken. Which means, in a region where the density of population is frequently low, that the number of people who speak some of these languages often does not surpass that of the inhabitants of a Dutch village.

The most wide-spread language of the centre of the island, the Bareë, extending over an area about ⅖ that of the Netherlands, is only spoken by approximately 40.000 people. In many parts of this island one need not travel far in order to pass into the domain of another language and geographically a language-zone is by no means always a unity: on a part of the north side of the neck of the island the inhabitants of the coast speak Tontoli, but along the coast one may also hear Tomini, Palu, Umalasa, Dampelasa, Tinombo and Buginese. Why Buginese, which properly belongs in the southwest of the island? Because the Buginese are sea-farers and traders and they colonised different parts of Celebes as well as of Borneo and the lesser islands.

Colonisation spread more than one idiom far beyond its original domain. The Malays in particular have always swarmed out as sea-farers. They were established along the rivers and coasts of Malacca and Sumatra on the important trade-route from the West to Java, the Moluccas and China. It is not surprising that at an early date the Malay state became a political centre. We know the language of this old country to a certain extent from ancient inscriptions: the literary language, based on a later form, was modernised and adapted as the official Malay in use by the Government, the present day schools and the modern Malay literature. Malay colonisation spread the language to other islands, and the Islam, the Portuguese and the Company all used this fairly easy idiom, disregarding its more complicated grammatical features, in order to make themselves understood all over the Archipelago. A special kind of Malay mixed with Portuguese words superseded the native languages on the coast of Ambon and Banda. Here it is the language of Christianity, elsewhere that of Islam.

The Company for its purposes used an adapted form of Malay which in written documents was somewhat better than that used in oral communications. Out of the daily intercourse between European masters and native servants of different speech, between Dutch merchants and Javanese, Sumatranese, Ambonese, etc., chiefly in the large trading-centres, a Malay idiom developed that shed the stricter forms and contained many elements from Portuguese, Javanese, Dutch and Chinese. It is a mere auxiliary language, only fit for communications of a simple and concrete kind.

This language is often called Low-Malay, a most unfortunate term, because it makes it seem to be a counterpart of the expression Low-Javanese, which denotes something entirely different. This is the ordinary Javanese language, used by friends and equals who converse without ceremony. In addressing superiors however certain words are replaced by synonyms, and in the intercourse with very exalted personages again other synonyms are used in mentioning the parts of their body, actions, possessions, feelings etc. This usage, not unknown even in our own language, has assumed exceptional proportions in Javanese. It must however be respected on pain of being considered rude and illbred. In the traditional old-fashioned Javanese society where every one knew his place it was comparatively easy to observe this custom, but in our times, now people of rather low origin by their education and position in a modernised society no longer consider themselves the inferiors of those who would be their superiors according to the old conceptions, this peculiarity of their language is felt by many to be very cumbersome. Better education at colleges and universities, where they were taught in Dutch and often lived in a Dutch milieu, has estranged many young Javanese from the language and thought of their parents. For foreigners this peculiarity of Javanese, along with its rich vocabulary and the difficulties of its construction, differing a good deal from our own, has been a deterrent, causing those for whom, because of their work and position, it would have been better to use Javanese, to resort to Malay or Dutch.

A common feature of all Indonesian languages is their lack of formal grammar. They have very little declension and conjugation; even singular and plural are not distinguished. This does however not necessarily mean that they are all easy. They have a definite word-order and make use of a large number of auxiliary words, the proper function of which it is often hard to master. In vocabulary the Indonesian languages also show a strong resemblance. Many words are identical throughout the Archipelago: *lilin* is "candle" in Malay, Javanese, Batak and elsewhere; *pisau* or *piso* is "knife" on Java, among the Bataks, in Malay, among the Dayaks on Borneo and even in the Philippines. Other words show regular differences in form: Malay *rumah*, Javanese *omah* "house"; Malay *ratus*, Javanese *atus* "a hundred"; Malay *bulan*, Javanese *wulan* "the moon"; Malay *batuk*, Javanese *watuk* "to cough". These and other regular similarities and differences are explained by assuming that all these languages are related, in somewhat the same way as German, Swedish, Danish, Dutch, English are related and are derived from a supposed Proto-Germanic language, each having in the course of many centuries developed its own peculiar features. It is further assumed that the mother-language of all the Indonesian tongues was spoken long ago, in any case before the beginning of our era, in the coastal regions of Further India, from where the speakers of this language or of this group of closely related languages must have swarmed out. We have no direct literary evidence of these early wanderings and migrations of the Indonesians. It may however be assumed that they took place at different times and in different directions and that, after the various tribes had settled on the numerous islands of the Archipelago, there was mutual contact between neighbours, which again complicated the differentiation of the languages.

Apart from this influence of sister-languages, more than one language in the Archipelago was strongly influenced from abroad. In the first place from India. During several centuries the Hindus carried their rich and varied culture to Java and other parts of the Archipelago and so also enriched the language with many loanwords. A number of these spread further from Javanese or Malay. A great many Sanskrit words have become part and parcel of the language, as in Javanese *desa* "village", *bangsa* "people", *rajah* "prince" and scores of others; sometimes they are not in current usage but confined to the literary language, as *buminata* "prince". Later Islam introduced many Arabic and Persian terms. The Arabic words chiefly refer to the Islam religion and Islamic law, such as *salat* "daily worship", *majit* "corpse". Commercial terms like *traju* "scales", *bandar* "commercial town" come from Persian. The close trade relations existing particularly between the Malay part of the Archipelago and the South of India introduced many expressions from the languages there current, and in the last centuries came an increasing number of European, chiefly Dutch, words. Some of these were introduced in the period of the first relations with the West. Not a few Portuguese expressions are still in current use: *sepatu* "shoe", *bendéra* "flag", *kreta* "carriage". Among the Dutch words adopted in the early days of the Company are chiefly words pertaining to the simple material things of every-day life, much used in the intercourse with subordinates: *duwit* from "duit" (coin), *sopi* "zoopje" (a drink), *bolsak* "bultzak" (a mattress). The many loanwords from Dutch that in modern times have found their way into the language reflect the deep and far-reaching influence of Dutch cul-

Papuan village on a bay in New-Gu

ture on the population of the Archipelago. From government and jurisdiction came words like *inspèksi* (inspection), *sèrtipikat* (certificate), *pos* (post), *opisjiil* (official); many other words were introduced in every-day modern life together with the idea they stand for: *dokter* (doctor), *oto* (auto), *otèl* (hotel) etc. The younger generation, that has a keen interest in Western civilisation and that publishes periodicals of its own, frequently forges new expressions which are a mixture of literal translations of some Dutch idiom interspersed with untranslated Dutch words.

Foreign influence has raised the cultural level of many parts of the Archipelago and enriched the spiritual life of many generations of its inhabitants. Especially Java owes a large part of its considerable culture to the Hindus, witness its architecture, its religious currents and its literature. It would however be a mistake to suppose that without this influence all literary development as permanent expression of spiritual life would have been lacking. To a certain extent it is possible to form an idea of the level of Javanese and Malay culture before the advent of the Hindus, by comparing, on the one hand, the cultural circumstances, still prevailing among those people in the Archipelago that have lived outside of the cultural currents, like the peoples of Central Celebes or the interior of Borneo, with, on the other hand, the data found in Javanese or Malay literature. The idea of "literature" should of course be taken in a very wide sense and not be regarded as tantamount to *belles lettres*; even legends and songs that have been handed down orally in a more or less fixed form should be counted. Such a comparison shows that, before the penetration of Hindu culture, these peoples probably knew adages, formulas, prayers, popular sayings, saws, couched in a free rhythmic form that could easily be remembered and recited. They are marked by correspondence of words, parallel construction and other stylistic features. Such ancient literary forms, by no means restricted to the peoples of the Indies, still survive among conjurors, priests and priestesses who are fixed by tradition; there are also remnants of this type in adages and proverbs and in literature.

In the old Malay society the *pawang* was conversant with the art of composing such texts. The *pawang* was an expert in many things requiring special skill: gathering honey, fishing, orientation at sea, medicine; he banished

Mission 6

diseases, and knew the powerful formulas and how to compose them. In Central Celebes there are priestesses who maintain contact with the world of the gods and who, when they send their souls out of their bodies in order to travel to heaven, recite a long litany as an accompaniment.

Among the more progressive peoples this literature of formulas was overgrown by a luxuriant growth of poems and stories in diverse modes. It is however clear that popular poetry, couched in a free metrical form and handed down orally, is a continuation of this style. The so-called *pantuns* of the Malay often have stanzas of four lines consisting of eight to eleven or twelve syllables with alternating rhymes. A somewhat free but very good English translation of one of them runs:

> The fate of a dove is to fly.
> It flies to its nest on the knoll.
> The gate of true love is the eye.
> The prize of its quest is the soul.

Very striking are the internal rhymes, and the assonances which sometimes become complete consonance. A critical European may ask what is the connection between the two halves of such a stanza? Sometimes it is not even possible to give a satisfactory sense to the first half. These *pantuns* were therefore formerly regarded as mere jingles and it seemed hard to understand that the Malay could listen to them with rapt attention. They satisfy however the same primary needs as similar popular poems do among other peoples; they are fit for rhythmical recitation, they are marked by parallelism, assonance and rhyme, and the subject-matter is of a nature to touch the heart of the people: love, melancholy, sorrow, mourning, mockery, banter in half or almost wholly enigmatic language, in circumlocutions, allusions, and references, often repeating the same thing with different words. It should be remembered also that according to the old religious conceptions in the Archipelago certain words should not be mentioned because of the specially dreaded or sacred character of what they stand for, further that proposing riddles prospers the growth in nature, in short that in this society the connection between the word and what it expresses is very close and the word therefore may exercise magical influence. This belief, combined with a playful pleasure in poetry and in listening, plenty of leisure, an intimate knowledge of the life of plants and animals, finally an instinctive insight into man's interior life, all these factors form a fertile soil for the creation of such popular poems.

Intimacy with nature and animal life is also seen in the great number of animal stories: on Celebes the little bittern is the hero, on Java and among the Malays and Atchinese the *kantjil* or *pelanduk* (dwarf-deer) whose ruses and cunning are told in many a tale. Another type is romantic stories; here one finds old native elements and Indonesian variants of well-known fairy-tale motifs, such as the miraculous birth, the foundling who is recognised, love for a dream-prince who marries a divine being, the prince errant in quest of his princess, metamorphoses, magic rings, battles between invulner-able heroes and monsters, a princess in a magic palace, etc. etc. They also betray foreign influences, chiefly Hindu and Persian-Moslem: in Malay litera-ture several mixed tales composed out of old native and Hindu elements are interlarded with names of famous persons and towns from the Islamic world, like Harun-ar-Rasjid, Mecca and Damascus. There are also many Javanese and Malay versions of Indian and Arabic-Persian works, mainly stories about the principal figures of the Koran and Moslim history. There is, for example, a long Malay story about Iskander, a figure created by Moslem-Persian imagination, whose proto-type is Alexander the Great.

The traditions about *adat*, regulating rights and duties of individuals and groups, ritual, privileges and penalties, juridical rules etc. were handed down orally. They were regarded as the heritage of the ancestors, received from higher powers, either a god or the first founder of the tribe in a hoary past. Historical traditions go back to the first beginnings: the origin of the people and its ruling house. The "oldest" history is a time-less, mythological pre-history, beginning with creation or the supernatural birth of the founder of the house from a bamboo, or a golden globe, or foam, and then the bio-graphies of himself and his successors which often are a concatenation of fairy tale motifs. In more recent generations one meets bearers of historical names, but the romantic-anecdotical elements predominate. The interest centres around court events, treated uncritically from the point of view of the court itself and inspired by the belief that chanting the deeds of the ancestors, representing cosmic forces, re-invigorates the power of the ruler. It is not so much history as ethnology and sociology that derive benefit from a study of these tales except when the events narrated are not too far removed from the author. So for example the Buginese have elaborate notes on important events. Historical figures who made a special impression, striking events that fell within the sphere of interest of the native population, found a pen to describe them. The careers of the Governors General Speelman, van Imhoff and Daendels, the massacre of the Chinese, the expeditions to Bali and Borneo in modern times, the Atchinese war, a big fire, all such things are described in Malay literature.

The Javanese produced a more versatile and more interesting literature than the other peoples of the Archipelago. Unfortunately so far only part of it has been sufficiently studied because there are but a handful of Javanese scholars, mostly Dutch. These few however have achieved a great deal and the veil has been lifted from much of the ancient Javanese literature and history, thus restoring for the Javanese part of their own cultural treasures. Javanese literature is by far the oldest in the Indies. Not counting some inscriptions furnishing important data for ancient history, the existing Javanese writings cover a period of approximately a thousand years. They are usually written on specially prepared palmleaves in oblong shape, called *lontar*. The earlier works are written in Old-Javanese, which is very different from the modern language, both written and spoken. It is full of words borrowed from Sanskrit and the Old-Javanese writings are largely translations or adaptations of Sanskrit works. These were religious books, containing summaries of Brahmanistic or Buddhistic doctrine, prayers, mythology etc. They were translated so as to enable the faithful, not sufficiently conversant with the language of the original, to recite and understand them.

About the year 1000 A.D. adaptations were also made of Indian epics, first in abridged form, in prose, but later certain parts were recast in metrical forms, borrowed from the highly developed court art of India. These poems are very obscure; several have been rewritten in later periods of the language and in other literary forms. The influence which these episodes from the great Indian epics, the Mahabhárata and the Ramayana, have exercised on Javanese culture can hardly be overestimated. Suffice it to mention the *wajang*, the famous Javanese shadow-theatre. Its repertory is based on these epics, but the interesting point is that the various episodes and even the characters of the heroes are treated with such freedom that they are barely recognizable. Why and how this has come about has not yet been sufficiently explained.

The origin of the wajang itself is highly problematical. Various theories have been advanced by way of explanation. Some have argued, on insufficient grounds, that it came from India; others, that ceremonies in honour of the ancestors manifesting themselves as shades are at the origin of it; others again, that the wajang was a performance of a primitive "men's house ritual" to which only the adult men were admitted. None of these theories seems to be quite satisfactory. In any case a wajang performance is regarded as something "out of the ordinary"; fixed by certain rules and traditions it is something sacred and solemn. A mystical force radiates from the acting of the divine ancestors; it introduces the Javanese into life's mysteries and shows him how to behave. To witness the scenes of this imaginary shadow-world is for him in the highest degree educational and edifying.

The best creative period of this old native literature is long past. The peak of New-Javanese literature was reached between 1600 and 1750, that of Malay literature also in the 17th century. Among the Buginese even in the middle of last century chiefly old women alone were well acquainted with the great mythical epic *I La Galigo*. This does not mean however that at the turn of this century Javanese and Malay literature were dead. Much of it was still recited and so came within reach of the great masses of illiterates. Stories from the wajang and mystical tracts were also widely read and had their place in a good Javanese education that found its inspiration in the past.

In modern times western culture has not passed unnoticed. The Malay world, with less background in an old civilisation of its own and more accustomed to look abroad, produced a century ago a fore-runner, Abdullah. This remarkable man was active on Malacca as language-teacher in British service; keenly interested in western civilisation he burned with desire to let his fellow-countrymen share in it and raise their spiritual level. He wrote something entirely new: an autobiography full of interesting details. There is moreover native journalism which, from its first beginnings in the middle of the 19th century has made great strides as a champion of progress. The style and language of these periodicals have been much simplified and are strongly influenced by their western models.

In order to forestall the danger that, with the rapid increase of literate graduates of modern schools, printing-houses would throw a lot of inferior reading-matter on the market, the Government established a Bureau for Popular Literature which had the task of providing good books at low cost. At first some stories from native literature were published in a somewhat castigated form. Later a great number of Dutch and other western novels were translated and adapted, for example works of Swift, Marryat, Tolstoy, Dickens, Dumas, Shakespeare etc. At the same time handbooks of useful knowledge were printed: manuals for gardeners, electricians, painters, nurses, bookkeepers; books on hygiene and popular medicine, on history and geography, popular almanachs, educational periodicals. Western novels enjoy a greater popularity with the Malay-reading public than with the Javanese.

The production of original literature in the native languages has also been encouraged by this Bureau. A number of novels were written by natives, generally with a strong bias and not free from sensationalism, though some compare favourably with many a European product. They are interesting as symptoms of the new life born from the contact of East and West.

CHAPTER 7

Some Aspects of Native Art

Prehistory shows that even before the advent of the Hindus the Archipelago could boast of considerable culture. Though in the palaeolithic period the population still lived in a primitive, nomadic state, during the meso-lithic period they came in contact with people of a higher culture. In the neolithic period descendants of people from Yunnan in South-China migrated from Further India to certain islands of the Archipelago sailing in out-rigger prahu's. It is now generally admitted that this happened about 2000 B.C. They successively reached Malacca, Sumatra, Java, the Lesser Sunda Islands, the Moluccas, Borneo and Celebes. Another branch of these people left their traces in the Ganges-delta of India; a third in China, Formosa and Japan, the Philippines forming a bridge between Borneo and Formosa.

These people who came to trade, automatically brought new cultural elements with them. The result was the organisation of village life, house-building, weaving, pottery and other forms of industry. Retail trade began between the various islands.

A second cultural wave came from Tonkin. This invasion introduced bronze and iron into the Archipelago. From the village Dong-son in Tonkin, an important centre of the bronze industry, this type of civilisation often takes its name. It probably flourished in the Indies during the last three centuries B.C. One of its characteristic features are glass beads that may have come along the trade route from the eastern Mediterrean to China and further, or, possibly also, are of local origin. They are found in the huge stone sarcophagi, belonging to the megalithic culture.

When therefore, in the 4th and 5th centuries of our era, the Hindus came to trade, they found people with a measure of culture. It was profoundly affected by Brahmanism and Buddhism. Religious centres were formed at the courts of local princes, in whose honour temples and monuments were erected. This influence lasted for many centuries, being particularly strong on Java. From about the 13th century on the architecture and sculpture showed a more distinctly Javanese character: there is a great difference between the plan and style of the Borobudur (9th century) and the Shivaitic temple at Blitar (14th—15th century).

Islam brought a new stream of culture. About 1500 A.D. most of the coasts had been islamised. The old Hindu culture was only preserved in the east of Java and on Bali. The new Mohammedan rulers however built their mosques in Hindu-Javanese style and gates, doors and pulpits were decorated with antique motifs of which the heathen character betrays itself even under the seal of Islam.

The advent of the Portuguese and Dutch again introduced a different culture. Then, under Dutch rule, Western influences constantly increased. Education, missions, foreign import-articles, tourism, cinema, world-exhibitions, explorations, the trade in curios, — all these, together with the traffic on water, on land and in the air and the communication by telephone, telegraph and radio, break the isolation and conservatism of the old native society. Only where the native princes still rule there are radiating centres of the old culture, as for example in the Principalities and on Bali.

In spite of all these changes very old forms of art exist even today. Take a Papuan who is fixing a heavy stone head to his wooden club. He first wets the top of the stone with water mixed with sand. Then he rotates a bamboo-joint on it so long till the stone is pierced. Now 4000 years ago the material for a green bracelet was pierced in the same way. In that neolithic period tree-bark was beaten into clothing with the aid of a stone hammer. The same was done in the Hindu-Javanese period with this difference alone that then the hammer was of metal, but the Toraja of Celebes today still uses a stone.

One of the most common ornaments on objects from the bronze period was the spiral and its various derivatives such as the spiral with tangent, the double spiral and the spiral-meander. This motif, more than twenty-two centuries old in the Archipelago, is still in use among certain Papuan tribes and on Mentawei, and on Borneo it is used in the brass-foundries.

The technique used on Borneo and in Minangkabau is a continuation of the old art of casting "with lost mould" from the bronze period, although today soldered brass wire, bent into spirals, is also applied. Clever faking is stimulated by the popularity of the antiques. One of the most characteristic products of the bronze period is the kettle-drum. Its shape may be compared with certain drums still in use in Alor at the buying of a bride. The Alor type is somewhat narrower and the wooden drums of New-Guinea, in the form of an hour glass, are narrower still. The kettle-drums from the bronze period are particularly interesting for their decoration. They also occur in Indo-China, the country from whence at that time this culture spread to the Indies. On one of these Indo-Chinese drums the surface shows a man playing a mouth-organ. This mouth-organ is also represented on the reliefs of the Hindu-Javanese Borobudur and this same instrument is still played on Borneo and by the inhabitants of Laos. That drum of Hanoi also shows a ship with the bow in the shape of a bird's head. Similar ships are found on the painted boards, used by the Dayaks in the festivals for the dead, when the soul embarks for the land of the shades just as, with the ancient Greeks, it was ferried across the Styx by Charon. These kettle-drums also have a tri-angular ornament which, in various transformations, is found on bamboo tubes, woven materials, brasswork and batiks.

We know that in the megalithic culture shrines were built in the form of terraces. This style of architecture was preserved on Java till the later days of the Mojopahit period. The mountain-temple on the Lawu, the Chandi Sukuh, is just such a pre-historic monument under a Hindu-Javanese varnish. On Bali, in the neighbourhood of Kintamani, even today such a building of pre-historic architecture is still in use. Traces of megalithic culture are also found on Nias, Flores, Sumba, and in the Solor-Alor Archipelago, and even in the immediate vicinity of Batavia.

Native art can not be properly understood by one steeped in the ideals of ancient Greece and the Renaissance, or familiar only with the standards of modern European society. A different key is needed to open the doors of this strange sanctuary of art.

First then one should realise that the natives know nothing of Art, written with a capital. Their artists are anonymous; they do not seek individual fame. Their object is merely to create things that may have beneficial effect and endow their owner with prestige in his community. Beautiful means powerful, artistic means strong, decoration means invigoration.

A frog on the surface of a drum served to suggest the idea of rain and so bring about rain. Whether the frog was beautiful or not was immaterial: the sole purpose was to compel the heavy clouds to let loose their burden of water. Beautiful pieces simply have more magic power than ordinary ones. Even in our civilisation there are some customs like the use of a silver trowel at the laying of a foundation-stone or the bestowing of a handsome presentation sword that are relics of conceptions still fully alive among the Papuans of today. In many parts of the Archipelago such ideas still persist in spite of Hinduism, Islam or Christianity.

Hindu culture introduced a full-grown art that was at the same time learning. Still the old equivalence of beautiful and powerful continued to prevail. In the 9th century at certain places of Java and Bali a great many clay models of a stupa were cast from bronze moulds so that the faithful could take these home as a charm or present them as a votive offering. Now inside these miniature stupa-models clay-seals, inscribed with some powerful magic text, were inserted, and the bottom of the stupa was then closed. Obviously the purpose of the maker could not have been the beauty of the script, since nobody could see it; it was merely that of making a powerful object that could convey blessings and avert evil.

In a Balinese inscription one reads that a *Mpu*, a holy man, made a certain statue. Did he think of beauty when he made it? Not at all. His object was to obtain long life and the statue was a means to that end. When in 1365 the Buddhist monk Prapañca composed a "beautiful" poem, that is one according to the highly complicated rules of the art, the purpose of the poem was to glorify, and thereby fortify, the prince, some of whose increased power might radiate on the poet who knew the sacred poetic lore. When towards the end of the Hindu-Javanese period near Banjuwangi a terra-cotta image of a goddess of fecundity was made, nobody thought about "Art" or the individual creation of the "artist", but what mattered was the idea of fecundity conjured up by this clay object. This is the way to look upon most creative art of the Hindu-Javanese period, whether it be the stately reliefs of the Borobodur, or the scenes of Rāma's heroic deeds on the

Chandi Lara-Jonggrang, or the story of Krishna on the temple at Blitar.

This idea of the efficacious, magic means permeates not only art as expressed in stone sculpture. A certain arrangement of precious stones, a certain shape in gold or silver, wood or woven material, a certain form of language, prose or poetry, may serve this purpose just as well. Also a movement, a dance, a sound, a musical composition which pleases the gods and compels them to do what is wanted of them. By means of the religious festivals the gods are forced down to the earth and held there, people on Bali think. It is something automatic, the effect of a cause, and the initiated controls that cause. Therefore he is powerful and honoured for his learning, not his art.

The same idea prevails on Mohammedan Java. Just as a prehistoric axe is efficacious, so are a Hindu-Javanese statue, writing or ornament. Hindu-Javanese culture is still alive; its gods and heroes still throng the screen of the wajang. The name of the ancient heathen capital Mojopahit still retains magic force. Somewhere in a Mohammedan mosque a gateway dating from the days of Mojopahit is placed and worshipped. The link with the past is felt and preserved. The wajang reinforces the bond with the ancestors, in spite of the fact that it frequently has degenerated into a public amusement and gamelan music is now broadcast by radio.

During the last fifty years native arts and crafts generally have been on the decline and some techniques have even disappeared. Efforts are being made to save and promote some of them. Under European influence a new Balinese pictorial and sculptural art is developing which is of a secular character. The silverwork industry at Jocjacarta has been revived; this industry adapts itself easily to European demand and in decoration it takes up the Middle-Javanese and East-Javanese motifs in stone.

At Jocja a school of dramatic and chorographic arts and music has been established, where every one, including Europeans, may study these arts under the personal direction of the most gifted and most distinguished members of the Javanese nobility. Jocja also boasts of a school of industrial arts with an European principal, under whose direction native masters are teaching the various techniques. Native princes are interesting themselves in the preservation of native art. They organise from time to time great dances at their courts at which native and foreign guests are entertained in the most lavish manner.

Theoretically Christian Missions have no desire to undermine native art. Since in most cases however the expressions of this art have to do with heathen institutions, in practice it is not always possible to live up to this theory. Occasionally some form of art is lost but another comes in its place. Images of the Trinity inspired by old Middle-Javanese motifs were made by a Mohammedan Sundanese and on Bali the Last Supper was carved in tuff by a native convert. This art-problem confronts the missionary movement in many other countries and should be viewed in that larger connection. Although the solution is still in an experimental stage, it aims at preserving native style and technique, inspired by Christian symbolism.

CHAPTER 8

Government and Islam

Islam reached the Indies comparatively late. The immense distances and the absence of intensive direct communications between the East Indies and the countries that form the nucleus of the Islamic world easily account for this late arrival. When it came, it was exclusively from India. In the 12th century it appeared first on North Sumatra; from there in the 14th century large parts of Java were reached. In the 15th century the process of Islamisation was nearly completed, though even today its expansion continues among peoples professing some dynamistic religion. It would be tempting to discuss why it was so rapidly adopted and how it was freely adapted to the needs of its new followers. Here however we are dealing with the fact of its existence as the religion of the large majority of the population. How many Moslims there are in the East Indies it is impossible to say exactly, as the census never gave separate figures for religions. It is safe to estimate that in 1930 of the 60 million inhabitants then constituting the population of the East Indies not less than 54 millions were Moslims. In 1940 of about 70 million people there must have been at least 60 million Moslims.

The continued existence of Islam in the Indies was no doubt seriously threatened by the advent of the Europeans. It is indeed almost a miracle that at the time of the conquest no attempt was made to exterminate Islam. The customary view of the age was that subjects should embrace the faith of their ruler and it would not have been surprising if the East Indian Company had attempted a compulsory mass conversion. It never did, — not from any lofty principle, but simply because it went to the Indies to trade and for no other purpose. It did not even aim at the acquisition of land; far less was it interested in the native population and its salvation, in spite of occasional outbursts of zeal on paper. The display of such interest would have cost

money and that was scarcely made available even for the inevitable expenses entailed by the establishment of Dutch rule. The first principle of the
directors of the Company was economy: what mattered were the dividends,
indispensable for waging the war with Spain. There was therefore no question of any large-scale compulsory conversion. Proselitising might in some
cases even be a hindrance to trade. Only where christianisation proved possible without much trouble, expense or resistance, as on the island of Banda,
it came about early. Elsewhere abstention was the rule. Even the means for
a more peaceful and therefore less expensive method of christianisation were
stinted. The building of schools was limited as much as possible, and a
scheme for sending out parsons was heavily curtailed. Public opinion might
have wished differently, but its voice was not heard in the oligarchic ruling
circles. And how little was known about the East Indies and the indigenous
population! For sure there were scholars like Thomas Erpenius, the first
Professor of Arabic at the University of Leyden, who in 1616 published an
Arabic New Testament and in 1622 an Arabic edition of the Pentateuch,
both destined for the propagation of Christianity in the East Indies, but in
the counting-houses of the Company's shareholders little heed was paid to
such men.

So there never was any religious compulsion in the Indies. Tolerance, in
this case, was the result of niggardliness and nothing to be proud of. However, there it was, and the vice of avarice prevented our colonial rule being
indelibly tainted by the sin of religious intolerance, so common in that age.
When later the means for compulsion existed the spirit of the times had
changed and tolerance was the natural attitude.

Legislature showed the first symptom of this modern spirit in the Instructions for the Governor-General of 1803, the 13th article of which prescribed
religious "neutrality". This article is still part of the Statutory Law of the
Dutch East Indies. The treatment of Islam was not altered one whit by this
clause of 1803: it remained free as before. There was only one restriction,
as in the past: the Mecca pilgrimage was frowned upon. In 1716 the transportation of pilgrims on Company's ships had been forbidden, and even at
the close of the 18th century a special government licence was still required
for a pilgrimage. This was "because such vagrants are only harmful on account of their following among the Mohammedans". It was thought, not

entirely without cause, that every hadji came back from Mecca as a fanatic and ever after was a parasite on the native population. This policy was now continued in so far that in 1825 and in 1831 regulations were enacted making passports to Mecca very expensive in order to prevent a large increase of pilgrims. For the rest the Government abstained from all interference with Islam.

Any other policy would really have been impossible. Islam was far too imperfectly known to enable the Government to devise a positive Islam policy. In the first half of the 19th century expert advisers were totally lacking. This may seem strange to us who know that Islam is not only a religion but also a social system with a law of its own containing many provisions for the organisation of the state, matters therefore of the highest importance to the Government. The fault lay not so much with the Government as with the degree of Arabic scholarship attained. That scholarship, starting with Erpenius and continued by a series of very capable men, was in some respects quite admirable. The trouble with it however was that it was too much concerned with showing up the falsehoods of Islam as against the truths of Christianity and with translating the Bible and Summaries of the Creed into Arabic. Later, in the 18th century, Arabic was chiefly studied as an auxiliary language of Hebrew. There was a single scholar, Reland, who was interested in Islam as a religion, but even he confined his studies to dogmatic problems and did not furnish any facts on which to build an Islam policy. In the nineteenth century Arabic studies took a great flight: grammar, philology, history, science, geography, poetry, each of these studies had the predilection of some scholar. Especially in the second half of the century scholarly attention turned to Islam, but it was not until the fundamental work of Snouck Hurgronje threw a flood of new light on Islam law that the foundation was laid for a true Islam policy of the Government in modern times.

This Islam policy, as conceived by Snouck Hurgronje and adopted by the Government, chiefly consists in a vertical division of Islam into two parts. One part is the religion in a western sense. This remains free, in accordance with our entire constitutional system. This point is strongly emphasised: it is not permissible to argue that, since our Moslims in the Dutch East Indies are slack observants of their faith, they should be made subject to rules and regulations in all sorts of matters closely touching their religion, if to do so happens to be desirable from the Government's point if view. This would contravene the principle of freedom of religion that should on no account be violated. Islam however is more than a religion in a western sense. It is a system, not only regulating the relationship of man toward the Supreme Being, but also all social relationships among the followers of Islam. From a western point of view this is not religion and therefore the principle of unlimited freedom cannot be applied to this part of the system. Higher general interests such as the protection of the native population or assertion of the Government's authority may make intervention necessary. Resistance to such intervention should be put down, if need be, even by force of arms, for here the Government may act with a clear conscience and it should not brook any flouting of its authority in the pursuance of its lawful task, be the offenders "clothed in a venerable religious garb".

In this theory then the faith itself, the dogma including eschatology, remains free, although Mahdi expectations connected with ratu-adil ideas may sometimes compel the Government to intervene forcefully. Free also in principle remain the chief religious duties, the so-called five pillars (ritual purity, ceremonial worship, religious tax, fasting and pilgrimage), though certain rules have been fixed with regard to some of these subjects. Free from interference also remain those parts of Islam in its social aspect that are regarded by the Moslims themselves as being of a religious nature, as for example the rights of the individual and family-law, especially with regard to marriage, and hereditary law. Though the principle of division might permit interference in such matters, such interference would certainly be felt by Moslims all over the world as religious constraint. It is therefore wise not to insist, to respect these convictions for the present and to keep open the way for gradual changes. It is hoped that people will not cleave forever to antiquated institutions such as polygamy and unilateral repudiation and Moslim law as it is at present should therefore not be codified. Just as in the past "adat" deviated from certain rules of Moslim law it may do so in future and them recognition on our part should be readily given. Finally no compulsion should be applied in cases where individual Moslims still observe such ancient rulings of Moslim law as prohibition against taking interest, refusal of insurance etc. It may be expected that social evolution will take care of such survivals.

Interior of the Mosque at Medan with Mohammedans at their pr

So far then Islam remains free, but no further. It need therefore not be respected in so far as it has a political character, that is in such questions as the Khalifate, Pan-Islamism and the Holy War. Pan-Islamism for example, both in its classical and its modern form of concentration and association of all Moslims under the leadership of the strongest Moslim state, is inacceptable to us. Interference of any foreign power or prince with the population of the Dutch East Indies for which the Netherlands East-Indian Government alone is responsible, may not be permitted under any circumstances.

These principles, adopted by the Government as the basis for its Islam policy, have proved quite satisfactory. They are perfectly clear and simple.

Two of the "pillars" of Islam, though free in principle, nevertheless are subject to a certain supervision. In the first of these, the "djakat" or religious tax, being in the nature of munificence, the purpose is merely to guarantee the character of the subscriptions as free gifts. All pressure or coercion in the collection of this "djakat", be it with the best intentions, should be absent. Native officials should never enjoy any profit from the proceeds of these voluntary gifts. In cases where this contribution is customarily collected from a central point and the proceeds form the most important revenues of the personnel of the mosques in the capital-towns of districts and sub-districts, the officials should guard against malpractices in the administration and division of these funds.

The second pillar, the *haddj* or pilgrimage, was made truly free by the new regulations. Snouck Hurgronje showed that in modern conditions there is no danger to be feared from the large majority of pilgrims. Owing to the easy connections every year a very large number of pilgrims can take part in the haddj, so that there is no longer any special glamour about them. A sojourn in Arabia of a few months moreover, can not turn these pilgrims into fanatics. They do not find there anything else than purely religious edification. They do not understand Arabic and their time is fully occupied with sightseeing. A prudent attitude is only advisable in the case of the so-called *mukims*, who frequently study several years at Mecca and naturally become imbued with purely Moslim political views, impossible to realise in the Dutch East Indies under our rule.

Pilgrimage having been made free owing to this new view of the problem, the old hadji examination dating from 1859 and accentuating the excep-

Mission 7

tional and politically dangerous character of the pilgrims was abolished in
1902. The passport for hadjis was not abolished, but instead of aiming at
restricting pilgrimage, it now served to protect the pilgrims and consequently
was made very cheap. This protection especially in Arabia was not superfluous. It frequently happened that women were sold into slavery and men
engineered into debt and then pressed to work as coolies on plantations in
the Straits, not to return till after many years, if at all. In the general interest hygienic control of the pilgrims also proved imperative. They may now
only embark in a number of so-called pilgrims-ports and on their return
disembark only in certain ports. For their own protection pilgrims are required to be in possession of a return-ticket. Directions have been issued ensuring proper provisions for their care during the voyage. In Arabia there
is the supervision of the Dutch Legation at Djeddah established in 1872
(first as a consulate) and at Mecca itself of the native Vice-consul. The control of returning pilgrims on Java and Madura has now passed from the
Dutch to the native civil servants.

The complete freedom of pilgrimage is not without its drawbacks. Annually relatively large amounts are withdrawn from the native economy. So far
however it has not been thought necessary to restrict the haddj to circles
able to defray its costs from an economic surplus. Not only native society as
such is not benefited by the haddj; very often it is economically harmful for
the pilgrims personally. The voyage is often very rashly undertaken; debts
even are incurred for it. Before their departure they are told not to count on
any financial support from the Government, should they get into difficulties
in Arabia, but this deterrent, meant for their protection, has insufficient
effect. The only exception to this general rule is that needy pilgrims do get
medicine free. In spite of this principle the Gouvernment in 1933 lent its
aid in the repatriation of several thousands of so-called "Destitutes". A
slight restriction of the freedom of pilgrimage was introduced in 1928 when
it was ruled that passports should not only be withheld to persons trying to
evade financial obligations or judicial examination, but also those from
whom extremist propaganda among pilgrims might be expected.

Complaints about the existing institution of religious jurisdiction were
long-standing and numerous. Java, having accepted Islam relatively late
and possessing but few scholarly Moslims, differs from some other parts of

the East Indies and the rest of the Moslim world in that it does not know a special judge called *kali* or *kadi*, but this jurisdiction is exercised by the *penghulus*, the directors of the mosques. These are at the same time advisers in the district courts and marriage-officials but the income they draw from all these functions together is generally inadequate. The complaints concerned chiefly the expense of the procedure, the inexpertness of the judges, the lack of appeal and the indefiniteness of the judge's competence. The state of affairs was somewhat improved by the institution in 1882 of priest-councils presided over by the penghulu. Though from an Islamic point of view this was an error, since Moslim law only knows of one judge, in practice it did not make much difference. The executive and the judiciary were by this reform much more strictly separated than before when the native "Regents" often meddled with jurisdiction.

Since complaints about religious jurisdiction continued, after protracted deliberations in 1931 a new ordinance was passed. The competence of the judge was defined and hereditary law withdrawn from it. The penghulu became sole judge, assisted by two advisers. Their salaries were made more adequate, so that they should no longer be dependent on the proceeds of legal expenses, now to be paid into the Government's treasury. Finally a Court of appeal was created. The introduction of these reforms has unfortunately been delayed by the depression. Juridically the priest-councils therefore still exist, but from 1937 on the new ruling about the question of competence has been applied to them so that they do no longer take on cases of hereditary law. The Court of appeal has also been introduced in 1938. Further improvement may be expected from the introduction of a guaranteed financial position and a better education of the penghulus.

The political doctrines of Islam obliged the Government to supervise Mohammedan religious teaching. In 1905 a system of licenses was introduced, to be replaced in 1925 by an ordinance recognising only repressive control. Under the old system supervision was restricted to *gurus kitab*, giving advanced teaching in the law, and *gurus tarekat*, teachers of a mystic fraternity. The new ordinance also embraces *gurus Koran*, giving very elementary religious instruction. This new ordinance is generally found very unsatisfactory.

The Government also gives grants-in-aid to Mohammedan schools.

During the very fundamental discussion on education in the "Volksraad" in the session 1938—1939 the Government expressly declared not to have any preference for education based on Christian doctrines. If Moslim schools, chiefly established by modern organisations, receive far less subsidy than Christian schools, this is only due to the fact that they have started so much later and their schools are fewer in number. The Government also stated as its policy the organisation of "neutral" schools for the benefit of Moslims in regions that are in the main christianised.

In all matters concerning Islam the Government is advised by a special Advisory Bureau. Its Chief reports to the Governor-General directly. The post has been held by eminent orientalists like Snouck Hurgronje whose influence has been far-reaching. At a time when it was very hard to know what was going on in native society the personal investigations of the Adviser and his staff were indispensable. In modern times with native press, native societies and native members in the Volksraad there are many other means of finding out native public opinion. Hence the character of the Adviser's role is changing. Nevertheless in some form or other the Government will always have need of the advice of good oriental scholars.

CHAPTER 9

The Place of Christianity

PROTESTANT MISSIONS

Every student or visitor of the Indies comes in contact with mission-work. Protestant missions, with which this chapter is to deal, are largely the activity of different groups or denominations of Protestant Christianity in the Netherlands. For a small part they are an enterprize of the Protestant church established in the Indies itself, known as the "Indian Church". Still another part is the work of Protestant communities in other countries, such as the U.S.A., Germany and Switzerland. This is because Missions as an activity of the Christian church are a common interest of all Christian churches and groups and therefore have an international character.

In a book that presents a survey of what is being done in the Indies and what vital forces are active there, for purely practical reasons missionary activity should have its place. The Indies show a complexity of dynamic forces: political, governmental, economic, social, cultural, and, not in the last place, religious. The fact that these forces are operating in a "colonial" world lends a very special character to the nature of the problems and the ideals cherished. Today the word "colonial" suggests far more than the relation of dependence, in which, politically and economically, part of the tropical world finds itself with regard to a government controlled by people of an entirely different race and different mode of life. Such a definition was true in the days of the East Indian Company and part of the 19th century, when the world was still divided into a number of spiritually autonomous zones existing each after its own kind. Now however the political and economic leadership of the ruling nation is no more than the factual basis of the colonial relationship. This relationship itself today entails a much more far-reaching task. Colonising today does not only, and not even in the first place, mean a more or less intelligent political and economic control, but it implies a process, impossible to arrest, of incorporating into a dynamic world-unity nations that for many centuries have lived by principles and forms of life now sapped at the very root, thereby compelling these nations to strike new roots and shape their lives in entirely new forms. In other words, every colonial world is at present in a stage of transition, profoundly affecting the sentiments, ideas and forms of life of the indigenous population. The colonial problem points to a profound revolution of life now in progress throughout the colonial world. Properly speaking it is first and foremost a huge educational, that is, a spiritual problem, or, better still, a religious and moral one. All activity in leading positions does not only carry a political or technical responsibility, but also one of spiritual leadership.

No one who seriously considers the spiritual and material wellbeing of the population of the Indies should ignore these fundamentals of the present colonial problem and each feature of the total picture of the Indies should be regarded in this light. From this point of view Missions with their various activities of a religious, medical, social and educational character will be seen in their true place.

Once it is realised that the present colonial problem is first and foremost a spiritual one that sets an almost superhuman moral task, it will be clear that Missions as a factor in the life of the Indies deserve serious attention. By its very nature missionary activity seeks to lay new spiritual foundations, to renovate and reshape life in accordance with guiding and absolutely authoritative principles and its work therefore deals immediately with the most pressing problem of the population of the Indies, which is to find a solid foundation for life and to acquire universal principles fit to serve as beacons in this modern era.

However, in order to understand the nature of such an enterprise as Missions, it is not only necessary to see it against the background of the living problems of the Oriental world in which it appears, but also against its own background. What after all, is the missionary movement? This question deserves to be examined.

Missionary activity is characterictic of all religions carried by the conviction that they have to preach a universal vital truth valid for all mankind of every time and clime. Religion, differing in this from philosophy, is always first concerned with the obtaining of indestructible salvation; knowledge and understanding, though not necessarily absent, are of secondary importance. The religions which most strongly show the urge to preach to the world, each in its own way, this indestructible salvation are Islam, Buddhism and Christianity. History teaches that it is most potent of all in the latter. Christianity by its very nature and origin is a religion of salvation. This salvation must be proclaimed and preached, for this salvation does not merely or mostly concern the individual person, but the entire world. An open-minded examination of the Bible, the charter of Christianity, will find this everywhere expressed. According to this Bible God has revealed His divine plan of salvation for the world and mankind in the person, the words and works, the life, death and resurrection of Christ. Whosoever seeks to know God, should look at Christ. One of those words from the Bible says that the reason of this revelation incorporated in Christ is that God loves the *world*. In other words: the salvation is for the entire world and must be proclaimed to the entire world. It should find expression in communities of men who find unity in their knowledge that they share in this salvation and let their words, thoughts and deeds be directed by it. Missionary activity, apostolate, going forth into the entire world with the proclamation of salvation and the purpose of founding such communities of believers sharing in this salvation is therefore part of the very nature of the Christian faith. It would deny its own nature and origin by not showing this missionary urge. This is therefore an ineluctable necessity for the Christian Church and for every one who does not understand Christianity from without but from within. To believe in Christ means at the same time to discover and to profess that He is the only legitimate Lord of every separate individual and of the entire world. Missionary activity therefore is not really prompted by any injunction of the Bible, nor by the desire to convince dissentients of the validity of one's own supposed truth, but it is the direct result of the nature of the Gospel. True, universal salvation, experienced as a divine gift, can not remain shut up, but must be carried out into the world. Within the scope of this point of view, proper to Christianity, improvement of the world and men, though it may and should be one of its results, is not the real object of missionary activity.

After these brief remarks about the background of missions themselves let us now examine the significance and place of missions in the totality of life in the East Indies.

The total number of native Christians in the Archipelago that are the fruit of Protestant missions amounts now to more than 1½ millions. The distribution of these Christians over the various islands is of course very uneven. The oldest Christian territory is Ambon with the neighbouring Moluccas. No sooner had the East Indian Company conquered Ambon from the Portuguese in 1605, than it undertook to care for its spiritual needs. Among the population it found many Roman-Catholic Christians under the care and direction of priests working under the high patronage of the Portuguese authorities. These small groups of Christians now became the object of Reformed-Protestant care and served as starting-point for the Christianisation of Ambon, Saparua and Banda. For several centuries now the Ambonese have been a people of Christian convictions and till the present day they are of great importance for the missionary work in the Moluccas, on Halmaheira, Buru and New-Guinea. Ambon always is the reservoir for pioneers and auxiliary forces of Mission-work and education. This small nation therefore is of great importance for the eastern part of the Archipelago and puts its stamp on life in these regions, partly because it is Christian, partly because it has been so long under Dutch rule. In the minds of most inhabitants of the eastern Archipelago the *agama-Ambon* (the Ambonnese religion) is *the* religion. As a matter of course the *guru-Ambon* is *the* teacher.

In 1935 a very important change took place in the situation of Ambonnese Christianity. Until that time the Ambonnese Christians formed a dependent, administrative part of the "Indian Church"; since that year they are an autonomous entity with their own governing body, the Synod, and have a federative link only with the "Indian Church". This autonomous Moluccan church numbers about 200.000 members, and with renewed zeal its governing body has set about the religious, moral and ecclesiastical education of its members.

New-Guinea that now attracts a good deal of attention for political as well as for scientific and economic reasons (explorations!) enjoyed missionary interest as early as the beginning of the second half of the 19th century. For about forty years missionaries worked there with scant result. It was the time when New-Guinea was still a totally isolated and forgotten island. By its incorporation into the great world-traffic and by the more intensive activity of the Dutch authorities, forces were set going which disturbed the Papuan way of living and made the population seek a new hold in life. An ever continuing movement towards Christianity began. Now there are in northern New-Guinea more than 60.000 Christians.

On Halmaheira and Buru missionaries have worked for some scores of years; on these two islands together there are about 40.000 Christians.

For a century now the northern part of Celebes, the Minahassa, has been another Christian centre. The neighbouring islands of the Sangihe and Talaud group also are almost entirely Christian. Together they number approximately 400.000 Christians. The church here is now also autonomous and has merely a federative connection with the "Indian Church". The christianisation of Central Celebes is proceeding satisfactorily and is merely a question of time. Further south on the island missionaries are also very active.

In the south-eastern part of Borneo there is an autonomous Dayak church, not large in numbers (12.000), but, thanks to the support of Swiss and German missionaries of the Basel Mission, a very active one.

On Sumatra the Batak Christians are very important. Nearly the whole of Sumatra is Mohammedan and in Atchin and the Minangkabau there are Islam centres of great devotion. The Bataks round the Toba-lake however had not been islamised. About the middle of last century they came under the influence of German missionaries of the Rhineland mission, at a time when this region still was practically outside the sphere of Dutch official activity. Splendid work has been done among this refractory but gifted and energetic people. The steadily growing church has been autonomous since 1930; it has no less than 400.000 members and has undertaken missionary work of its own in the north of Sumatra. Ever since 1865 the Rhenish mission has also been established on the island of Nias, where it had a very dramatic history.

On Java with its dense Mohammedan population of 42 millions, missionary activity is varied. Its medical and educational work strikes the outsider most. There is some slight activity among the Madurese but more among the Chinese.

The East Indian Company never tried to introduce Christianity on Java. After 1800 the Government at first, fearing Islam, was averse to any efforts in that direction. About 1850 however it was found that on eastern Java, apart from any organised missionary activity, small groups of Christians had sprung up, that needed spiritual care. This was the beginning of Mission work on Java. At present there are 60 or 70 thousand Javanese Christians with their own autonomous churches on West, Central and East Java, in spiritual and material respect aided by the various missionary organisations.

On the Lesser Sunda Islands Protestant missions are active on Bali, Sumba and in the Timor-Archipelago. The work on Bali was undertaken by the native church of eastern Java; that in the Timor-Archipelago by the "Indian Church". Here about 150.000 Christians are now being organised into an autonomous church with a federative connection with the "Indian Church".

All this missionary work was undertaken by societies specially organised for this purpose or by some churches that regard missionary activity in a non-Christian world as their self-evident task. They need not be enumerated here. They are assisted in their work, requiring a thorough knowledge of people and language, by specially trained emissaries of the Netherlands' Bible Society. These men help the missionaries to find their way in the foreign world and prepare translations of the Bible and biblical text-books. The so-called "Indian Church" is of great importance for the development of native Christianity. This is the established church, organised by King William I from the remnants of the old Company's church. It now has two sections: the church of the European Protestant Christians (that is Europeans and Indo-Europeans of mixed blood), and the different native churches, each having their own synod and a measure of autonomy. In 1935 the church was disestablished, the state retaining certain financial obligations towards the church which however is free to direct its own affairs. The importance of the "Indian Church" for the development of Christian life in the Indies lies chiefly in the fact that Europeans and natives are united in it without difference of race or origin and this church creates the possibility that all native Protestant churches will some day grow into a unity.

The principal forms of missionary activity are: the propagation of the Gospel by word of mouth or by publications, religious and ordinary education, youth-work, work for women, hospitals and medical care, all kinds of social work. More than three hundred missionaries, about fifty doctors and more than a hundred women-assistants are engaged in this mission-work and devote themselves to the spiritual and physical needs of the population. Many hundreds of natives work as pastors of congregations, evangelists, teachers, nurses etc. Like all human endeavour this work is far from perfect but the driving power behind it is the desire to bring the Indies into living contact with the best that Europe has received and to renovate individuals and community through the life-forces of the Gospel. From a general point of view the eminent importance of mission-work is the fact that, by dint of its religious-moral character, it collaborates fundamentally towards finding the solution of the main problem of the Indies: the spiritual and moral renovation and activation of the native population. This work arises from the need to serve God and one's neighbour according to the deepest needs of that neighbour.

Formerly the dominating figure in mission-work was the European missionary. As a result of his own activity and that of his assistants communities of Christians grew up under his direction. Though the missionary as such has not disappeared, this picture is rapidly changing. In the native autonomous churches the full accent lies on the word autonomous. They carry the full responsibility for nurturing and expanding their own spiritual life and they in their turn undertake mission-work in their non-Christian environment. Thus more and more the problem will arise, how in an oriental fashion, in keeping with their own character, these churches will develop into a true Christian church. With this problem in mind in 1934 a theological college was founded, with the purpose of recruiting from the native world men capable of leadership in this new period of great opportunities and responsibilities.

ROMAN-CATHOLIC MISSIONS

On January 27th 1922, at Bandung, in the park opposite the palace of the Commander-in-Chief of the army, the life-sized statue was erected of the well-known Roman-Catholic missionary in Atchin, father Verbraak. The Government presented three guns towards casting this statue. "And they shall beat their swords into ploughshares" (Micah iv, 3). A symbolic action indeed! In the cultural work of peace which the Government undertook especially after the sanguinary Atchinese war, Missions also had their share.

In the 19th century for many decades Roman-Catholic Missions were almost exclusively interested in Europeans and "Indo-Europeans" (of mixed blood). There was no strategic plan for missions on a large scale. Catholics in Holland were only mildly interested and there were few trained men. The Jesuits who entered the mission-field in 1859 and were alone until 1903, did what they could to supply every demand for missionaries. Various circumstances caused such a demand in different places.

Missionary work on Flores was the result of a contract between the Netherlands and Portuguese governments in 1854 stipulating that the Roman Catholics living on that island were to be attended by Catholic priests. Journeys on Timor brought to light remarkable remnants of earlier missions. The population recognized in the Catholic priests the missionaries of yore and there were many applications for baptism. On the island of Banka in 1853 a mission station was founded at the request of Catholic Chinese coolies. Later, for the same purpose it was extended to the west coast of Borneo. In other places the government officials encouraged the starting of missionary stations in the hope that Christianity would have a beneficial influence on the development of the population. Great prudence was observed whenever the initiative came from the population, but in many cases it was felt that the requests should not be denied. The fact that in the Minahassa on Celebes in the 'seventies nearly three thousand people applied to travelling missionaries for baptism was the beginning of missionary work there. A few Bataks studying at Batavia and others who came in contact with missionaries at Medan took the initiative that led to the founding of the Batak mission.

Even for mission work among the Javanese the first impulse came from the population itself. Among Dutch mission circles and even among Catholics in the Indies the conversion of the Javanese was held to be impossible. It was very curious indeed that there was so little interest in the Javanese living, as it were, nextdoor. Not until a deputation of Javanese in the district of Semarang came to ask in person for missionaries was mission work begun there about 1900. The common fallacy that no Javanese, being Mohammedan, would ever become a Christian, soon vanished on nearer acquaintance with large groups of the population especially in the south of central Java.

From the turn of the century on, the encouragement from the Government in some cases and the unmistakable eagerness of the native population in others, completely changed the attitude of Catholics at home towards missions in the Dutch East Indies. The "call from afar" evoked a warm response in the mother country. The occupation of the mission fields, the increase in numbers and the improvement in calibre of the Catholic converts, especially during the last twenty years, has been beyond anything that could have been dreamt of in the last century.

Here the crucial question arises: is it possible to influence the soul and conscience of Oriental peoples as deeply as is required by the foreign "western" religion? How does the missionary succeed, while his countrymen have so much trouble with improvements of a technical, economic or social nature merely touching the externals of life?

The task of missions is conceived on such a high plane that it does not aim at a merely humanitarian goal. Their charitable works, however valuable in themselves, their purely cultural activities, though already a sufficient title for claiming a share in the common national task, are not their final object. Missionary activity is only satisfied if it can plant the tree, not if it can only tender the fruit. It wishes to impart the religious conviction, for only thus can the fruits of our civilisation permanently thrive.

To establish convictions then is the difficult task of missionary work taken as a whole. But the sphere to which convictions belong, though never unintellectual, is not purely intellectual either. No one who understands the preaching of Christianity as an expounding of Christian truths merely addressed to the intellect, grasps the meaning of missionary work. In order to infuse into the native a new insight, especially of religious matters, one should have his confidence and gain his sympathy. A prerequisite for this is to know him.

The study of language, customs and ideas is therefore the first condition for success. Comparatively few missionaries have completed a university course in language study or ethnology; nor is a theoretical knowledge of the different religions and their methods of propaganda valued overmuch. Without neglecting these auxiliary means the missionary prefers to study the living object in mission work itself and to acquire the linguistic knowledge in the concrete environment of his own mission field. One of our best linguists always had a living Javanese sitting by his Javanese dictionary, who did nothing but compose sentences; in this way for many years the meaning of words and sentences was explored. To learn the language in this way is at the same time to handle a key to the mysteries of ideas and customs.

The study of a living language is the study of the habits of thought. Only a knowledge of the language qualifies the missionary for observation of the conduct of the people among whom he has to work, and leads him to adapt himself to their character.

This principle led to the founding of mission study hostels for the future missionaries of the Javanese mission on Java itself. There the young recruits from Holland together with their native colleagues prepare themselves for their future task in a suitable environment.

A few examples may illustrate what has been said about the native character and the adaptation which is the result of proper understanding. A Hollander, disposed to be straightforward and consequently apt to be wanting in tact, has less appreciation for the tact and circumspection valued so much by others. A propos of the so-called lack of sincerity of the native this difference was once aptly characterised as: "For us the first law of the tongue is: do not ly; for the Javanese it is: do not offend." We, hyper-civilised Westerners and very matter-of-fact Dutchmen attach great value to the formation of capital even on a small scale. We are apt to overlook the fact that the Javanese is first and foremost a member of his community and that we ourselves are strongly individualistic. We do not understand why the Javanese does not save. But long intercourse with the native makes one realise, without entirely excusing the shortcoming, that Western thriftiness may come into conflict with his fixed social habits. The family bond is of such close and valuable intimacy that a thrifty person often would be regarded as a miserly egotist and perhaps be expelled altogether.

The adage "never the twain shall meet" is primarily true of the difference between East and West in views and convictions. If we were to see this as an essential difference, we should have to abandon mission work in oriental countries, since faith is a conviction. We must not suppose, however, that a conviction is only established as a result of reasoning or a purely intellectual process. One may explain to a Javanese that the God whom he knows and serves should be known and served in the way which He Himself has ordained. He may admit that the exposition of Christianity is beautiful and grand. He may nod approvingly. You flatter yourself that you are making good progress. But if finally you ask him what the thinks about it he will reply: "Yes, this is a fine religion for Hollanders, but we are Javanese . . ."

From his tone it is clear that his opinion is unshakable, firm as the mountains of Java. If the argument is continued with special emphasis on the unity of God and therefore of all religion, he does not go into that. Therein lies his strength. He will reply: "You are clever, we are stupid, we are only Javanese. Your religion is more beautiful than ours; it is the religion of the Hollanders, and we are Javanese . . .!"

What is at the back of all this? The Javanese is a slave of tradition, of his *adat*. His religion is part of that tradition, that *adat*. He is not used to reasoning about such matters. He follows the *adat*. It is unheard of that any one should try to invalidate the *adat* by argument. If he were like us, one could say that his *adat* against our arguments is like an armour which repels or blunts our arrows. But he is not like that. His adat as defensive weapon is rather like an aura enveloping him. One shoots one's arrows or bullets right through it without any effect. With him there is no collision at all.

We are used to standing alone, relying on our own judgment and deciding for ourselves what we want to do. The Javanese is not primarily an individual human being; first and foremost he is a Javanese, a member of the Javanese people.

So by a study of the people, by living contact with the natives, rather than through books with fine descriptions of Hinduism, Animism, Magic etc., what was strange at first becomes more natural and intelligible.

The Javanese, — and the other peoples of the East Indies are just the same — is not irreligious, but the great masses never absorbed intellectually the various forms of religion that swept over these parts. Christianity is not confronted by a reasoned, definite, religious system. This is an advantage for mission work, though the difference in the way of reasoning appears as a great obstacle especially to the beginning missionary.

How is the native led tot religion?

At the express request of the East-Indian Government in 1886 a new missionpost was started on the Kei islands. The missionary selected for that task, Father J. Kusters, turned out to possess the sturdy qualities needed for that difficult enterprize. The choice of the first mission station was almost fatal. He established himself at Tual, the only habitable place which, however, was a centre of Mohammedanism. He made trips to the surrounding islands. Disappointment followed upon disappointment, enough to break the courage of the boldest man. At last a letter came from Batavia, with the advice that the mission had better be altogether abandoned. Then the missionary's will, firm as a rock and his unshakable faith revealed themselves. "Give me another month," he entreated his bishop, "and if then the good Lord does not bring relief, let me go, though with a broken heart." His plan of campaign was ready. With apostolic joy and courage he once more went to Langgur and resorted to medicine and prayer. "And," he wrote not long afterwards, "next morning many sick were cured of their fever and I could begin with the labour for their souls." This kind of argument both East and West understand. But the little prahu which carried the missionary to victory was at the same time his cross. Often he had to stay for weeks in a miserable hut, harassed by ants and mosquitoes, those tropical "wild animals", more redoubtable than the romantic tigers and panthers! With great patience he succeeded in forming good Christians. An occasional visitor would with intense surprise hear Christian songs ringing through the forests or far off in the fields. If the people embarked to work elsewhere for some months they first would come to ask for the sacraments and a blessing. On their return their first trip would be to their beloved missionary and his little church.

In many parts of Europe, long since christianised, the position of Christianity would be very different, if its propagation had only been by preaching. The great question that dominates the work of conversion in the Indies is, what Christianity has to give to those people.

The „Missigit" of Medan, one of the finest Mohammedan mosques in the East Indi

The native is poor and indigent. Not in the sense of the impoverished individual, living among the well-to-do and so always having a chance of improving his lot. Out there the entire population is poor. The desa, the entire region is indigent. There is no means of progress.

With this situation the Christian missions are confronted. They come, if not with riches, yet with a desire to give and share. Christ enjoined upon the missionary to put his natural talents into the service of His love. The Mission should help those people in all their human needs: in their sickness, by furnishing medical aid and nursing; in their ignorance, by supplying schools and education; in their poverty, by improving agriculture and promoting industry; in their faults, by moral training. But all this activity should be a revelation of love. Only when this becomes palpable does it compel people to love in return. In this way hearts become accessible to the truth of Christianity.

Among the inhabitants of the islands of Flores and Timor mission work now is mass-conversion. After a slow preparation of about half a century the number of Catholics grew from 40.000 in 1917 to 279.000 in 1938. Most of the difficulties mentioned before have here been surmounted. A few of the natives have already been ordained as priests and are completing their studies at the seminary of Toda-Belu. Gradually the mission work is becoming independent of the home-country. In the heathen parts of New-Guinea, the Moluccas and Borneo, although the difficulties have only been partially surmounted, strong centres have already been formed.

For all mission work, especially that among the more developed peoples the watchword should be: "He went about doing good."

When father Fr. van Lith started the Java-mission, he asked himself: What does the Javanese expect of me? The Javanese, poor and backward himself, was living in a fertile country where rich Hollanders and educated Indo-Europeans had chances of getting on in the world which he lacked. Javanese history tells of intrepid seafarers, powerful kings, who long held sway over the entire Archipelago. There was once a well organised government. In the literature and the ancient monuments one may still admire the artistic sense of former generations. In the rich language the traditional intelligence of the people finds its expression.

Such people need education. The school opens to the Javanese the way to an adequate subsistence and a suitable position in society. Is the school, therefore, not exactly the work of love that the Javanese needs and wants?

Since the Government in those days frequently was not able to open a sufficient number of schools for Javanese children desiring to get on, mission work tried, as best it could, to supply that want. The great popularity of these schools is proof of the particularly cordial relationship existing between teaching staff and pupils. The schools are good indeed and the teachers receive special pedagogical training to qualify them for their task.

The intensity of the mission work may be illustrated by a few figures. In the period from 1870 to 1900 the number of R. C. native Christians increased from 11.000 to 26.000, that is, in thirty years it was only doubled; in the next twenty years it was trebled and amounted to 72.000. Between 1920 and 1930 the mission staff increased from 93 to 272 priests and the number of baptized increased proportionally from 72.000 to 233.000. This figure was again doubled in the last nine years: in 1939 the total of native Christians amounted to nearly 478.000.

The majority of these Christians are found on Flores and Timor, but the Moluccas and New-Guinea also make a good showing with their 40.000 Catholics. In the apostolic vicarate of Menado there are 25.000, at Padang 10.000, on Borneo about 10.000 and on Java more than 35.000.

The growing generation is being prepared for life at more than 1600 schools with over 142.000 pupils and 4000 teachers. This education is largely charity, since more than 600 of these schools receive no government subsidy.

Charitable work for the benefit of native society is chiefly carried on in 45 hospitals, large and small, with more than 2000 beds. The number of visits to clinical hospitals is more than 700.000 and district nurses pay more than 70.000 visits a year.

In the general policy of raising the level of the East Indies Missions with their cultural and educational activities have become indispensable.

There are now native priests and even a native bishop.

Mission work is weaving a close bond between ourselves and the people over-seas. This was well expressed by a Javanese student-priest when in

1922, at the first international mission congress at Utrecht, he said:

"We are Christians and Catholics. It is the name Catholics that unites us intimately with you. It is the same name that bridges oceans and levels mountains; it is the same name that makes our eyes see, not the colour of the skin, but the blinding glory of the divine childhood; it is the same name that removes differences of character and customs. We are neither unknown nor strangers to each other, but brethren and sisters of the same Master, with the same Father, and the same Mother, the Church, with the same desire and the same goal."

CHAPTER 10

The Conquest of Distance

AT SEA

As in every Archipelago thickly dotted with islands within sight of each other, from early times on there was a well-developed navigation in the East Indies. It was carried on by the population in their prahus that in great numbers sailed the straits and inland seas. The advent of the Westerners interfered with this. The United East Indian Company, desirous, above all, to maintain its trade monopoly, for many years, often by very drastic measures, curtailed the navigation of prahus. Not until the end of the 18th century, freed from this oppression, could it expand again, and it was chiefly the Buginese and Makassarese, excellent sailors, who profited from this opportunity.

By modern standards this traffic of prahus in terms of tonnage and turnover was not large. These vessels were small and slow; only once a year, with the monsoon, could they set out on long trips. The Dutch authorities, after 1816, reasserting themselves in the Indies, scarcely took any notice of them; nor did this kind of interinsular navigation, in the first half of the 19th century, interest European businessmen. Interest was centred almost exclusively on fertile and populous Java and the possibilities which it offered for the home-country to get rich returns by means of compulsory cultivation and an almost monopolistic trade-organisation. The contact of this principal island with the other islands was not promoted but rather, like trade in general, thwarted by an number of restrictive measures.

The result of this policy was that, when in 1819 Singapore was occupied by Raffles and opened as a free port for all import and export, it soon attracted a large part of the traffic of the Outer Islands. Raffles' creation

supplied the need of a free centre for all Archipelago traffic. Chinese merchants, finding facilities at Singapore, soon developed the British port into
the great emporium of South-East-Asia. As early as 1824 it was reported that
native vessels more and more were passing by the Dutch East Indian ports in
order to supply their needs at Singapore. Neither Riau, lying opposite, made
a free port in 1828, nor Makassar, made a free port in 1846, could hold their
own against it. As far as the eastern islands of the Archipelago import and
export were centred on Singapore.

Every year the prahus of the Buginese would sail up the roadstead in
fleets, laden with the products of the islands, for the most part sold to China.
In exchange they purchased Western wares, usually made in England, such
as iron and textile products, for their return cargo. But larger ships with
European rigging, chiefly schooners, also took part in this traffic. They
mostly belonged to Arabs and Chinese. On Java and Madura, at Palembang and the large ports of Borneo these "coasters" soon became so numerous that they exceeded the prahus. When in 1854 the Government began
to issue sea-briefs to ships built abroad, the number of large vessels of more
than 500 tons, mostly barques and brigs rapidly increased. Part of these
were owned by some European merchant-adventurers.

About the middle of the century the influence of liberalism gradually
brought about a freer economy in the Indies and more interest for the
Outer Islands. Makassar, Menado, Ambon, Banda, Ternate, and other
places were made free ports and several ports, hitherto closed to all shipping
other than Dutch and native, were opened to foreign flags. The only effect
of this measure, for the time being, was, that the suctive power of the Singapore trade, becoming more active with navigation of its own, could make
itself felt further in the Archipelago without any let or hindrance.

At the same time steam navigation entered the East Indies. The first
steamboat, owned by a private firm at Batavia, had been operating since
1830 along the north coast of Java. For a long time it remained the only
one; in 1850 there were no more than two besides about ten belonging to the
government navy, used at the same time for the transportation of passengers,
mail and packages, especially between Batavia and Singapore, connecting
up with the British overland mail from Europe.

In the following years several more firms began to operate steamships, at first for the transportation from port to port of their own goods, later chiefly in the service of other mercantile houses. In the interinsular trade navigation began to separate itself from commerce, formerly, as a rule, practised in combination. This shows that there was an entirely new task for the steamship in the navigation of the Archipelago. Being independent of wind and weather and having a regular speed it could achieve something that was impossible for a sailing-ship, namely, to maintain a regular service on fixed sailing-dates by which not only the communication between the islands was speeded up but also all uncertainty about times of sailing and arrival was removed. In this way the distances in this vast archipelago, if not conquered, at least became a calculable factor in communication.

It is significant that steam navigation, being a Western invention, was also first operated by Western companies. The initiative in interinsular traffic that in the first half of the century had largely passed into Chinese and Arabic control, was thus regained by Westerners. Partly this was made possible by the support given by the Government. The authorities soon realised the enormous possibilities for private steam navigation in the vast domain under their control, and saw that they could now relieve the ships of the navy from the task of carrying mail, passengers and troops. In 1850 it was decided to entrust a former naval officer with the organisation of a steam packet navigation service from Batavia to the western coast of Sumatra, to Singapore, to the west coast of Borneo and via the north coast of Java to Makassar and the Moluccas. As it was not certain that the enterprise would pay, the Government gave an annual subsidy, which, in return, ensured it a reduced rate for Government cargo and passengers.

Starting with a fleet of four small iron screw steamships, the packet service gradually expanded. However, these were the years when steam navigation was technically still far from perfected, and in the long run it failed to give general satisfaction. Moreover, the subsidy was very high. When therefore in 1865 the contract expired, and tenders were called for, the service was assigned to a British firm that was the holder of the lowest. As a Dutch firm with the next-lowest tender only asked one cent per sea mile more than the British, so that the annual difference in the Government's subsidy would only have amounted to 400 guilders, a great deal of hostile criticism of that decision was heard. It was however quite consistent with the economic liberalism of the age not to discriminate between nationals and foreigners, and to favour under all circumstances the interests of the consumer, that is, the shipping party, above those of the producer, that is in this case, the transporting party. Of considerable moment also was the consideration that British steam navigation in those days was far ahead of ours and that therefore better service might be expected from a British firm than from a Dutch one.

The new company on the whole lived up to these expectations. It gave such general satisfaction that in 1875, with a decreased subsidy, its contract was prolonged for another fifteen years. In 1890, when its services came to an end, it owned about thirty steam ships and operated eleven lines in the Archipelago, most of which covered long distances.

In the meantime a fundamental change in the communication of the Indies with Europe was brought about by the opening of the Suez canal in 1869. Not only did the passage through the canal bring the route to the Indies entirely within range of the steamship, but also it was considerably shortened and facilitated. It became feasible for small lightly-built ships that could never have weathered the stormy voyage round the Cape. Now, sailing from European ports in the favourable season, these could reach the comparatively calm waters of the Mediterranean and the Indian Ocean without much trouble. The result was that a lot of cheap and old ships were sold East in order to traffic in the quiet tropical seas of the Archipelago in the employ of some adventurous owner. This caused an enormous increase of ships in the East Indian waters. Says Joseph Conrad in The End of the Tether: "The piercing of the Isthmus of Suez, like the breaking of a dam, had let in upon the East a flood of new ships, new men, new methods of trade. It had changed the face of the Eastern seas and the very spirit of their life . . ."

However, not only the number of steamships increased. Many large sailingvessels, no longer needed elsewhere, also went East. Statistics show the following figures:

in 1868 15 steamships, 122 schooners, 33 brigs and 123 barques
in 1878 38 steamships, 215 schooners, 30 brigs and 92 barques
in 1888 54 steamships, 212 schooners, 22 brigs and 67 barques.

It must have been a grand sight on the Indian seas: the full sails of the schooners and barques in the light against the blueish green coasts finding their way in and out between the islands across the ever-moving surface of the water!

In the eigthies the steamship definitely took the place of sail-borne vessels. Within ten years, between 1875—1885, in the Outer Islands alone steam navigation was doubled. Chinese and Arabic and even progressive native owners began to follow the Western example. About 1895 the total tonnage of steamships exceeded that of the large European rigged sailing-vessels, and about 1905 that of all registered sailing-vessels including the very small ones. Taking into consideration the greater speed and frequency of steam-ships it is clear that several years earlier the steamship had definitely con-quered the sailing-vessel. Speaking in terms of tonnage of vessels departed, in 1910 steamships had more than 95 % and sailing-vessels not quite 5 % of the inter-insular traffic!

In the first years after the opening of the Suez-canal it was however Singapore and not the Dutch East Indies that drew the greatest profit from this revolution in the world of shipping. Just as in bygone days Batavia had been the first important port of call in the Archipelago for ships coming from the Cape, now Singapore became the great port for all traffic coming from Europe and headed for the Indies and Eastern Asia. Not only for the sale to China of native-grown products was it in the eighties preferred to East-Indian ports, but also for the transit-traffic even of the products of the Eu-ropean estates it generally offered a better freight-market than these, and so deflected traffic.

The Singapore trading-houses, shortly after the middle of the century, had begun to follow the native prahus with their own ships and travelling agents. This was possible because, by virtue of the navigation laws of 1850 the British flag in the Indies, except for coastal navigation, had been put on a par with the national flag, and also because more and more ports (the so-called "native ports" and "freeports") were opened to it. The influence on the islands of the Singapore trade penetrated ever further. Through the power of their kongsi-organisation and the attraction which their system of advancing money had for the population, the Chinese, and also the Arabs, succeeded in ousting the commercial navigation of the Buginese and other merchants. With their own agents in the principal places they frequently controlled the economic situation as far as the Moluccas in the eastern part of the Archipelago. The prahu shipping, in so far as it continued to exist, was then made subservient to them by advances of money and had to restrict itself more and more to the fetching and distributing of cargo in the vicinity.

Between 1870 and 1880 on the east coast of Borneo and in North Celebes (the Tomini Bight) Singapore trade with its own ships and agents was definitely established. Using at first schooners and brigs the owners soon realised the advantage of steamers and organised more or less fixed lines for traffic along seacoast and riverbank in the Archipelago. The communications of the islands with Singapore became so frequent that, much to the advantage of trade, freight-rates could always be kept low, while opportunities for shipment to Java were infrequent and the tariffs of the packet service remained high. For fine descriptions of the curious coastal trade of these Singapore-based ships one should turn to the novels of Joseph Conrad who, in 1887, as second mate of the steamer "Vidar", owned by an Arabic merchant of Singapore, made five voyages to the east coast of Borneo. With a masterly pen he re-created life on board ship in the Indian waters and the atmosphere of the ports and coastal settlements. His books give an excellent picture of this primitive trade on almost virgin coasts and of the predominant part in life, played by the regular arrival of a small old steamer from Singapore.

After 1880 Government circles realised to what extent trade in the Outer Islands had passed into the hands of the British. In view of possible political complications such a condition of affairs was judged dangerous. The difference between the ever growing activity of Singapore and the ports of Java serving mainly for direct European import and export was striking. Around 1890 technical improvements were made in several ports: at Tanjung Priok breakwaters and quays were built, at Padang and Belawan Deli harbours and quays were constructed, but the pivotal problem remained unsolved, how to deflect the trade of the Outer Islands back into national channels.

The twentieth century brought the solution of this problem. A new self-confidence together with a general change in the spirit of the times, no longer dominated by an extreme liberalism, induced both Government and private individuals to interfere with a situation that had become more and more undesirable. This century did not so much bring the conquest of distance, which had already been made by steam, but rather the defeat of foreign control.

The medium through which this end was attained was the organisation in 1888 of the Royal Packet Company, replacing the old company of 1865 that had been in British hands. Its contract expired in 1890 and was not renewed. The predominance of Singapore in the trade of the Archipelago was ascribed by many to the deliberate policy of that company. Though this was certainly not true, it was a fact that, by concentrating too much on the fixed contract-lines gravitating round Batavia and the other Javanese ports, it had neglected to establish communications with Singapore and so had lost most of the cargo from the Outer Islands. Upon the organisation of the new Dutch company there was a general demand from the ports that lines on Singapore should be established. The fact that Singapore was the great emporium for the products of the Outer Islands could not be ignored.

By meeting these demands the Royal Packet Company regained indeed much of the lost ground. Its regular sailings and its excellent organisation soon made it very popular and preferable to the often irregular ships from Singapore. Chinese merchant-owners gradually stopped competing and used the Royal Packet Company (K.P.M. for short) for the transportation of their goods.

But there were also other reasons for its success. The opening up of the Outer Islands brought about an enormous increase in the production of pepper, copra, sago, rubber etc. In the eastern part of the Archipelago it was chiefly copra, produced by the natives themselves, that revived trade. This was a new article and, unlike most forest-products of the islands, its market was not in eastern Asia, but in Europe and America where it is used in the soap, oil and fat industries. Now Singapore had no special hold on this trade. The K.P.M. succeeded in controlling the transportation of this article from East Indian ports abroad by offering special privileges for through-shipment to Europe. Makassar developed into the principal port where the copra from the eastern islands was transshipped, and gradually the trade in the other products of that part of the Archipelago gravitated to Makassar. It became independent of Singapore, and regained its old importance as a centre for import and export.

In the long run the direct influence of Singapore was restricted to western Borneo, eastern Sumatra and the islands between these coasts where the small ships of the "mosquito fleet" are still sailing off and on. In the twenties and thirties of this century traffic here developed enormously because of the increase in the production of native-grown rubber.

In this same period ports at Tanjung Priok, Makassar, Surabaya, Belawan Deli, Sabang and Telok Betung were also improved. In ports like Ambon and Ternate the quays however are still too small and antiquated. Most of the so-called ports in the East Indies are in fact nothing but open roadsteads in more or less sheltered bays on the coast where the large ships anchor and where the communication with the shore is effected by means of small barges and prahus.

Thus, by an alert and energetic policy and manysided activity the K.P.M. succeeded in nationalising shipping in the Dutch East Indies and warding off the preponderant influence of Singapore in these regions. It even opened lines on Asia, Australia and Africa. It now has about 150 ships, more than 60 lines in the Archipelago and about 100 local offices. It controls all ship-ping on the sea and along the coast fiom Sabang to Merauke. Its network of shipping lines is at least as important as the railwaysystem on the great continents. It encourages enterprize in distant regions and has even taken over the cash-advance system of Chinese shipping, giving enormous short-term credits, thus playing an important part as a banker. The Government, recognising the place which the K.P.M. had gained for itself, each time, on the expiration of the term, has renewed its contract.

When about 1910 the major part of shipping in the Archipelago was controlled by the K.P.M. there was no objection to opening the Indies even wider than before to foreign flags. In 1912 they were admitted to coastwise navigation between ports that were open to general trade. Only when in the years of crisis after 1930 an excessively strong Japanese competition arose and in certain parts of the Archipelago the economic life threatened to be-come dependent on foreign shipping it was again found necessary to restrict this freedom. In 1936 a number of ports, chiefly in the eastern part of the

Archipelago, were closed to foreign flags and coastwise navigation was reserved for Dutch ships only.

Nowhere the development of the K.P.M. traffic is more characteristic and its economic and social function more important than in this eastern part of the Archipelago. In this extensive domain of sea and islands it forms the principal means of communication for the exchange of goods and transportation of passengers. For the larger islands too, as yet little developed and without either railroads or motorroads, the ship is generally the only means to bring about coastwise traffic between their various parts as well as with the outside world. Steaming from roadstead to roadstead, from island to island it fetches the products and carries the imports of all kinds necessary for daily use: furniture, manufactured goods, pottery, petroleum, foodstuffs, luxuries both for natives and westerners.

To these distant coasts the ship also brings the trade of Chinese and Arabic pedlars who on board ship display their wares in little stalls and on land set up each time their market booths. At the same time it also acts as a floating credit-bank advancing to engrossers or small planters the money needed for trade or production until the moment of sale enables them to pay back. For other reasons too its regular arrival is a welcome event for the community in these remote settlements for it means news, mail and newspapers for the official, the missionary, the commercial agent. For a short time it draws these and their families into the orbit of the civilisation of which they form part, thus inspiring them with new energy for their work in the coming period of seclusion.

Laden with the produce of the district: with copra from many islands and coasts, with ratan, gums and ebony, with maize and rice from the coasts of Celebes, with spice from the Moluccas, cattle from the Lesser Sunda Islands, pigs from Bali, rice from Lombok and Sumbawa and also, more to the west, with forest-produce from North- and Central Borneo, with rubber from South- and West-Borneo and Sumatra, pepper from Banka, with coffee, pepper, sago, timber, fish, palm oil, fibres from the various coasts of Sumatra, with rice, sugar, tobacco, coffee, rubber, kapok from small shipping ports on Java, with salt from Madura, coal from Sumatra and Borneo, — the ships of the K.P.M. daily return to the large ports of Makassar, Sura-

baya, Tanjung Priok, Belawan Deli, Singapore, where they unload either
for local consumption or for transhipment to the steamers of the transoceanic
lines.

The K.P.M. maintains long shippingroutes in the Archipelago, as for
example from Makassar to the Moluccas and beyond to the frontier zones
of Dutch New-Guinea, Humboldt's Bay and Merauke, and from Surabaya
to North-Borneo, keeping the ships en route for weeks on end, and also very
short ones, from Singapore or Belawan to the eastcoast of Sumatra, a trip
completed in a few days. Its lines probe the coasts like feelers. With Java
as a centre it casts a web over the entire archipelago, which also aids the
Government in firmly maintaining its authority. Its ships cross wide seas
to remote groups of islands on the fringe of our dominion, but in Borneo
and Sumatra they also sail up the rivers from jetty to jetty for the export
of produce and the supply of articles of consumption, thus creating traffic
by water where on land no communication with the outside world has yet
been established.

With its fleet of nearly 150 units the K.P.M. thus exercises the most widely
diverging functions. Its steam- or motorships transport travellers, mail or
tourists, serve as cattleboats or cargoboats for the transportation of petroleum, coal, salt or fish. In size they vary from 500 to 5000 registered tons,
not counting the ships connecting up with the foreign lines, of which the
largest measure more than 14.000 tons. But whether on river-, sea- or ocean-
traffic, the Westerner finds the accommodation he requires, with the greatest
degree of comfort naturally on the large passenger ships, equivalent to mail
steamers, maintaining the communication between the large ports within
the Archipelago or with Australia, New Zealand, Africa and Eastern Asia.
The travelling Chinese and Arabic trader for his part finds on board the
care and food he likes; so do the crowd of native passengers who, often in
entire migrating families, huddle pleasantly together on the decks in the
midst of their goods and chattels. They mostly prefer the quieter and faster,
though more expensive trip on a western ship to that on some old uncomfort-
able steamer of a Chinese company or the uncertain passage in the native
sailing prahus.

The K.P.M. accounts for about one half of the total interinsular shipping. The oil-companies have their own tankers and motor-freighters. Then

there is, especially in the western part of the Archipelago, still a considerable amount of foreign shipping. A very special feature however of the general shipping movement is the increase of the prahus of Buginese, Makassarese and Madurese. Large sailing-vessels like schooners, brigs and barques, as everywhere else, have practically disappeared, but these small sailing-craft have profited from the general economic development. They fetch and distribute goods in places not touched by the K.P.M. and even make long-distance voyages competing against the K.P.M. by low freight-rates. They are especially important in the eastern part of the Archipelago. However, though they are at present certainly more numerous than they ever were in the past, they make up only 2 % of the total interinsular traffic. This very clearly brings out the enormous development of navigation in the East Indies and the preponderant part played in it by steam-engine and motor, products of Western technique. Yet the lover of the picturesque cannot but hope that the beautiful colours and lines of the small native prahus will for many years continue to grace the ports in the Dutch East Indies.

ON LAND

Roads

When the nineteenth century dawned even on Java there were only dirt roads. There were few bridges. The East Indian Company confined its influence to the coast and did not go far inland. The principal settlements on the coast communicated by sea and in the bad monsoon all communication was generally interrupted.

It is the "iron marshall" H. W. Daendels who created the first real road on Java. He became Governor-General in 1808, and a few months after his arrival he ordered the building of a hard road from Buitenzorg via Bandung to Sumedang. Soon this became part of a great post road from Anjer to Banjuwangi along the entire length of the island. More roads followed so that, during the British interregnum, (the later) Sir Stamford Raffles found some good roads inland. The "culture-system" promoted the building of roads, generally by compulsory labour. Natives were not allowed to drive cattle or transport goods on these hard roads; for these purposes there were parellel dirt roads. The hard road was chiefly intended for the horse-post which was leased out. At regular intervals there were relay stations, called pendopo's, where horses were changed. At steep inclines buffaloes were available to take over the heavy work. Rafts ferried the coaches across the large rivers; wooden and bamboo bridges were supposed to exist across the smaller rivers, but heavy banjirs ofter washed them away.

In the course of the 19th century these conditions gradually improved. About 1900 there were on Java and Madura 20.000 km of hard roads and country roads with 250 arched bridges with a span of more than 10 meters, 1500 small arched bridges and nearly 10.000 bridges with iron sleepers and wooden covering. But many of these bridges were of temporary construction and some important river-crossings were still lacking.

Since then much has been done. After 1910 compulsory labour was no longer employed for the building of roads but regional road-taxes were introduced and labour was paid. Especially after 1914 many roads were built on a uniform plan. The increased motortraffic made entirely new demands that were quickly met. By the end of 1938 Java had 9000 km of asphalt-roads, 14.000 km of hard roads and 4000 km of dirt roads.

Sumatra got its first hard road in 1834; it was the famous road across the Anei chasm. It was connected up with roads built in the longitudinal valleys of the Barisan mountains and the Padang plateau. The rough mountains along the coast prevented for a long time the building of roads across the island. On the east coast traffic on the large rivers was able to penetrate deep inland so that roads were less necessary. However, in the seventies and eighties a road was built from Palembang to Tebing Tinggih, cutting the journey from 30 days down to 5. With the development of Deli a great network of roads was built around Medan, but it was several years before this was connected up with the other roads. A road building programme of 1916 provided for a longitudinal road through the entire length of the island from Telok Betung on the southern tip to Kota Raja in the north, and for transversal roads from Medan to Sibolga and Padang, from Palembang to Benkulen, etc. All these roads have since been built; they have naturally stimulated the economic development and also tourism in this beautiful country.

In 1938 there were on Sumatra 8000 km of hard roads, of which nearly 1000 km of asphalt roads. In Minangkabau moreover there were under special administration 1555 km of road, of which 142 were asphalt roads. Except on Bali, Banka, Billiton and some parts of Celebes and Borneo roads on the other islands have not yet been modernised. Much is being done to mend this state of affairs. Altogether on the Outer Islands there were in 1938 about 3600 km of asphalt roads, 26.500 km of hard and 12.000 km of dirt roads.

Nearly all the roads in the Dutch East Indies are well beaconed under the good care of the automobile clubs.

Railroads

The Dutch and East-Indian Governments have often been blamed for the late appearance of railways in the Indies. Not entirely without cause. The need was felt for the increased transportation of produce to have better roads than the dirt roads running along the hard post-roads, while, moreover, there was a dearth of draught-animals.

It sometimes happened that, for want of transportation, government coffee lay mouldering in the godowns of the Principalities while the ships that were to carry the product oversea waited for months for their cargo on the roadstead of Semarang.

For a time a plan was under consideration to establish on Central Java a huge waggon park with four thousand buffaloes. But a calculation showed that such a scheme was not workable. A herd of forty camels sent out at the request of the East Indian Government could not be acclimatised. Nor did experiments with lamas and donkeys have any better luck. The idea was conceived by one Minister of Colonies to encourage the raising of buffaloes, to forbid their being slaughtered and to accustom the Javanese to a diet of goat's meat, but his Governor-General opposed the plan.

From 1840 on the idea of building railways was very much in the air. Several people applied for concessions, but there was much difference of opinion about the profitableness of the proposals. Moreover, there were no reliable maps so that no proper calculations could be made. There were some people who foresaw the most evil consequences from the building of railways: in a pamphlet of 1872 a former government official solemnly declared that it would lead to the downfall of our sovereignty.

Finally in 1863 a concession was granted for the building of a railway

in Central Java and ten years later the line Semarang-Jocja was completed. Its total length was 256 km. It had a gauge of 1.435 m. For other lines a gauge of 1.067 m was decided on, the first one completed being that between Batavia and Buitenzorg.

The private company that had taken the initiative in building the Semarang line at first had to cope with immense difficulties and twice very nearly went bankrupt. Although later it completely recovered and became a flourishing concern, its initial troubles had frightened capitalists. The Minister of Colonies therefore proposed to build government railways and his plan was passed by Parliament in 1875. A line was built from Surabaya to Pasuruan with a branch line to Malang. The results were so encouraging that several more lines were built. In 1894, by linking up the existing lines, Batavia and Surabaya were connected by rail, although between the two terminal points there still was a track of about 60 km with a wide gauge, necessitating transshipment and changing trains. By building a third track between Solo and Jocja this difficulty was removed in 1905. Various improvements and shortcuts were made in modern times so that since the end of 1934 the entire distance between Java's two principal cities may be covered in 12 hours. The trains are air-conditioned and there are daily night trains with very comfortable sleeping-cars.

At present Java has about 3000 km of railways in government ownership and nearly 2500 in private hands.

On Sumatra the first railway was built in Atchin for military purposes. This was in 1876. Later it was extended and linked up with the Deli system for the transportation of its rich produce, such as tobacco, tea, palmoil, rubber, etc. On the west coast of Central Sumatra there is a separate railway net, built in 1891 for the shipment of coal to Padang. Its length is 264 km. Finally there are also railways in southern Sumatra. These were built in order to open up that fertile region, practically without roads, and to promote emigration from Java. Since 1925 there is a through connection from Batavia via the Sunda Straits (steamboat ferry) to Palembang. The total length of these lines is 645 km. All in all Sumatra has 2000 km of rail.

On Celebes a short light railway was opened in 1922 from Makassar to Takalar. The competition of the coastal navigation however was so strong

Mission 9

that this line proved a failure and was suspended. On the other islands there are no railways. Plans for lines on Borneo, northern Celebes, Bali and Lombok were laid aside in the depression years after 1929. Moreover with improved roads buses and trucks are able to supply the limited traffic needs.

The building of railways powerfully stimulated the development of the regions traversed. This was manifest in eastern Java, in Bantam, in the Preanger districts, but nowhere more clearly than in Deli and southern Sumatra. Not only did the railways open possibilities for emigration and develop the cultivation of native crops, but they also enabled Western enter-prize to lay out vast estates. Without the mass-transportation by rail sugar and other products could never have been cultivated in such huge quantities.

The rates for freight and passenger traffic are very moderate. Natives used to pay one cent per km, and since the depression reduced their circum-stances they travel free after the first 400 km, so that a trip from Surabaya to Batavia, a distance of 800 km, costs only four guilders. The rates for the higher classes are also lower in proportion than in Europe.

The Dutch East Indies now have 7400 km of rail. The lines are all in excellent condition and are a testimony to the energy and powers of orga-nisation of the Dutch. Until the depression most lines were paying well. The unchecked competition of motorbuses and motortrucks, as everywhere else in the world, has recently created a grave pioblem for which so far no satisfactory solution has been found.

IN THE AIR

The necessity of rapid communication in a farflung Archipelago, measu-ring from East to Wset more than 5000 km, where a handful of people have to carry out vast and responsible tasks, is obvious. It is therefore generally recognised nowadays that the Dutch East Indies cannot get along without air transportation.

It developed from modest beginnings in 1928. Then the air-lines Batavia-Bandung, Batavia-Semarang, later continued to Surabaya, Batavia-Palem-bang-Singapore, connecting up with foreign services, and Batavia-Medan via Palembang and Pakanbaru were started. On most of these lines the service was infrequent. Only once a week there was a connection with Singapore and Medan, and once daily with Surabaya. Now this line runs two services each way on three days a week. What this means to the business-man at Surabaya who has to carry on negotiations with the Government at Batavia, is self-evident. It is possible to be there and back in one day with ample time for business. Many people remember the time when the trainjourney between these two cities still took two days!

The air-net may be divided into two parts: one which aims at drawing the Archipelago itself closer together, and one which connects it with other trans-pacific countries. Both tasks are equally important and naturally the linking up of the home-service with the foreign service is a matter of careful planning. The K.N.I.L.M. (Royal Netherlands Indian Air Company) succeeded very well in doing so. The lines to Singapore were linked up with one to Saigon, no doubt to be pushed on to China in the near future; there is an important line to Sydney, and lastly a line was opened to Manilla. Now the Pan American Airways fly from San Francisco via Manilla to Hongkong and Singapore, and also branch off to New Zealand, where they join the line Sydney-New Zealand. The connections from the Dutch East Indies fit in splendidly with this air-net. At the same time they open up remote and rather isolated parts of the Indies. There is, for example, the connection Bali-Timor Kupang, from where one crosses over to Port-Darwin in Australia. The connection with Manilla touches at important ports like Banjirmasin, Balikpapan and Tarakan on Borneo. Singapore and Saigon may be reached by different lines. There are the K.N.I.L.M. lines from Batavia and Palembang and from Central and North-Sumatra, that is Pakanbaru and Medan. But there is also the new line to Pontianak and the tin-islands. Further more there is the connection of the Royal Dutch Airline (K.L.M.) from Penang via Medan and Singapore to Palembang-Batavia. The connection with the European line of the K.L.M. is of course of essential value. Practically all places of importance in the Indies are now via Batavia, Palembang, Singapore and Medan, connected up with the airline to Europe, which again links up with all European capitals. But this K.L.M. line also provides direct communication of the Dutch East Indies with Siam, Burma, British-India, Iran, Irak, Palestine and North-Africa.

By the joint service of K.L.M. and K.N.I.L.M. the rapid connection Europe-Australia has been established, which brings London and Sydney within only seven days' distance of each other.

Finally there is the important air-net for the eastern part of the Archipelago: Celebes, the Moluccas and New-Guinea. Makassar, Menado, Ternate, Ambon, Bandaneira and places on New-Guinea like Babo, Fakfak, Manokwari, the Lakes and Hollandia at the extreme north-eastern tip may all be reached now in two days from Surabaya. Twice a week one may travel from Java to New-Guinea. It goes without saying that the linking up of these remote parts of the Indies with the air-lines that span the Pacific, the Far East, the Near East and Europe is of the utmost importance for their future development.

Small units like the aeroplane have the immense advantage of much greater frequency than ships. This, combined with their speed, makes the air-service such a boon in a country like the East Indies. High Dutch officials, from the Governors-General on, regularly travel by air on their official tours. An immense territory may be visited in a short time. In calamities help may be sent rapidly. Engineers, business-men, doctors all profit by it. The planes are generally booked full which shows that air-travel does indeed supply a want. It is rapid, cool and comfortable and distances are devoured that otherwise take many days.

The opening up of New-Guinea, now proceeding, would be unthinkable, if, along with navigation which takes care of the transportation of heavy cargo, aeroplanes could not carry back and forth experts, mail, reports, transport sera and medicine and so, drawing New-Guinea within the vicinity of Surabaya and Batavia, remove its isolation. The same holds true for the oil centres on Borneo and the commercial centres on Celebes. Everywhere the aeroplane fulfills the welcome task of bringing all these local centres closer to the great focuses of administration and commerce on Java.

Further technical development will steadily extend the task of the K.N.I.L.M., for it may be expected that problems will be solved that so far present technical difficulties. One of these is the connection with South-Africa via Madagascar. Here is still a wide field for Dutch enterprise.

IN THE AETHER

Radio-telegraph and -telephone

The telegraph is the means *par excellence* of rapid communication and its need is most felt when distances are so great that ordinary correspondence takes weeks and months. The East Indies therefore need an efficient telegraph-service, not only for the use of the public, but how could the Government keep up its contact with its officials unless it had at its disposal a means of rapid communication like the telegraph?

Now the building of an efficient network of telegraph lines is a very costly enterprise, especially in the tropics, where suitable lines have to be cut in inhospitable regions of mountains and forests. Moreover many sea-cables between the islands were necessary. The laying and keeping in repair of these cables that had to be constantly renewed was very expensive. Most cables did not pay. In 1922 the total length of sea-cables in the Indies was 12.567 km. When the radio began to show ever better results it was decided to stop laying new cables and gradually to change over to radio communication. The development was so rapid that in 1938 no more than 382 km of sea-cables remained. The overland wires in the interior of Sumatra and Borneo, which used to be frequently destroyed by landslides, inundations, falling trees and wild elephants, were also abolished.

In the tropics the ultra-short wave of 20—60 meters is used. For long distances this is more satisfactory than the long wave of far more powerful transmitters and there is less atmospheric disturbance. At more than 80 places in the Outer Islands there are now transmitters with receiving-installations, so that all of these can now exchange telegrams. Moreover at a great number of small places there are receiving-stations principally for governmental use, and gradually senders are also built at these stations. But even a receiving-station alone is a great improvement on the time when such places were visited once every four, six or eight weeks by some steamer.

Batavia is the principial centre for all these radio-connections. The transmitters have been built on the Bandung plateau. They relay to all the important places in the Outer Islands, which, in their turn, are the feeders of the less powerful stations in their neighbourhood. Makassar and Amboina are the most important transmission-stations for the Archipelago. Every day the powerful Malabar station at Bandung which maintains the communication with Holland and was built during the first world-war, sends out official news. In places that have no newspapers the local official makes this news further known to the population. Before radio-receiving sets were general this way of spreading news was an immense improvement over the old slow methods.

The *radio-telephone* also developed along with the radio-telegraph. In March 1927 for the first time a voice from Holland was heard in the Indies and in May the spoken word from the Indies became clearly audible in Holland. In January 1929 radio-telephonic communication between Holland and the Indies was opened to the public. In 1931 a radio-telephonic station was opened at Medan, inaugurating the inter-insular telephonic communication between Java and North-Sumatra and a few months later telephone-subscribers in North-Sumatra could not only get subscribers in Java on the 'phone but also those in Holland and in all countries with which Java was connected. The following year the telephone system of the Deli Railway Company was also connected up so that East-Sumatra as well can hold radio-telephonic conversations. By building a radio-telephonic sender at Makassar in 1933 and one at Palembang in 1936 North- and South-Sumatra were likewise connected by radio-telephone.

The radio stations in many other places in the Archipelago are gradually being fitted for radio-telephonic use.

Radio-broadcasting

Before April 1st 1934 the radio in the Dutch East Indies gave but little satisfaction. Few people listened in because long-distance reception was generally bad or impossible. The heavy atmospheric disturbances make it impossible to listen even to local music broadcast on wave-lenghts above 150 meters and at great distances the disturbances interfere with all sound so that one can not hear any senders above 100 meters wave-length. For the Indies one has therefore to make use only of wave-lenghts from 16—60 meters. Senders of that type were then rare or unknown. Short-wave receiving-sets were expensive.

In 1933 the Netherlands-Indian Broadcasting Corporation (N.I.R.O.M.) obtained a concession from the Government, with the obligation to organise within a certain period of time a program for the Western population as well as one for the Oriental population and to make this perfectly audible. This meant that, under circumstances that from a radio-technical point of view were exceptionally difficult, two programs should be made audible at the same time over a territory extending in the direction North-South over a distance equalling that from northern Germany to southern Italy and West-East equalling that from the extreme western tip of Ireland and Spain to far into Asia Minor.

On April 1st 1934 the N.I.R.O.M. began with four senders, at Batavia, Bandung, Semarang and Surabaya and in the course of that year the number was increased to seventeen. Five senders had the general (Western) program for West-Java, six for East and Central Java and the remaining six took care of the Oriental program. On January 1st 1935 it was found that on the whole of Java, with few exceptions, broadcasting was perfectly audible. Gradually the area was extended and on September 30th 1936 the entire Dutch East Indies were satisfactorily served by the N.I.R.O.M. Senders were increased in number and made more powerful; by the end of 1939 28 senders were in use, some of them being so strong that they may be easily heard in Europe. 37 different frequencies have been allotted to local broadcasting organisations and radio-dealers and, since all of these try to make themselves audible at the greatest possible distance, a good deal of organisation is necessary.

The number of listeners-in that in January 1933 did not amount to quite 5000 had in January 1940 increased to nearly 90.000 and it may be supposed to be well over 100.000 by now.

The enormous significance of the radio for the general public is obvious. People living at distant, isolated places who used to be deprived from all such cultural advantages, are now able to listen in to educational courses, religious services, concerts, theatricals and addresses by Government officials and others. International football games, played in Europe, excite such interest that every living-room becomes as it were part of the public tribunes where every goal made by one's nationals is cheered as loudly as on the football-field itself. Besides this there is the daily press-news, eagerly followed by everybody. Those who used to be out of everything, and after weeks or months received their newspapers with stale news, now can keep abreast of all that happens from day to day in the more inhabited parts of the globe.

CHAPTER 11

The Conquest of Natural Resources
Western Energy and Technique

THE STRUGGLE FOR AND AGAINST WATER

As in most regions within the equatorial rainbelt, while the population was sparse and the land largely covered with tropical forests, agriculture in the Indies was *ladang* cultivation. This method consists of cutting and burning the forest in suitable places and, without any further tillage of the soil, planting alimentary products, that is, in the Indies, chiefly dry padi. Such *ladangs* usually only serve a short time, as after a few years the yield diminishes to such an extent that new terrains have to be opened up. The crop is entirely dependent on the rainfall which is limited to one definite rainy season and so planting is only possible during that season.

This *ladang* agriculture is only able to provide food for comparatively small numbers of people and remains very primitive. Only when after a long time the deserted *ladangs* are once more covered with forests can they again be used; sometimes they remain permanently unfit for use and are lost for agricultural purposes because the fertile topsoil is washed away or the soil is covered by parasitic grasses forming the well-known alang-alang plains. The population must therefore dispose of ever fresh territories and repeatedly found new settlements surrounded by large areas of uncultivated soil. As the population grows denser, in the long run there are not enough fresh forestlands available and it is compelled to keep these lands in use much longer or even permanently and apply new agricultural methods which may ensure sufficient crops even under such circumstances.

In the densely populated regions of the Indies, such as Java, Madura, Bali, the period of *ladang* cultivation is long past, but on Sumatra, Borneo and New-Guinea even to-day it frequently occurs.

The transition from *ladang* cultivation to permanent cultivation of the same fields has everywhere been chiefly made possible by the replacement of the dry padi cultivation by the wet or sawah padi cultivation. This takes place on fields that during the entire period of cultivation until just before the harvest are entirely submerged by water; this water is held there by levelling the fields, larger or smaller according to the original incline of the terrain, and surrounding them by small dykes. Since a sufficient submerging of the sawahs cannot be guaranteed by the rainfall on the sawahs alone, even with the plentiful though mostly very irregular tropical rains, sawah cultivation can only yield good results if by an artificial water-supply, that is by irrigation, the needs can be met. With the transition to the wet padi cultivation therefore the struggle for water began.

The most primitive way to get water is, to drain it off, by means of small channels, from fields behind and slightly higher than the sawahs. The water-supply then increases and may be sufficient even when there is little rainfall. It remains however dependent on the rainfall in the immediate vicinity and, because this frequently fails for fairly long periods even in the rainy season, this system of irrigation often remains entirely unsatisfactory. A definite improvement is only achieved when the water is supplied by channels that through their affluents reach out into the mountains and so always contain sufficient water for the sawahs dependent on them. Irrigation from such channels at the same time has the inestimable advantage that the water contains silt and salts abundantly furnishing the crops with the indispensable fertilisers. Especially in the Indies where the mountains largely consist of late volcanic soil rapidly corroded by the abundant rainfall, the water of most rivers is very rich; this exceptionally fortunate circumstance explains the fact that, while fields not irrigated and washed by the heavy rains quickly lose their fertility, irrigated fields retain their fertility throughout the centuries and naturally poor soil even may improve considerably through irrigation. If the rivers contain water in the dry season also, there is the additional advantage that even in that period the fields may be irrigated and planted. Though this is generally not done with padi requiring plenty of water, it is feasible for other crops, the so-called east-monsoon crops, requiring less, and so the annual yield of the field is considerably increased.

At first the struggle for water had to be waged with very simple means: low dams in the smaller rivers in the hills, built by piling up loose stones of which the rivers themselves yielded an inexhaustible supply, were sufficient to conduct the water into the small irrigation channels. As the population increased and larger terrains in the plains had to be brought into cultivation, ever larger rivers had to be tapped. Since the beds of the larger rivers in the plains generally do not contain stones, dams there were built with bamboo and wood and by means of these dams the water had sometimes to be raised up several meters and to be conducted to the sawahfields in long channels. Such dams however cannot resist the devastating force of the banjirs, frequent during the west monsoon: either they are washed away by the swollen stream so that no water at all is diverted into the channels or, if they withstand the pressure, far too much water flows into them, silting up the openings at the mouth with large quantities of sand and stones and scouring and damaging the channel beds. Only by incessant hard labour on the dams and channels is it at all possible to maintain irrigation with such primitive means and the farmers have to toil without respite for the preservation of water that in itself is abundant enough. In laying out their dams and channels they show great perseverance and skill, but their technical knowledge remained elementary and throughout the centuries it does not seem ever to have advanced. While in architecture brilliant examples of the achievements of Java's inhabitants in the distant past may even to-day be admired in the beautiful temple ruins, in irrigation, though untold millions have slaved at it, no remains from the past are extant, with the possible exception of a few very old channels.

Only by the introduction of western technique constructions were made, strong enough to serve for long years, and was it possible to replace the ephemeral works of loose stones, wood or bamboo by permanent constructions of masonry, concrete and iron.

About the middle of the last century the situation on Java had become such that the Government felt the necessity, in the interest of agriculture, to have irrigation works built by its engineers and to depart from its former policy of leaving the responsibility for irrigation entirely to the farmers themselves.

On account of the great increase in population, then already noticeable, and consequently the ever growing extension of agriculture over the vast coastal plains, in the struggle for water, apart from many lesser ones, the larger rivers had also been harnessed for irrigation purposes. In spite of the farmers' willingness, under the direction of their chiefs and the officials of the Civil Service, constantly to perform exacting labour requiring innumerable hands and a great deal of material, the difficulties which they encountered were so great that conditions at many places became intolerable. This was, to a large extent, also due to the circumstance that in native irrigation works not sufficient attention was given to the essential provision for draining off the water. Existing drains frequently were made unserviceable as such by dams built in them in the interest of flooding; new draining-channels were never built; the most that was done was to prevent inundations from the rivers here and there by the construction of light dykes. Hence failures of crops both by scarcity of water and by floods were frequent and extensive.

At first the assistance of the government's engineers was limited to incidental cases. Where help was felt to be most urgent native constructions, the maintenance of which clearly was beyond the power of the natives, — generally dams in rivers that fed larger channels, — were replaced by permanent constructions, and in regions repeatedly harassed by floods the draining-system was improved. Though the resulting improvement was considerable it was not enough. By building a major construction here and there, all the difficulties of conducting and separating the water through the primitive channels with their defective devices for separating and tapping, the inefficient water-control etc. were not eliminated. With the increase of participants in the use of the available water it was felt more and more that with such primitive works an economic husbandry of water was impossible and a fair distribution out of the question. Before long therefore it was realised that the ever growing demand for water could only be met by entrusting to a special staff a much wider and more intensive control of the supply and distribution of water. Thus, from 1885 on, the incidental assistance was gradually and carefully replaced by permanent control. Beginning with those regions where improvements were most urgent, it was steadily extended so that at the beginning of this century it already covered a large part of Java. Now for years it has become so intensive that it may be said that on Java all the available water has been placed under technical control. At first this control had to make the best of the very imperfect means provided by native irrigation, but gradually improvements were effected and a beginning was made with the construction of complete, technically well-equipped, new works.

This intensive water-control was achieved by dividing Java into so-called irrigation-zones. Each irrigation zone comprises the basin of one or more of the larger rivers and totals several hundred thousand hectares of arable land. At the head of each zone is an engineer with a large staff of technicians. Apart from the control of the supply and repartition of water, he is entrusted with the construction of new works and the maintenance of the existing ones.

When Dutch engineers began to apply western technique to irrigation their first hydraulic constructions were modelled on those with which they were familiar at home. They even went so far as to use Dutch materials, such as Dutch bricks, carried to Java as ballast in the sailing vessels. Before long however an architectural type was evolved that made use of local materials and styles. These first constructions, though solid enough in themselves, were sometimes, for want of good maps and charts, built without sufficient knowledge of the lay of the land and the details of the irrigation system and so the results were disappointing. After the systematic control of irrigation had been undertaken by the Government, the engineers soon made themselves thoroughly familiar with all the secrets of irrigation methods and the initial defects were remedied and in future avoided.

To build all the works necessary for an irrigation region is a very extensive operation. Through a main channel fed by the reservoir the water is conducted further and, by means of locks, tapped off into secondary channels which carry it to the secondary sections. These are subdivided into smaller tertiary units, each of which receives water from a tertiary channel tapping the secondary one through a lock. The size of these tertiary units is so modest that the final care for further small works may in general, provided there is the necessary supervision, safely be left to the farmers themselves. The most convenient size is from 100—150 hectares.

All cultivated lots within this region should be able to receive water as well as drain it off. Since the level of the irrigating channel must be higher, but that of the draining channel lower than the field concerned, a second system of channels is necessary, which finally emerges into a river or the sea.

Now for all this very detailed maps, clearly indicating all variations of elevation, are indispensable. Such maps have to be drawn by the irrigation service itself. By careful observation, extending over a long period of years, numerous data have to be collected about the volume of water available in the different seasons, in order to fix the acreage that may be irrigated by a river. The planning and execution of a sound irrigation system is therefore an extremely slow and painstaking work, but only in this way is it possible to guarantee a regular and fair distribution of the water over the smallest units and a good drainage of the rainwater.

When, at the beginning of this century, the systematic construction of modern irrigation works began, first the existing native works were improved. These had to do with irrigation from smaller and middle-sized rivers for irrigation regions of at most ten thousand hectares. The reservoirs, built in the middle or upper course of the river, where the bed has been scoured out fairly deeply, nearly always consist of a weir of masonry, damming the river and so raising the water up sufficiently to be conducted into the tapping-channel. Generally a few meters are sufficient for that purpose. These weirs naturally raise the water level in the river during banjirs, but so long as the beds are deep, whatever damage might occur may be averted by short dykes. The irrigation region is extended as much as possible to include sawahs formerly dependent on the rainfall or not irrigated at all. With the better modern equipment rivers that could not be tackled with the primitive native means can now be made serviceable. This is particularly the case with the larger rivers in the plains, which, full of fertile silt and with an abundant water-supply, so far were flowing through the coastal plains without being used for sawahs that were hankering after water but had to be content with very insufficient irrigation dependent on rainfall or minor streams.

At the same time in the hills, where numerous native irrigation works often supplied small regions almost too abundantly with water, constructions were built to prevent waste, and ensure the water supply for the lower districts.

The tapping of water from the large rivers in the plains can not be effected by means of the ordinary fixed weirs. During the western monsoon the water level of these rivers often rises to or above the banks. A further raising of this level would have to be offset by very long and high dykes. The weir should therefore be built in such a way that at low levels it presses the water up to the required height but at high levels does not cause any further stowing up. This is done by making a weir consisting of solid pillars between which there are openings that can be shut at will by sliding gates. In the Chi-Tarum river for example there is a weir with four openings twenty meters wide that can be closed by heavy iron rolling shutters of six meters high. When the gates are up the banjir water may pass through freely without unduly raising the water level.

The reservoirs in the large rivers of the plains generally provide water for very extensive irrigation regions; that of the Chi-Tarum comprises an area of 71.000 hectares, that of the Chi-Manuk of 80.000 hectares and that of the Tangerang of 52.500 hectares.

On account of the very flat formation of the coastal plains and the extremely high water levels which may occur in the rivers, the drainage there was generally poor and the ricecrops were often severely damaged by water. The improvement of irrigation was therefore coupled with a struggle against superfluous water. The coastal towns also repeatedly suffered from lack of drainage and extensive and costly works were constructed in order to protect such cities as Batavia, Semarang and Surabaya against the water.

The irrigation from some rivers presents the difficulty that the ground is so situated that the water can not easily be stowed up to the required level with the ordinary means. This difficulty can only be solved by pumping the water up. In other countries wide regions are supplied with water by means of pumping, but in the Indies this method of irrigation, as a rule much more expensive than that by means of a weir, until recently was not applied for the irrigation of sawahs. This method had however for many years been applied for the less exacting irrigation of sugarcane plantations where, with the aid of pumping-stations, in the dry season water, that otherwise could not be used for irrigation purposes, is pumped up from riverbeds and water-channels. Only during the last few years pump-irrigation for the water-supply of sawahs has been applied in a region of 20.000 hectares in the "residency" of Banjumas, which receives water from the Seraju by means of an electrical pumping-station.

The supply of water discussed so far was mainly concerned with the western monsoon irrigation of the indispensable staple-food crop, the padi. In the eastern monsoon the available water-supply is considerably less but then also there is great need of irrigation water, since then, at least on the lower ground, all planting without irrigation is impossible. Crops of the eastern monsoon however are also extraordinarily important, not only for the food-supply, but as an economic factor as well. Moreover the cultivation of sugarcane, the chief crop of western enterprise, requires water in the eastern monsoon and is even entirely impossible without irrigation. Although the crops of the eastern monsoon and sugarcane need much less water than padi, on account of the far smaller supply of the rivers in the eastern monsoon the demand for water then is even more urgent and the struggle for it even fiercer. In many regions there is a bitter dearth of water in the eastern monsoon. Western technique provided the means of improving this state of affairs. During the western monsoon the abundance of water in the river is frequently greater than is needed for immediate irrigation purposes. Rather than to allow this water to flow down to the sea unutilised, part of it is collected in large reservoirs, formed by building high dams in suitable riverbeds in the hills, which back the water up several scores of meters and form collecting basins of millions of cubic meters. With this water, collected during the western monsoon, the scarcity in the eastern monsoon may be supplemented. There are already many of these reservoirs on Java, where, on a small scale, the farmers used to apply this method of old, and during the last twenty years many more, and among these some of the largest, have been built. The total contents of these reservoirs now amounting already to 400 million cubic meters, will certainly be much larger in future.

This struggle to make the best possible use of all available water was combined with constant efforts to increase the acreage. As the population increased, by breaking virgin soil, forests and marshes, ever new fields were made available for tillage. During the last forty years on Java and Madura the total area of sawah fields was augmented from 2.700.000 to 3.350.000 hectares; that of the dry fields from 2.900.000 to 4.600.000 hectares.

There is however a limit to the quantity of land as well as the quantity of available water. Large areas of forest in the hills have to remain intact since deforestation would unfavourably affect the watei supply of the rivers, while also for the supply of timber much forest must be respected. With a further increase of the acreage of about 1.000.000 hectares the utmost limit will be reached on Java and Madura that have a total surface of 13.200.000 hectares. A large part of these fields however will never have the benefit of irrigation water; these dry fields are chiefly located in the hills and because of the milder climate, without irrigation and particularly if — as becomes more and more customary — they are manured, they can yield very satisfactory harvests. Not of padi however; this staple-product, rice, will always be confined to irrigated fields. The final maximum production of rice will therefore not depend so much on the available acreage as on the available volume of water and this is dependent on the final results of the hard struggle for water by means of the irrigation technique. The results of this struggle so far are that, while in 1900 there were scarcely any complete technical irrigation works at all, in 1910 the necessary works for 100.000 hectares, in 1920 for 519.000 hectares, in 1930 for 883.000 hectares and in 1940 for 1.300.000 hectares were completed and in full use, which, in other words, is equivalent to an area of two fifths of the Netherlands.

The struggle for and against water is not merely confined to Java and Madura. In the Outer Islands it began at about the turn of the century and was carried on with ever increasing energy during the last few years. The need of alleviating the pressure of population on Java through emigration to the Outer Islands, — Sumatra, Borneo and Celebes, — and therefore of opening up these regions as production areas for the gigantic and ever increasing quantities of rice needed for the population of the Indies, was a strong incentive for carrying the battle to these countries of inexhaustible possibilities.

It is self-evident that this struggle for and against water has demanded considerable financial sacrifices. From 1900 to 1940 there was a total expenditure of 270.000.000 florins for projecting and executing new and keeping up old works.

Apart from irrigation there are other purposes for which water supply is of vital importance. Fortunately the quantities involved are not so enormous as for irrigation.

In the first place there is the need of providing waterpower for electricity, which in the Indies is almost exclusively produced in this way. For this purpose it is necessary to have water dropping from a great height. The waterpower stations therefore are always in the hills; the water is gained from the mountain torrents and conducted to the powerhouse with the aid of constructions that show much resemblance to irrigation works: mostly it is necessary to build storage basins so as to have enough water available in the dry season. The water is used but not used up and below the power-house it can again be utilised for irrigation purposes. All constructions of this kind were built during the last forty years. In the government's power-houses alone, though they supply only part of the total electrical energy produced in the Indies, much of it being in the hands of private concerns, in 1938 135.000.000 kilowatt hours were produced.

Finally the city-waterworks make a demand on the available water supply. During the last forty years all large and a number of smaller and even very small places were provided with excellent aqueducts for drinking water. On the Outer Islands all important towns also have good water-works and there and on Java more are constantly being built.

THE GREAT PLANTATIONS

These pages will deal with the great plantations, founded with western capital, run on western lines and controlled by western people, mostly Dutch. There is no exaggeration in the appellation "great". These planta-tions are great as units; even a small one comprises an area at least ten times that of a modern farm in the newly reclaimed polders of the former Zuyder-zee; the larger ones are a hundred times that size. Their number is also great: both on Java and on the Outer Islands there are about 1200, that is 2400 in all. Their total area is large: on Java 600.000 hectares and in the Outer Islands 575.000 hectares, that is in all 1.175.000 hectares or 11.750 square kilometers, which is 15 % more than the total agricultural acreage of the Netherlands and one third of their total surface. Great is also the yield of tropical crops: in 1939 it amounted to 2¼ million tons with a value of about 300 million florins.

Mission 10

Great again is the social-economic significance of these plantations. One figure will illustrate this: the great plantations furnish labour for, at a moderate estimate, 1¼ million natives, which is twice the number of the total agricultural population of the Netherlands.

They are indeed great in every respect!

Nevertheless there are some misconceptions about these plantations.

There is, in the first place, a very general misconception, that the pioneers of these plantations with their capital, their energy and their organising power have seized the existing native agriculture; that, in so far as it seemed advantageous, they have rationalised it, and that therefore they have exploited in a western way the age-old agricultural assets. Against the undeniable economic advantage of this more rational exploitation there is therefore supposed to be the social disadvantage of undermining the autonomous, though more primitive, activity of native agriculture. It is however a fact that not a single one of the important products of the great agriculture was formerly cultivated by the natives. In so far as they are being cultivated by them today, it is a result of the example given to the population by the great plantations. The very important cultivation of coffee and rubber form an illustration of this assertion. The products which the Dutch found in the Indies and which excited their great interest in these regions, namely pepper, cloves, nutmeg, spices in general and some other exotic products, never were incorporated into the western agriculture on any large scale. Coffee, tea, quinine, rubber, fibrous plants (sisal, cantala), cocoa, oil palm trees were introduced either by the Government or by the western planters. There is no question of part of the traditional native agriculture gradually having been forced to give way to western, capitalistic, large-scale industry with its advantages and inevitable drawbacks. On the contrary, western plantations supplemented and enlarged the basis of economic life in the Indies which, as will be shown, could not possibly have got along without them.

Another general misconception is that the western plantations have their origin in the former compulsory cultivation of certain products. The western planter, it is supposed, simply stepped into the shoes of the Government, when this system of compulsory cultivation, known as that of van den Bosch, was abolished and the free cultivation of these products was expressly denied to the native farmer who had the oldest title to it. This presentation of the facts is, in general, untrue. It is quite obviously false in the case of new products like rubber, export-tobacco, fibres, palmoil, which were started long after the compulsory cultivation system had vanished. But even in the case of the older products like sugar, coffee, tea and quinine there is only a small particle of truth in this assertion. Even during the compulsory cultivation the Government, for sound reasons, contracted with European industry for the extracting of sugar from the sugar cane grown by the natives. The abolition of the compulsory system therefore confronted this industry with the problem of how to procure the sugar cane without pressure on the population. The compulsory cultivation of coffee that had become a very important source of revenue to the Government was carried out by the natives on fields belonging to them. When compulsion was abolished the population entirely abandoned the cultivation of this product, in a great measure as a result of a catastrophic leaf blight, which allowed the cultivation of Arabian coffee only on some high fields in the hills. The European large-scale private cultivation of coffee that now began had to respect the population's right to the use of their own fields and therefore had to look for entirely new land for its plantations and adopt new methods. As for tea and quinine, though the credit is due to the Government of having been the pioneer in their cultivation, they had never anything to do with the system of compulsory cultivation. To say therefore that upon the abolition of the compulsory system the western planter merely stepped into the Government's shoes is really too simplistic a view.

A third misconception concerns the way in which the western planters acquired the land needed for the cultivation of their products. In order to clear this up, a little excursion is necessary.

It is often believed that against the benefits which the great plantations yield to all concerned there is the drawback that they use land formerly tilled or at least tillable by the natives for their own agriculture. What however is the case?

When the compulsory system was in full swing, private individuals who wished to practise large-scale agriculture, apart from other difficulties, had but few and inadequate means at their disposal for acquiring the necessary land. The Government had no powers to sell land on a large scale; sale or lease of land by natives to non-natives was forbidden. The only alternative left to western private enterprise was, either to take on lease waste land from the Government or try to persuade the natives to grow on their fields the products which it was prepared to put on the market. On such foundations it was impossible for large-scale agriculture to thrive. Lessee rights formed a poor basis for a financial project: they could not be subject to either transfer or mortgage and did not offer any security to the planter or his investor. The second method was equally unattractive: one would be entirely dependent on the skill and good faith of the native farmers with whom such agreements were to be made. There would be no control over these people and it would be impossible to introduce rational business methods, vital for any enterprise involving large capital. In neither way could western large-scale agriculture prosper. Yet this was urgently necessary. Not only, as people sometimes believe today and certain political circles then took for granted, for the benefit of those would-be planters who were out for making a fortune. It was demanded by the entire economic development of which the signs were unmistakable. Whatever criticism one may level at the compulsory system, it is a fact that it braced the economic life and stimulated the increase of population. When therefore in the middle of the 19th century compulsion began to be reduced and made less severe, and when finally total abolition, though gradual, was decided on, it was imperative not to allow the newly gained economic activity to die down. The only practicable solution was large-scale agriculture by private concerns, but, in order to succeed, this had to be given a solid basis.

The result was the Agrarian Law of 1870. The main principle of this law was the ruling that all no-man's land was at the Government's free disposal. Moreover this law had the double purpose of giving security and freedom of movement to the growing large-scale agriculture and of guaranteeing to the native population its title to its land. To this end it was decreed that all waste lands of which the Government may freely dispose, could be given in hereditary lease for a period of 75 years, and that, subject to certain rules, natives could lease their lands to non-natives; further, that no cession of land could infringe the rights of tenure of the native population. The sale of land by natives to non-natives was, as heretofore, forbidden.

For the one-year crops, such as sugar and tobacco of which every year the entire yield is harvested, a short lease is sufficient, though, in the case of sugar, because of the expense of modern factories, the term should not be made too short. For the cultivation of these crops this law therefore created the possibility of leasing land from the natives. This was necessary because the possibility of cultivating these crops on the dry lands at the disposal of the Government is very limited. The two products named, as well as the new cultivation of rosella (that is the Java-jute, from which guni-sacks are made), are raised on irrigated fields. Rarely will the natives not have rights of tenure on such irrigated fields, since they use these for growing rice, their favourite crop. If these lands are wanted for large-scale agriculture there is in general no other possibility than, observing the restrictions imposed by law, to try to lease these lands from the population. By far the largest part of the area, occupied by large-scale agriculture, consists however of virgin soil, broken by the planters themselves, on which previously the natives grew no crops at all and from which the benefit was little or nothing. With the exception of the short-lease lands for the one-year crops, covering about 150.000 hectares annualy (that is approximately one eighth of the total area of western agriculture), the plantations of this large-scale agriculture are therefore an addition to the cultivated land, wrested from the tropical forest, and economically comparable to the land-reclamation that will be the result of the Zuyderzee works in the Netherlands.

To say then, that the great agriculture uses about 1.000.000 hectares for the cultivation of perennial crops, means that 1.000.000 hectares of waste land have been reclaimed and planted. This reclamation is nearly always a conquest of the primeval forest and must be constantly defended tooth and nail. Should this defense relax, the result would be no more doubtful than what would happen to our Dutch land-reclamations should we neglect dyke-repairs: tropical nature which is relentless and has no respect for human labour would in a short time regain its conquered territory. The defense is the more difficult because the plantations are widely scattered. There are indeed regions where they adjoin each other, where entire mountain slopes or plateaux have been brought under cultivation, but such cultivated zones are but islands in the midst of the merciless, wild, tropical nature.

Though these islands of western exploitation are scattered over a large part of the Archipelago, naturally the western planter first chose the island of Java as the field of his activities. There, of old, he was most at home. The Dutch Government's administration there was already very intensive at a time when scant attention was given to the Outer Islands. On Java the planter found to a certain degree the protection of a well-ordered society, without which economic development is scarcely conceivable. There was already a fairly good system of roads, at least in the inhabited regions; a beginning had been made with the building of railways. There was peace and order, and life and property were secure. An ever increasing population could furnish the labour required for the reclamation of the land and its future exploitation. This point deserves to be examined a little closer. It is often made to appear, that this increase of population made it simple for western capital to start and develop their plantations, as if, in other words, this merely amounted to a very obvious exploitation of an ever increasing surplus of cheap labour. It is true that in the last quarter of the 19th century, when the great plantations were started, the Javanese population increased annualy by several hundred thousand souls. Looking at this increase from a merely statistical point of view, one is inclined to conclude that the western concerns could draw from an abundantly flowing source of labour. This however was far from being the case. The beneficial results of the Dutch administration, improving irrigation and so extending the acreage available for alimentary crops, were already widely felt, and made it possible to provide an adequate food-supply for the increasing population. The Javanese with his traditional preference for the cultivation of alimentary crops continued to be primarily interested in this and most of the new mouths could provide for themselves in their own environment. The Javanese desa, if not in depth, was developing considerably in breadth.

Under such circumstances it is clear that for the western plantations, laid out on waste land, there was no question of an easy and cheap exploitation of the population surplus. On the contrary, the pioneers often had to take a great deal of trouble to recruit the necessary labourers and to persuade them to settle down permanently on or near the plantations. A chronic shortage of labour was one of the chief obstacles which the pioneers encountered. These difficulties were only gradually overcome through the increasing birth-rate of the native settlers. The situation was somewhat different for that kind of western agriculture such as sugar and tobacco that was dependent on the lease of irrigated fields belonging to the natives. This is an intermittent lease, in other words, it is not allowed to use the same land during an un-interrupted number of years for western agriculture. The western planter is obliged by law, as soon as he has garnered his harvest, to place the land at the disposal of the owner for his food crop. This explains why the western planter, on starting the cultivation of sugarcane and tobacco (formerly also indigo), established himself as it were in the midst of Javanese life. Here however the question of labour also frequently presented difficulties, in the past as well as today. The supply is very variable, dependent on seasons and circumstances. The Javanese rice-cultivation requires many hands, particularly for the harvest, and the natives prefer it to any other agriculture. If it happens that, owing to whims of the climate, the period of the greatest labour on the ricefields coincides with the greatest demand of labour by the western planters in the same region, the latter will experience a shortage of hands. He then has the greatest difficulty in getting his fields tilled and planted on time. Frequently labour has to be recruited from distant regions where the shortage of hands is less serious, and in the period when the cul-tivation of sugar reached the peak of its development, experiments were made with expensive mechanical ploughs to replace manual labour in case of necessity.

Nevertheless, taking all in all, the western planter of annual crops does on the whole succeed in securing the necessary labour. This is not so much the result of a chronic over-supply caused by the steady increase in popula-tion, as of the fact that this form of agriculture has become part and parcel of Javanese life. Every traveller in the Indies observes that the relations of the natives and the western planter are very close and friendly. There are far more interests to unite than to divide them. Though there may be occasional squabbles about the distribution of the precious irrigation water, about the fields in use by the natives and those on which the planter has his crop standing at the moment, these incidents are of no account com-pared to the predominant interest of both parties in the total volume of water and the preservation, improvement and extension of irrigation works and weirs. The timely and abundant irrigation of the nursery beds of the natives' rice crop is of vital interest to the Javanese farmer, but at the same

time it does not leave the planter indifferent, since the more the harvest of
the native crop is delayed by scarcity of water, the later the land becomes
free for the next crop of, let us say, sugarcane. Both parties also are equally
interested in the combat against blights and diseases. They have innumerable friends and foes in common. It is certainly true that in courting common friends and fighting common foes the western planter often takes the
initiative and shows the greater energy, but it is equally true that in the
long run, as his understanding matures, the Javanese is quite willing to
follow his lead.

Now is it true, as is sometimes contended, that in this so much smaller
sphere of conflicting interests, the will of the economically stronger western
planter predominates? An affirmative answer to this question would wrong
the excellent Dutch administration. For in all these controversial points the
Government is on the lookout, carefully weighs the interests involved, guards
against arbitrary action, and protects the weak against the strong, should
these be inclined to go too far. As soon as there is the slightest danger of this
kind, the Government intervenes and the carefully planned, preventive
regulations, devised over a long period of years, forming strong bulwarks
against any violation of the boundaries fixed in the common interest,
are innumerable. It is scarcely conceivable that there exists any other
country in the world, where the Government so jealously watches over
the general interest as in the Indies, and where such a vast knowledge and
experience of the life and vital needs of the people have been stored by the
Government.

But, it may be objected, the western planter no doubt is interested in low
wages. What about this? Does there not lurk here an opportunity of exploitation by colonial capital that might be injurious to the population?

The answer to this question lies in an analysis of the character of wage-
labour performed for the plantations by the natives. Let us first look again
at those concerns that have their plantations on lands leased from the natives or are at least located in the midst of Javanese rural life. In the original
Javanese society the proletarian was unknown, as is generally the case where
agriculture is the principal means of subsistence. The landtenure of the
Javanese is extremely cut up; large landholdings are exceptional. Labour in
other people's employ naturally also occurs among the native agricultural

population, but, apart from the fact that remuneration of such services is often in kind, the relationship between employer and employee is quite different from that in the West. These wage-labourers are therefore by no means proletarians in the western sense of the word. Now it is a striking fact that, wherever western large-scale agriculture has been introduced, proletarisation of the population also scarcely exists, if it exists at all. Hence wage-labour there has also a different character than in the West.

The people who enter the service of the western planter may be divided into two main groups. In the first place there is the large group of those who are only temporarily in the service of the westerner, that is only during the period, chiefly that of planting and harvesting, when the greatest amount of work has to be done. Now it is a curious but very fortunate circumstance that for those products with which we are here chiefly concerned, this period in general coincides with the time when there is least work in native agriculture. This period therefore offers the natives the opportunity, if they so desire, to earn additional wages on the plantations, and this addition to their income was the more welcome as the demands made on life by the natives gradually became higher, and their own village life could no longer furnish everything that was wanted, things such as clothes, better furniture, more expensive objects of utility, social intercourse, in short, all those things that lend colour and interest to life and that can only be obtained when there is a fairly developed system of monetary exchange. The relationship of these people to the plantation is therefore intermittent and entirely free. Any kind of contract stipulating the length of service is absent. There is the most complete liberty. If it does not please the labourer to work on the plantation there is nothing to compel him. If he does not wish to earn an additional income, if he can do without it, or if he simply wishes to have a few days off, nothing prevents him from staying at home. It is all left to his own sovereign judgment; it is largely a question of how far he needs an additional income and what is the purchasing value of the money earned.

This is of course all somewhat theoretical and it will be clear that the operation is not always so smooth. In times of economic crisis the fall of prices of the necessities bought for money often lags behind the fall of prices of the products of western agriculture and the lowering of wages. It may therefore happen—as it did happen during the depression years, — that, greatly to the detriment of the population, a disparity occurs between the purchasing value of the wage-money and the wages themselves, and that consequently there are complaints about low wages. On the other hand it should not be supposed that the planter reacts to every drop in prices by lowering wages. In practice the equilibrium achieved will be maintained until the economic pinch absolutely forces him to a reduction of wages, but even then it remains to be seen whether the population is willing to perform the labour at these lower wages. The employer certainly cannot independently fix the rate of pay if he wants to be sure of a sufficient supply of labour. Apart from the unforeseen consequences of such an unprecedented crisis as that of 1931—1934 against which employers can never entirely safeguard their employees, experience shows that generally both parties succeed in agreeing on a rate that satisfies both.

Let us now turn to the second group of employees. For recruiting labour, assignment and supervision of work, payment of wages etc. natives of greater intelligence and better training are wanted as overseeers, or *mandurs*. Moreover the complicated technical equipment of, let us say, a sugar plantation, cannot do without a number of native mechanics, the so-called *tukangs*, working chemists, clerks etc. All this is skilled work, that can not be done by drifting labour. Technical skill and experience are needed and these can only be acquired by years of training and practice in the same industry. Such people are in the permanent service of the western employer and resemble therefore more wage-labourers or personnel in the sense in which we understand this relationship. Although many of them still own their ricefields, yet they have become more detached from the desa. Often they live in the immediate vicinity of the factory that provides houses for them. Without having severed their contact with the desa, for their income they are largely dependent on the plantation. They have, in fact, reached a higher level of life than the desa can offer. Persons who want something else than the quiet, self-contained life of the native farmer, here get their chance. The plantation is the centre from which a differentiation in the community gets its impetus, and, however idyllic the picture of this native community may be, in the long run, as contacts with the outside world become more frequent, it does not satisfy its more progressive members.

The wages of this kind of people, being their chief or only income, should of course be adequate. Naturally they vary according to the fluctuating purchasing power of money. Employers however abide by a certain wage-scale that guarantees a decent livelihood. It is clearly to their interest not to let their technical staff deteriorate. In an extremely elaborate plant like a sugar-factory, in technical and chemical respect perfected in its minutest details, run by a handful of Europeans, no one will be foolish enough, for the sake of momentary gain, to risk losing the services of a personnel that often has a complete mastery of the most intricate working methods.

In this entire question of wage-labour and wages the interests of employer and employee are therefore in the main parallel.

The question of labour in the Outer Islands however is quite different and far more difficult. When, particularly during and after the governor-generalship of van Heutsz, Dutch administration was systematically extended to the other islands, opportunities were gradually offered there that previously did not exist. Our knowledge of land and people increased enormously and a detailed inventory could be made of large parts of the Outer Islands that had been practically unknown. It was found that, though especially on Sumatra the soil was not as fertile as on Java, there were regions, here and there, that could be brought under cultivation. At the same time it was realised that, for further pacification and penetration of the Government's authority, such a cultivation that always entails economic development, would be an indispensable adjunct of the administration. Large-scale agriculture as a stimulant to economic development is particularly necessary there, where the cultural level of the population is not high enough for it to be brought directly to greater economic activity through the benefits of a good administration. This implies that in those regions there certainly was not that abundance of cheap labour that is often supposed to be indispensable for western large-scale agriculture. The population either did not exist at all or lived in such primitive conditions that one could not count on its labour. It had no need of additional income; nor had it any desire to leave its own villages and settle down in the vicinity of the plantation in order to earn there in future the whole or part of its living. It was completely satisfied with the primitive existence it had led for centuries. It did not understand the idea of wage-earning. In other regions, where life was less primitive and a monetary system of exchange had already penetrated, the population had sufficient means of subsistence in its own agriculture so that it seemed superfluous to go to work on the new plantations. Hence it was impossible to depend on the supply of part time workers, as in the lowland agriculture in the great population centres of Java, nor could it be reasonably expected that before long a sufficient number of native colonists, willing to work, would settle on or near the plantations. There was no other way than to recruit labour from elsewhere, and this way was naturally followed. It is not strange that the first pioneers, the tobacco planters on the east coast of Sumatra, who started their plantations before our administration had been firmly established, began by recruiting Chinese. On the east coast of Sumatra there was far more contact with Malacca than with Java. On the Malay Peninsula Chinese labour was generally resorted to, and the great Chinese population reservoir lay not far off. Gradually Javanese were recruited, and in 1938 of the 332.000 labourers on all the plantations in the Outer Islands there were only 26.000 Chinese left.

Thus a close connection was established between the great agriculture of the Outer Islands and Java for which it now became an important economic factor. No less than 300.000 Javanese men and women find in the Outer Islands a means of livelihood that Java did not offer. In an expanding society like the Javanese there are constantly people who for some reason or other find it hard to retain their places and there are others, the most energetic ones, who believe that they have better chances elsewhere. They are by no means the scum of society. It is significant that in the residency of Kedu, the home of many labourers for the Outer Islands, illiteracy is less than elsewhere. The opportunity to emigrate to the Outer Islands offers what should be a very welcome adaptation to the changes taking place in the structure of native society.

The maintenance of such an army of labourers, recruited elsewhere, naturally presents peculiar difficulties. It is necessary to say a few words about the very special provisions made in the Outer Islands for this purpose. As stated before, on the east coast of Sumatra, in Deli, large-scale agriculture was started at a time when there was scarcely any question of effective Dutch rule. This only came after the economic development set in motion by the first tobacco planters. No wonder therefore that at first there were no labour regulations. If the immigrant labourer had no protection from the Government, no more did the employer have any guarantee that the labourer, recruited at great expense, in the form of recruiting costs, travelling expenses and the inevitable advance of money, would supply his labour during the time of the contract. This unsatisfactory state of affairs was ended by the introduction in 1880 of the so-called "coolie-ordinance", regulating rights and duties of both parties, thus creating security for both, which was the more indispensable so long as the corrective and compensating influences of a well-developed society were lacking. This coolie-ordinance among other things contained the provision that it was punishable by law to desert the service, without valid reason, before the expiration of the contract, just as a sailor is punishable who deserts his ship before the end of the voyage for which he has signed up. This is the "penal sanction" about which so much has been written. It would take too long to pause for a description of the battle that has been waging for many years around this question. The issue is, in any case, no longer of actual interest, for by recent modifications of the ordinance it was ruled that penal sanction may only be applied to an annually decreasing percentage of contracts. The tobacco planters had already decided earlier to abolish it altogether.

The planters, for that matter, had realised at an early date that it would be unwise to exact the harsh letter of contracts, be they guaranteed by law or not. Long before the Government established a Labour Inspection, they had themselves made provision for excellent medical care for the labourers, good and ever better housing, children's welfare, education, general hygiene etc., in short all those things for which in these remote parts one could not fall back on society. They gradually created the atmosphere necessary to give the labourer and his family, come from afar, a feeling of home and thus to make penal sanction superfluous.

A rough estimate of the wages paid to natives by large-scale agriculture in 1938 shows a figure of approximately 100 million florins. This is 33 % of the total export-value of the products of these plantations, 20 % of the total import of the Dutch East Indies and 60 % of the total export-value of the export products produced by the population itself. These comparisons demonstrate sufficiently the importance of this figure. It amounts to this, that by means of large-scale agriculture potential labour may be converted into products that can be sold abroad in exchange for others not produced by the Indies, but more and more needed by an ever developing society.

We omit further financial details as too dry and technical. If a guess may be hazarded as to the total amount of capital invested in the great plantations, it would be about 2 billion florins. The average profit of the shareholders probably is not more than 6 or 7 percent, which may be called moderate. Nevertheless the Dutch public is always keen on investments in East Indian stock. The total amount invested in the colonies is certainly not less than 5 billion florins, which is about 20 % of the total estimated national wealth. This keenness is not only due to cold calculation of what seems profitable. The public has confidence in the country, in the government, in the industry of the people and in the diligence and ability of the men who direct affairs.

Who are these men? Apart from a small number of foreigners, hospitably received, they are Dutchmen, born in the Netherlands and in the East Indies, trained at our excellent educational institutions here and yonder: agriculturalists, technicians, chemists, managers. They all join young and generally remain on the job till the end of their working career. They get to know all the tricks of the trade; familiar as they are with the practical side of all problems they are also interested in their scientific side. They will undertake to survey and lay a road through a primeval forest or on a steep mountain slope; they do not hesitate to build a bridge; they know how to get the water on to their fields and off of them. They know the people with whom they have to work and speak their language fluently. But they are also ready to go into the most intricate problems of their business and its technique, they are able to follow and turn to good account the arguments of the scholars from the experimental stations. They are hardworking men and their working hours under the tropical sun are a good deal longer than at home. They are justly proud of the results of their work and vie with one another in the constant improvement of these results: a finer and better product, a higher return pro hectare, a lower costprice. An intelligent and enthusiastic kind of people whom it is delightful to meet. These people are more ashamed of an untidy, poorly yielding plantation, of an unsatisfactory product, of the loss of workpeople that could have been prevented, than they are of low dividends paid by the managing-director. That, they say, is his business, but we are responsible for the plantation. Keen as they are, they are ever ready with plans for improvements and expansion, and though occasionally their ardour carries them too far, it is generally best not to restrain them too much.

Before the great depression began there were about 12.500 Europeans engaged in large-scale agriculture; it was then reduced to about 8000, that is a ratio of 1 to 150 of native labour. The excellent organisation and the judicious selection of the humbler native collaborators make up for this small number of Europeans.

A word should be said about the experimental stations. At an early date the planters realised that they could not do without scientific advice. The Government of the Indies, since the beginning of the nineteenth century, has had in its employ scholars who have more than once rendered valuable service. As large-scale agriculture in expanding often encountered great difficulties it felt the need of the regular advice of scientific specialists. So a number of experimental stations were established where all the technical problems of large-scale agriculture were studied. The results of these experiments have often been astounding; more than once they entirely revolutionised the methods followed by the planters, through methodical plant-selection better results were obtained, pests were successfully combatted, the technical manufacturing methods were improved, in short, it is largely owing to the work of the experimental stations that the great plantations in the Indies may boast of a high degree of efficiency.

MINING

The Hollander is not a born miner, and it took some time before he began to be interested in the subterranean treasures of the East Indies. Steam navigation created the need of coal and in 1846 the first coal was mined on Borneo. In 1850 an ordinance was published opening to the public the opportunity of acquiring mining concessions. The first concession granted was for tin on the island of Billiton, where, in spite of immense difficulties and dangers even from pirates, in 1853 the first return of 652 pikul of tin was produced.

Nevertheless for several years progress was slow. There were discouraging facts like, at one place, the massacre by the natives of the entire personnel of a coalmine. Only after in 1883 a concession for petroleum had been granted on the east coast of Sumatra did the real development of mining begin.

Let us first look at some statistics. In 1938 there were 114 concessions for the mining of different ores, 160 for petroleum and other bituminous substances, 29 for coal and 9 for other minerals, as well as 148 for the quarrying of various building materials. The mineral production for that year amounted to:

tin	27.800 tons
gold	2.400 kgs
silver	18.000 ,,
bauxite	245 000 tons
manganese	9.700 ,,
phosphate	33.000 ,,
sulphur	16.000 ,,
diamond	1.600 carats
coal	1.456.000 tons
petroleum	7.400.000 ,,
mineral gas	1.227.600 ,,
asphalt-limestone	6.200 ,,

Besides these there were smaller quantities of copper, nickel, platinum, wolfram, monazite and iodine. Artesian water, because of its salutary effect on public health, should not be forgotten either in this enumeration of the earth's riches.

Geologically the Indies are a late formation. Volcanic action is still very intense. There are about 400 volcanoes of which 80 are still active. From their efflata corrosion has formed the fertile soil and from their gases sulphur deposits were formed. A large part of the soil consists of rock belonging to the tertiary period. For the occurrence of minerals the importance of this formation is in the first place this, that its sedimentary formations con-

Sawah landscape in the Preanger region (Ja

tain considerable deposits of petroleum as well as coal, while in the igneous rock ores were formed, the chief of which are gold and silver. Coal in the Indies generally has a high percentage of gas, so that it is very suitable for burning in ordinary factory-furnaces without forced draught. For consumption in engines and ship's boilers with forced draught some precautions should be taken. A fault of this coal is that it triturates easily; about 30 % of the coal dug is less than 30 mm in size. Further trituration takes place during transportation and it is quite a problem, as yet but partially solved, what to do with this coaldust. Though some of it is used in various ways, a large part of it must still be thrown aside as unmarketable.

It is a lucky circumstance that most coal veins in the Indies are very close to or even emerge on the surface. To reach the coalbeds it is therefore not necessary to build deep and expensive shafts, but as a rule tunnels are sufficient or, if shafts are necessary, no great depth is required.

The coalbeds themselves are often of great depth. At Ombilin (Sumatra) there is one of 7 meters, at Bukit-Assam (Sumatra) of 12—20 meters. At the latter place the coal comes right to the surface so that no tunnels or shafts are necessary at all, but large quantities may be dug in open pits. Nearly the entire production of the Bukit Assam mine — 456.000 tons in 1938 — was extracted in this way, and there is no reason why this should not go on for many years.

Bukit Assam and Ombilin (517.000 tons) both on Sumatra, are Government property; together they supply about 65 % of the total production. The other mines, all in the south and east part of Borneo, are private concerns.

There are also considerable coal deposits at various places on Java, on Celebes, on New Guinea and several of the lesser islands. The total amount of good boiler coal in the Archipelago is estimated at 5—6 billion tons.

Petroleum, already known in ancient history, only acquired practical utility when it became possible, by distilling and a treatment with sulphuric acid, to prepare oil fit for lamps. In 1859 the first oilwells were drilled in Pennsylvania.

Less than ten years later, in 1868, on Java there was some experimental drilling. Although a little oil was found, the quantity was not sufficient for

Mission 11

exploitation. Better luck attended the concession granted in 1883 at Langkat, Sumatra. In 1890 the first oil was obtained there by the newly founded "Koninklijke Nederlandsche Maatschappij tot Exploitatie van Petroleumbronnen in Nederlandsch-Indië" ("Royal Dutch"), at present a household word all over the world. The interest in Indian oil now rapidly increased. Other companies followed suit. The production, in 1895 only 95.000 tons, rose to 434.000 tons in 1900; in 1904 it already exceeded one million. Yet in those initial years the oil industry was far from prosperous. A serious drawback was the high percentage of gasoline for which at that time there was no market and there was no other way of getting rid of this useless by-product than to burn it. The great number of independent companies not only led to strong mutual competition, but also made it more difficult to hold one's own against foreign competition. A sudden and unexpected drop in the production of the "Royal Dutch" gave tangible proof that a comparatively small business enterprise is menaced in its very existence by the utterly incalculable capriciousness characteristic of nearly all deposits of minerals. The way to meet this difficulty inherent in all mining is to have so many chances that winnings outweigh losses.

These considerations caused the Royal Dutch to initiate a policy of concentration and combination of the different interests, culminating in 1911 in united control of the entire production of crude oil and its refinement in the hands of its daughter company, the Bataafsche Petroleum Maatschappij, with a capital of 80 million florins.

In 1938 the total production, including that of gasoline from mineral gas, amounted to 7 million tons. The export value of oil and oilproducts was over 161 million florins. Though this output represents only 3 % of the world production of oil, the Dutch East Indies, after the U.S.A., Russia, Venezuela and Iran take the fifth place as oil-producing country. 65 % of this share is produced on Sumatra, 20 % on Borneo, 10 % on Java and the rest on Seran. These quantitative figures however do not demonstrate sufficiently the special importance of the East Indian oil. This lies in its peculiar character, which, irrespective of other local differences, invariably shows a high content of low-boiling components. On an average it contains not less than 50 % of gasoline and kerosine, sometimes as much as 70 %. Some of these oils also contain large quantities of paraffin wax for which product, along with Burma, the Dutch East Indies is one of the most important producing countries of the Far East.

The "Bataafsche" (B.P.M.) now owns on Sumatra the refineries Pangkalan Brandan and Pladju (near Palembang), on Borneo Balik Papan and on Java the oil-centres Wonokromo (near Surabaya) and Tjepu. The Standard Oil is represented in the East Indies by the Nederlandsche Koloniale Petroleum Maatschappij with establishments at Sungei Gerong (near Palembang) and Kapuan. Several fields are exploited jointly by the Government and the B.P.M. as Nederlandsch-Indische Petroleum Maatschappij. For the exploration of oil on New-Guinea the Nederlandsche Nieuw-Guinea Petroleum Maatschappij was founded by the B.P.M., the Nederlandsch-Indische Petroleum Maatschappij and the Nederland-Pacific Petroleum Maatschappij in cooperation. The last-named company is a combination founded by the Standard Oil and the Texas Oil Corporation.

The wide dispersal of oil-fields on the different islands necessitated concentration of the refining of the oils produced. Use is made of pipelines many hundreds of kilometers long, built by the latest technical methods. Good motorroads connect the fields with the refineries. In New-Guinea and elsewhere air-prospecting as well as the newest geological methods of exploration of the fields are used with good results. In this way during the last few years extensive territories have been explored that would have remained largely unknown had the older methods of geological expeditions been employed.

The strongly varying character of the East-Indian oils stimulated industry to a selective refining with the aid of the most modern and efficient methods. This is for example shown by the fact that, while in 1939 the refineries handled 29 % more than in 1938, 32 % more market produce was obtained. The Dutch East Indies often were the experimental field for new methods. So it was there that the first Edeleanu factory of the world was founded at Balik Papan for converting the soot-forming oil of Borneo into a valuable lamp-oil for the oriental market. The latest cracking plants and a factory for the manufacture of aeroplane-gasoline were erected here. The manufacture of propane, butane and gasoline from mineral gas was studied and perfected in the Indies before these methods were applied in other countries. As a result the East-Indian oil-industry has acquired a degree of elasticity enabling it to meet great fluctuations in the demands of its markets. A number of secondary industries such as sulphuric acid factories, drum and tin factories equipped with the most modern machines, make the industry partly independent of the import of ready-made materials.

Most of the output of the refineries is destined for export. The major part of this is collected centrally in tank installations of the various companies situated on the small islands in the neighbourhood of Singapore, where they are blended into market qualities according to local specifications and shipped to Europe and America or to the markets of the Far East. Part of these products is shipped by tankers directly to Australia, while another part, chiefly piece-goods, is carried directly from the producing centres to Penang and the ports of the Far East. The various islands being so widely scattered a well equipped tankfleet is indispensable for an efficient oil-industry in these parts.

Asphalt which is one of the refinery products of crude oil at many places also occurs in natural deposits. It is extracted as asphalt-limestone.

Some waterwells occurring in oilfields contain iodine in sufficient quantities for exploitation. So far this is done only on Java in the district of Surabaya.

It is customary to speak of *gold* mining in the Indies. This is not quite exact. Most gold-ore deposits contain a high percentage of silver, varying in different mines. Silver generally prevails in quantity but gold in value. But there are exceptions: in the now exhausted mine of Tambang Sawah in total 2500 kgs of gold was mined for a value of more than 4 million florins and 182.000 kgs of silver for a value of about 8 million, so that this really should be called a silver mine. In the same mine the ratio of both metals is not always the same; as a rule silver will increase at lower levels.

There are however gold-deposits of another type that contain almost no silver. They are chiefly important on account of the alluvial beds on which formerly the native gold-production of Borneo and North- and Central Sumatra was based and where now the mining-company Bengkalis dredges gold.

As early as the second century A. D. Ptolemy knew that the Indies produced gold and old Hindu and Chinese records also mention it. Traces of this old activity in the form of tunnels, shafts and stone implements may here and there be found even today. Later the East-Indian Company also was much interested in gold, made surveys and for a number of years, though with little profit, undertook the working of the old mine of Salida, on the west coast of Sumatra, that was already known in Hindu times.

The rise of modern gold-mining in the Indies dates from about 1895. As a result of grossly exaggerated rumours about the value of a few happy finds a real gold fever began. It only cooled down after several millions had been lost in expensive prospecting. Not more than 9 out of the 200 companies founded in the first 25 years managed to achieve regular production and only two of these have been paying regular dividends.

In 1938 the production was nearly 2400 kgs of gold and more than 18.000 kgs of silver with a total value of more than 5 million florins. Since 1900 the total production was 119.000 kgs of gold with a value of 200 million and 1.150.000 kgs of silver with a value of nearly 53 million florins.

By far the most important ore in the Indies is *tin*. In 1939 with an export of nearly 32.000 tons the Indies supplied 17 % of world-consumption of this metal. They were only surpassed by Malacca with 57.000 tons and closely followed by Bolivia with 28.000 tons. In 1938 when the export was only 21.000 tons the net profit amounted to 25 million florins, 21 million of which flowed into the Government's exchequer.

The production of tin is centred on the islands of Banka, with 15.564 tons in 1938, Billiton with 10.501 and Singkep with 1655 tons. Native mining at Bangkinang on the continent of Sumatra produces 17 tons. Judging from geological formations it is not unlikely that tin ore will be found in other places along the east coast of Sumatra and possibly in the western part of Borneo.

Tin is chiefly obtained in alluvial beds, by means of dredging and other mechanical devices for moving earth.

The exploitation at Banka is entirely a Government concern. That on Billiton, formerly in private hands, is now also partly owned by the Government. This concentration of all tin production in the hands of only two participants, whose interests are closely parallel, makes the industry very flexible, so that, without great shocks, it is able to adapt itself to the needs of expansion or reduction of production, according to the dictates of an ever changing market.

An American once said: "With tin it is either feasting or fasting." He meant to describe the uncontrollable capriciousness of the tin market, showing extremes such as at Banka, in 1926, a profit of 56 million florins and in 1932 a loss of nearly 2 million. Such fluctuations are now no longer possible, owing to an international agreement between the seven chief tin-producing countries: Belgian Congo, Bolivia, French Indo-China, Malacca, Dutch East Indies, Nigeria and Thailand. This International Tin Control Scheme aims at keeping the fluctuation of prices within reasonable bounds by regulating the production.

Tin-mining is of special importance for the Indies because the Government for 84 % is interested in its production. Its considerable profits are therefore largely used for public welfare.

The largest part of the tin-ore of Banka is smelted in foundries on the spot; the rest, as well as that of Billiton and Singkep, is shipped to Holland, where it is smelted at Arnhem.

Bauxite is an aluminium-ore. It occurs in the Riau Archipelago in an extensive layer of 3 or 4 meters depth. The ore is of excellent quality. It is still exported but there are plans on the way for founding an aluminium industry on Sumatra and Java.

Manganese-ore, though occurring on several islands, is only extracted at two places on Java. The production is not large but the quality is good.

The mining of *phosphate* is a recent development. It is also limited to Java. The mineral occurs in limestone crevices and has probably been formed by a combination of this stone with phosphoric acid produced by guano-deposits.

The mining of *diamonds* is entirely in the hands of the natives. At present it is only practised in the southern and eastern districts of Borneo. The production has gradually decreased from 5600 carats in 1875 to not more than 900 carats on an average during the last 25 years. This is probably less due to exhaustion of the mines, than to the fact that, as the Outer Islands were more and more opened up, the natives abandoned the exacting and uncertain work of mining for the cultivation of various crops, thus securing a larger and surer income for less labour.

Other minerals than those named are not yet regularly mined. A little *copper*, some *platinum* are obtained as by-products of some gold-mines. At

Billiton and Singkep *monazite* and *wolframite* are obtained as by-products of tin.

Antimony-ore, occurring on Borneo, Celebes and Java is mined by the natives for their own use as a cosmetic. *Mercury*-ore in the form of cinnabar is collected by the natives on Sumatra and is appreciated as an anti-syphillitic. The deposits of these ores and others such as *lead, zinc* and *bismuth* are not sufficiently large to make a systematic exploitation profitable.

Plans were often made for the mining of the very considerable quantities of iron-ore, found in the Indies, but were each time frustrated by technical and economic difficulties. Shortly before the outbreak of war new plans were under consideration which, apparently, had encouraging prospects.

In south-east Borneo, on the Pulu Laut Archipelago, in the Lake-district of Central Celebes and on some islands of the Moluccas large areas are covered with a layer of iron-ore, several meters in depth, so that mining should be easy and cheap. The quantity on the mainland of Borneo and two islands near the coast is estimated at 400.000.000 tons; that in Central Celebes is about three times that quantity.

Though these ores are not of a superior quality, — the iron content being 45—55 %, — they may very well be used for making iron and steel.

Another type of iron-ore, called haematite and magnetite is also found at several places in the Indies. The percentage of iron in this ore is high, more than 60 % on an average, and the ore is on the whole very pure. The deposits are however not large and very irregular. The largest one is found in the Lampong Districts where about 2.000.000 tons are visible on the surface.

It was chiefly from ores of this type that the natives formerly obtained the iron for making their tools and finely chiseled weapons.

Finally there are, as beach formation on many islands of the Archipelago, magnetic iron sands. Some concessions for this have been granted on the south coast of Java in the residencies Kedu and Banjumas. It is calculated that there is about 35.000.000 tons of this ore, which, at an average grade of 57 %, would yield 20.000.000 tons of iron. The ore also contains 9—14 % of *titanium*.

In the Lake-district of Central Celebes *nickel*-ore occurs of the same type as that in New Caledonia. The possibility of mining this ore is now being examined. There are also deposits of *chromium*-ore, which might be important for a future steel industry in the Indies.

In speaking of the treasures of the earth one special category, that of building materials and suchlike, is often forgotten. This should not be, not only because of the part which they play in daily life, but also because they form the basis of industries which, though working only for the home market, contribute none the less to the general prosperity. Pottery, brick- and tile-making are real people's industries particularly on the thickly populated island of Java. Trass, limestone for hydraulic mortar and other building materials are abundantly found in the Indies. The cement factory near Padang is run entirely on western lines. Other such industries, for which the materials are available, will certainly be established in due course.

The total trade value of the mineral production of the Indies amounted in 1938 to 280.000.000 florins. In mining proper 3000 employees and 60.000 workmen found a living.

THE INDIAN FORESTS

"Netherlanders! Be astounded! Hear with amagement what I have to tell you. Our fleet is destroyed; our commerce is languishing; our navigation is being ruined; we buy timber and other necessities for shipbuilding with handfulls of gold from the northern countries, and meanwhile on Java we let our navy and mercantile fleet stand with their roots in the soil! Yes indeed, the Javanese forests have timber enough for building in a short time a considerable navy and moreover as many mercantile ships as we need ... The forests are state-property; better pay the Javanese for cutting and transporting, which will not cost much but will satisfy the Javanese; then there will soon be timber in plenty; and if then able and faithful men are made overseers of the forests, and see to it that the forests are cut, burnt and cleared regularly and new trees planted, then Java will yield for centuries all the timber that our Commonwealth may need for its navy and mercantile fleet ..."

In these terms Dirk van Hogendorp addressed the States of Holland in 1799.

His words have come true. Not only in the sense which he had in mind, but in a much fuller sense. Forestry on Java has attained a splendid development. So long as we keep in mind that before 1800, and even fifty years after that, we grievously failed in our care for the forests and thereby in our duty towards the population, we may be justifiably proud of the results of more than a century of regular forest-administration on Java.

Van Hogendorp only thought of the timber-supply. Naturally, in densely populated lands like Java and Madura this is a matter of great importance. But of even greater importance is the care for the maintenance of the fertility and agricultural possibilities of the soil. In these matters, particularly in the tropics, the forest plays an indispensable part, so much so that, according to many geological, agrarian and sociological experts, a good forest service should come before anything else.

Let us first examine this second and more important rôle of forestry.

It is true that in former times we failed to take care of the forests. It would however be unjust to blame our ancestors overmuch, for in those days the realisation of the importance of forests was rare and could scarcely interest Hollanders, coming, as they did, from a flat country with little forest. We can only regret the former neglect and try to remedy its evil effects. The founders of our colonial empire were so busy fighting their political enemies that they did not take time for measures against another equally dangerous foe, viz. water.

Water, not bent on conquest but only on devastation, is more dangerous than any army.

In two ways water tries to rob us of our ancestral land: through floods or through erosion and landslides. Floods can only be destructive on land that lies lower than the surrounding country, so that an entire country will never be devastated in this way. But it is a different matter with erosion and landslides. Practically no part of the country can withstand the force of these enemies; neither mountains, where the top-soil is washed away, nor plains which are covered with sterile mountain debris. The conquest by an army is more or less sudden; the devastation by water is slow, almost imperceptible at first, but it is thorough and final. The land conquered by an army remains habitable; the land devastated by water turns into a desert.

The great sneaking danger of erosion was formerly not clearly understood and probably people thought that things would not take such a bad turn. This was an error. With erosion, especially when there are geological and climatic conditions as in the East Indies, things take a much worse turn than people think. Erosion causes far greater disasters than any flood, but its action is less obvious, stealthier, and more thorough.

It is the forest that, in the first place, can set bounds to the erosive action of water. As long as the mountains are wooded there is practically no danger of washing off and sanding over and consequently of destruction of the country's fertility and habitability. As soon as the forest disappears there is an ever growing menace of devastation to the land. The Government therefore should keep a constant watch over the condition of forestation.

The Dutch East Indies have a forest area of 120 million hectares, that is about 40 times the total area of the mother country, and two thirds of the land area of the Indies. There is no doubt whatever that a considerable portion of these woods may, without any objection, be converted into arable land for the native population or plantations for European agriculture. It is however not a matter of indifference where the woods are cleared. While in some regions part of the forest may safely go, in others destruction of the forest would be disastrous. This is chiefly dependent on geological and topographical formation.

Now in many cases forests have vanished without anybody giving a moment's thought to this question. Natives were permitted to go ahead and convert as much forest into arable land as they thought fit and nobody worried about the consequences. In assigning lots on long lease to European planters the necessary care and foresight have also at times been sadly lacking. Both on Java and in the Outer Territories there are many examples of this unbridled deforestation. The "dying land" in West-Java in the upper reaches of the Chimanuk, Chilutung and Chikeruh, above Madjalengka is a case in point. Not long ago, in East-Java, the Provincial Council submitted a scheme of reforestation, providing for 5 million florins for the rebuying of certain land from the natives, and a further sum of 14 million for reforestation!

Much damage was done in this respect in the 19th century by the Government coffee cultivation and the subsequent occupation of the deserted plantations by the native population.

About 60 years ago a beginning was made with reforestation of the bare mountain slopes in the former residency of Bagelen. Since then much has been done. Though, until recently, deforestation still exceeded reforestation, it may now be said that on Java this disastrous denudation has been completely stopped, while in the Outer Territories the question is under examination. The conviction has grown that the future of the Dutch East Indies is at stake and great efforts are made to vanquish the many technical, political and economic obstacles.

On Java a point has been reached where practically all forest that must be preserved has been designated and beaconed off. Apart from teakwoods the area comprises nearly 2 million hectares of forest, a considerable portion of which however is not yet or not sufficiently grown and must therefore gradually be reforested. Through purchase or exchange this area will here and there have to be enlarged with land that, contrary to the public interest, was converted into arable land. On Java and Madura the menace of the all-destroying erosion has now fortunately been averted and the care now taken of all forests on mountains and slopes guarantees that in future this fertile country will not again be exposed to danger through ignorant negligence. Sins of the past have here been retricved.

Other benefits of a hydrological nature have probably been obtained at the same time. Though so far it has not been possible to furnish exact proof, the general conviction is that the reforestation of the denuded mountain slopes favourably affects the water-supply of the sources of the rivers, so that more irrigation-water is available. Hence, reforestation goes on *pari passu* with extension of sawah-acreage, and naturally the cultivation of sugar is thus also benefited. It is interesting that the native population, generally rather averse to restrictions on breaking waste land, is firmly convinced of the utility of the mountain forests for a greater supply of irrigation water.

In the Outer Islands the conservation of the forests is still in its initial stage. In many regions, up to 1930, the urge to clear wood for plantations or arable land was so great, especially on the part of the natives, that the authorities were often inclined to give in so as to avoid difficulties with the population. The impression is sometimes created of an unbridgeable

chasm between the interests of the population and the aspirations of the
Forestry Department. This is absurd. The Forestry Department has no
desire but to serve the interests of the population and the only real contro-
versy existing is between the inhabitants of the mountains and those of
the plains who often do not see eye to eye. The mountain people wish to
have the sole say over all forests in order to be able to convert them, at
will, into arable land, while the farmers in the plains dread disasters as a
result of deforestation. Since in practice forests in the mountains are designated for conservation, there will be difficulties with the mountain-people who
as a rule will protest against any forest-reservation limiting their freedom
to open up new land.

In the directly governed territories, comprising about half of the Outer
Islands, the consent of the population, often only obtained after protracted negotiations, was indispensable for any measures introduced and the
future is not yet safe. In the self-governing territories, though the matter
was often far from easy, in some cases the autonomous ruler was willing to
cooperate so that vast areas of forest could be earmarked for conservation.
On Sumatra 15 % of the surface is now reserved as forest, on Borneo 2 %
and on the eastern islands of the Archipelago also 2 %. On Java the percentage is 21, and it may be hoped that the same favourable state of affairs
will eventually be achieved in the Outer Territories, so that, as some one
aptly put it: "the forest for man's sake will be protected against man."

Though the conservation of mountain forest is undoubtedly the primary
duty of the Department of Forestry, it achieved its greatest success in other
lines of activity. There is the question of timber, first broached by Dirk van
Hogendorp. It may be stated without reservation that the production of
timber from the djatiwoods, known as Java-teak, is now guaranteed for any
length of time and the annual output of timber for the next hundred years
will steadily increase. Nearly a century ago when the first two foresters arrived on Java, they tried to create some order in the cutting of djati-timber.
Now all djati-forests, together 800.000 hectares, have been carefully sur-
veyed and taken stock of, and no more — in fact much less — is cut *per
annum* than will grow. Where trees are felled, new trees are planted, and
it may reasonably be expected that the new woods will yield more and better

timber than the old primeval forests. The production of djati-timber was also increased by opening up the formerly almost inaccessible forests by forestpaths and, after 1900, by a network of rail-tracks with a total length of 3000 km, requiring many expensive bridges and other engineering works. This greatly facilitates the transportation of timber, reduces freight costs and makes it possible to cut timber in places where formerly it did not pay. More than two thousand houses have been built for the foresters and their staffs, great timberyards with sheds and administrative offices have been constructed, saw mills erected for the handling of waste timber, all forests have been carefully marked out in order to avoid boundary disputes with the population. Simple motor roads for the inspecting officials have been built, logging streams improved and everywhere the personnel for the direction and the execution of the forestry activities has been augmented.

Though all these improvements entailed large expenditure, forest administration has been a profitable business for the Government. While at the close of last century the net profit was barely 1.000.000 florins *per annum*, from 1920—1929 it was, on an average, nearly 5.000.000 *per annum*.

Apart from timber the djati woods on Java also yield large quantities of firewood (1.300.000 m³ in 1929, 612.500 m³ in 1938). Much of this is used as fuel by the railway engines on Java. Besides more than 20 million kgs of charcoal for domestic use is produced.

The mountain forests on Java contain no djati trees; they are called wild wood forests. Most of the trees of many hundreds of different species yield no marketable wood. Some however produce valuable timber or firewood: the total yield is 40.000 m³ of timber and 300.000 m³ of firewood. Part of the charcoal mentioned above comes from these forests; also 10 to 20 thousand kgs of bark for tanning and dyeing, as well as many millions of bamboo poles, chiefly used for building tobacco sheds. Considering the vastness of these forests these yields are still insignificant, partly because there is a great deal of inferior wood, and partly because the forests are so located that transportation of cheap wood does not pay. The Forestry Department therefore aims at constant improvement of the condition of these forests by planting valuable timber fit for industrial purposes and protecting it, as much as possible, against suffocation by inferior wood.

Good results are expected from a species of pine, *Pinus Merkusii* which greatly resembles our red fir. Experiments are in progress with many other species, some yielding tan bark and resin. It may safely be predicted, that in future these wildwood forests of Java will supply an ever growing proportion of the total produce of the forests.

Four main causes hamper the wood production in the Outer Territories. They are: the difficulties of transportation, the heterogeneous character of many forests, the lack of labour and the political difficulties about tenure and disposal of the land.

At present the Outer Islands yield about 1.000.000 m³ of timber, 1.000.000 m³ of firewood and 50.000.000 kgs of charcoal *per annum*. In 1938 Sumatra produced 65 % of all timber, Borneo 33 % and the islands of the eastern part of the Archipelago the remaining 2 %. Nearly all the firewood and charcoal came from Sumatra.

It can not reasonably be doubted that in future this wood production will be increased manyfold. The forests are on the main route to Australia, China and Japan, where woods are scarce, and these countries will therefore certainly become large-scale consumers of our timber. Some specially valuable species such as ebony and ironwood will probably find a profitable market all over the world.

The forests of the Outer Islands also yield other valuable products such as ratan, copal, damar, various species of getah, tanbark, oleiferous seeds, kajuputih-oil, etc. in 1938 amounting to a value of more than 6 million florins.

In Atchin there are extensive pinewood forests that are separately managed. In 1938 they yielded about 3.700.000 kgs of resin (*colophonium*) and 1.126.000 kgs of terpentine. There is a great project to establish a factory for the making of coarse paper for packing agricultural products etc.

In conclusion a few figures about the Forestry Service. Its personnel numbers nearly 4000 men and there are well over a hundred forest inspectors with university training. Three fourths of these are stationed on Java; the rest in the Outer Islands. The Service pays about 8.000.000 florins in wages annually. Since the djati forests on Java requiring the greatest amount of work mostly are located in the less prosperous parts of the island, this high item for wages is the more significant.

This is only a very brief sketch of the work done in forestry. Much has been accomplished by which, especially on Java, the permanent supply of djati-wood has been guaranteeed and, which is of even greater importance, the land has been safeguarded against the ruinous effect of erosion. In the Outer Territories much remains to be done but our feet are firmly planted on the right road. We need not fear that posterity will reproach us for neglect, but rather may we hope that it will speak appreciatively of what we of the twentieth century did to preserve the fertility of the land and raise the prosperity of the people.

CHAPTER 12

From Four to Forty Four Million Souls on Java

This striking caption indicates the increase in population for Java and Madura during a period of approximately 130 to 140 years. It is a somewhat unusual mode of expression. It would have been more normal to state the comparative density of population per square kilometer. The title of this chapter would then have been: from 30 to 330 souls per square kilometer. Though statistically perfectly correct, such a statement, suggesting a development which does not exist, would have been very misleading.

In Ratzel's well-known theory density of population is related to economic development. At the bottom of the scale are hunters and gatherers with only a few souls per km²; at the top mining and industrial centres with 400 or more. In between these two extremes lies an entire gamut of economic evolution. Such a relation seems natural; we can hardly imagine the growth of population of Holland in any other way. First came the thinly scattered tribes with hunting and sparse agriculture; then a gradual intensification of that agriculture, amelioration of crops and cattle; stock-breeding and dairy-industry developed; trade and crafts began; towns were founded, various occupations were differentiated, the dwellings, formerly of wood, were replaced by permanent brick houses. Along with this development labour became more productive and the level of prosperity rose, owing to the rich variety made possible by division of labour. The result of this was an increasing density of population facilitating again further development. In addition there came in the 19th century the miracles of technique both in production and transportation which brought about a marvellous acceleration of the process. In industrial and mining centres and in the great

cities enormously dense local accumulations of people were formed.

Nothing of all this is apparent in the native society of Java and Madura: the increase of population is not combined with evolution of any kind. The densities now registered in a population of forty four millions already occurred at a time when the total number was estimated at four millions or less. In 1815, when with a view to the introduction of his land rent Raffles held a census, the estimated total was $4\frac{1}{2}$ millions, that is an average of 35 souls per km². In some rural districts however the density was 880, and in others only 9 per km². It is not too hazardous to suppose that even 1500 years ago, at the beginning of the Hindu domination, such a wide divergence also existed. Now what is the explanation of this apparent incongruity?

The Javanese was a riceplanter and sawahfarmer even before the Hindus brought their culture to Java. He does however not produce his rice for the sake of profit, but in order to supply the sober needs of himself and his family. The family is the basis of his agriculture and his own supply is his end. This sets natural limits to his activity and therefore also to the acreage required. Sawah cultivation is very intensive: the regular irrigation enables the soil permanently to yield a comparatively rich crop, and since the farmer only needs a harvest which can nourish him and his family for one year, he is content with a small plot of ground. The result is that in the fertile valley and plains of Java complexes of sawahs are formed that make an extremely dense population possible. In the higher mountain districts the method by burning, called ladang cultivation, is used; stretches of the primeval forest are cut and burnt away in order to form for a few years a field for the dry cultivation of rice. This procedure is subsequently repeated further on in order to give the soil time to recover and to grow new forest. It goes without saying that in this way the farmer needs a large acreage in order to continue his agriculture without interruption and that therefore with this kind of cultivation the density of population cannot be otherwise than small. This explains the difference in density between Java and the Outer Islands, and this same difference must have existed on Java, when in wide regions ladang cultivation co-existed with sawah cultivation.

The increase in population during this period, without western influence, was somewhat as follows. Wherever the population, free from calamities, was able to cultivate their fields for a time in peace and quiet, their numbers rapidly increased, until they threatened to exceed the limits that could be provided for by agriculture. Then it became necessary to open up new fields and to form daughter-villages. Thus the complexes of dense population extended ever further over new regions.

Did then this agricultural community during and after the Hindu domination not evolve in any way? Certainly it did: various arts and crafts and a rich cultural life flourished in those centuries. But this development had more a social character than an economic one. That is to say: the end toward which production, labour and interest were directed was not the utility of the products to the producers as separate individuals, but the significance which these products possessed for their owners as social beings, as members of a community, in the eyes of their environment. It was not the individual but the social value that mattered. A bull was not appreciated as draught-animal, a dwelling and clothing not as protection, a weapon not as an instrument of war, but they were first and foremost and sometimes even exclusively means to heighten and strengthen the social prestige of their owner.

These social needs, this feeling of dependence on the opinion and standards of the environment, this communal tie which bound the members of local communities together, were the driving forces in the development of oriental society; it drew its vitality from this religious communal sense. In these local communities which, for all their smallness and feebleness, were yet autonomous and organic entities, the social needs were much more pressing and important than the simple and modest economic needs.

The western Government, whose exclusive interest was focussed on economic objects and which was inclined to appraise all social phenomena and institutions solely at their economic value, had no eye for this different conception of life. It only stated the economic poverty and cut away as arid vine or parasitic growth what in reality contained the lifesap of these small communities. This attitude of the Government caused a shrivelling and shrinking of the self-sufficient little worlds of the oriental village community which led to stagnation and even dissolution.

There is still another factor which is responsible for this process of stagnation. The villages were aristocratic republics, based on unequality. The leadership of the local gentry was accepted as a matter of course. The gentry represented the element of social development within their community, they were the moving power in the cultural life of their environment. Under the influence of western rule however this aristocracy became more and more estranged from its social environment; it was incorporated into the western sphere, it adopted a western economic point of view and was lost to oriental society. It severed the close life ties with the village and became citified. The villages, robbed of their gentry and the social force proceeding from it, were consequently atrophied socially and culturally. They became bodies without a head, ships without a rudder, organisms merely vegetating on sap and strength gathered earlier, but no longer capable of further growth. Yet they must continue their struggle against the western economic influence which impoverishes, dissolves and undermines them.

The most striking feature of oriental society in the East Indies is its cultural stagnation. This stagnation however does not mean cessation in the increase of population. On the contrary, western influence promotes the numerical growth of the population. The reasons for this are easy to understand.

While in the European countries, owing to birth-control, the birth rate has become a fluctuating factor in the increase of population, this is not yet the case in oriental society. The bachelor and the widower do no more occur than the spinster and the fecundity of marriages is left to Providence. The death-rate on the contrary always was an extremely fluctuating factor in oriental societies, owing to sudden and violent numerical leaps in mortality. Civil wars, natural calamities, famines, epidemics time and again wiped out the increase which the population had gained and the constant steep rise and fall of numbers resulted in keeping the population practically stationary.

Here was a fertile field of beneficial activity for the western Government. Nor is it necessary to think in the first place of preventive medicine, of hygiene and sanitation; of even greater importance were the securing of peace and order, the suppression of civil war and despotism, the opening up of communications leading to the expulsion of famine, the prevention of floods and the economic water-supply by means of technical waterworks, the fight against diseases and pests in the crops. But the services of western medicine in the battle against epidemics such as cholera, pest, and influenza or endemic diseases such as beri-beri and malaria also contributed to checking the erratic leaps in the death rate of the native population. Consequently, while the rate of increase was fairly constant, periodical relapses failed to occur. An occasional outbreak of these diseases, checked immediately, ably, and forcefully, proved from time to time how fearfully in former times these plagues must have scourged a defenceless population.

These then are the two factors which determine the population question on Java: on the one hand the stationary oriental society, stagnant in a cultural and economic sense, and on the other, the uninterrupted increase of population. The result is something that may be called static expansion. In the mode of life of the population there is no apparent development. The sawah cultivation of the Javanese farmer of to-day can not differ much from that in the Hindu period; his house of bamboo or wood can scarcely be much different from that built by his ancestors 1500 years ago; the cultural achievements which society may boast of largely date from a hoary past; the agriculture on a small scale, the cultivation of the traditional crops and according to the traditional methods remains the exclusive occupation of the masses, and in the newly opened up distant regions it does not differ in any way from that in the oldest centres of habitation. The increased population therefore can only exist by expanding in breadth over an ever wider territory.

This static expansion has been going on for more than a hundred years. It is of a more individual character than the migrations of entire groups or districts that formerly used to take place. Raffles still mentions the depopulation of Bantam, Batavia, Cheribon, Demak. This did not only occur in order to escape from natural calamities and epidemics, but even more in order to flee from the oppression and tyranny of kings, chiefs, servants of the Company and the Government. The lack of proper means of communication limited these migrations to short distances, no further than the neighbouring provinces. Kediri and Madiun were populated from Kedu and the Principalities and served in turn as starting-point for migration further east. The difficulty in these migrations is the bridging over of the initial period. In the more recent individual migrations important works employing labour and at the same time opening up new regions, such as irrigation works and railways or roadbuilding, serve to furnish the necessary support towards starting an independent existence in a new environment. The colonists are usually not married or have left their families behind. Western plantation companies have also encouraged such migrations by offering the opportunity to tide over the initial years by wage-earning. Thus several hundred thousand Madurese succeeded in establishing themselves along the north coast of East Java. At the census of 1930 from 10 to 16 % of the inhabitants of Java's eastern provinces proved to be natives of other parts.

Needless to say this static expansion entails many privations. It will only be resorted to in cases of extreme necessity. These colonists are nowise pioneers in a better and more leisured existence, but in the new environment they content themselves with the same meagre living and before long these colonised territories will show the same density of population as the land of origin. Purely rural districts with a population that gets its living mainly by agriculture sometimes reach a density of 15 to 1600 souls or more per km^2, which means that 15, 16 or more persons must live on 1 hectare of arable land.

It will now have become clear why this chapter started by calling the statement, that the density of Java's population in the course of years increased from 30 tot 330 souls per km^2, entirely misleading. Though Java is now practically full up, even the last figure has little value, since with an agricultural population only the arable land comes into account and it depends therefore on how large a part of the land is fit for agriculture whether the density figure happens to be higher or lower. Java is privileged in this respect, for about 60 % of its surface consists of arable land in free hold of the native population and another 5 % has been allotted to western plantation companies in long lease or hire. The Outer Islands do not present these favourable conditions; not only is a much larger part of the soil there unfit for cultivation but in the remaining part the condition of the soil does not permit the population to lay out unaided large-scale irrigation systems. Extensive cultivation by burning must therefore be resorted to, and this practice requires a great deal of land. This explains why the average density of population is not more than 11 per km^2, and in the ladang regions even not more than 7 per km^2. In the real sawah districts however there are here also densities of 400 or more.

Java then is now full up and this makes further increase of population on this island and on Madura a grave problem, which causes the government more anxiety than it does the native population itself. The latter is not conscious of the problem and would bear the eventual consequences: impoverishment, undernourishment, diminishing power of resistance, with patience and resignation. Since approximately 35 % of the population are employed in some trade, an annual increase of 500.000 souls means that every year a livelihood must be found for 175.000 hands, but for the natives it means no more than that the number of mouths to be filled increases with one in every hundred. To them there seem to be many other problems of a graver nature than this.

All this does not yet give an adequate picture of the problem of population on Java. It still has another aspect: that of the money-need of the natives. They need money not only for the payment of taxes, but also for the buying of various necessities, from the occasional expenditure for clothes to the daily purchase of salt, lamp-oil, tobacco, dried fish etc. which are not produced by the desa itself. The money required for the satisfaction of these needs disappears from circulation in the village. The economic rule for monetary exchange being that the same quantity exported must be imported from abroad, against this monetary expenditure there must therefore be revenues from the monetary circulation outside the desa. From what source do the natives of Java then receive these monetary revenues? The answer is very simple: not in the first place from the sale of their products which are largely intended for their own needs, nor to any large extent from the lease of their land to western plantation companies, but first and foremost from the sale of their labour on the western market. Since 1930 these last two sources of income however have badly diminished. The Government has placed a far-reaching restriction on the principal cultures such as sugar, tea, rubber and quinine, and other cultures such as coffee and tobacco have been reduced on their own initiative. This has diminished the need of labour. The labour-markets both of towns and of the Government have also shown a rapid and considerable decline. A far smaller number of hands is consequently needed in western industries. Moreover those that find employment have to be content with halved wages. Thus the wage-earning capacity is affected in two ways and the population has become far too much dependent on the sale of its products which have, however, also much gone down in price and have but a limited market.

This development of affairs presents two grave dangers. The first is that the population that cannot get along without some money in hand, will fall hopelessly into debt. The second, that it will sell too large a proportion of the crops cultivated for its own use, which may compel it afterwards to buy again (but with what money?) or suffer undernourishment and so jeopardise its power of resistance.

This is unquestionably also one of the aspects of the population problem dealing with the relationship of the population to its livelihood. The pressing scarcity of money in native society is the result of the disturbed balance between the oriental and western spheres of the colony, not, in this case, by the increase of the native population, but by the reduction of western economic activities that have to provide the dense population with a livelihood.

This side of the population problem demonstrates clearly that every measure that will find a solution of this problem should fulfill two requirements. Not only should it create in sufficient measure new means of livelihood for surplus population, but it should also stimulate the share of the native population in colonial economic activity so powerfully that it can provide in its own monetary needs.

Let us now review the principal measures taken.

First there is irrigation, which may be described as reclaiming work by the Government. For the technical irrigation works built by the Government have added 1,2 million hectares of sawah to the agricultural area or they have at least considerably improved the quality of these irrigated fields and so made the labour of these sawah farmers more productive. This greater productivity has not only been achieved by securing a more abundant and more regular yield of the main crop, but also by making it possible for the farmer to use his sawah in the dry season for a secondary crop. On Java the irrigation has however reached its limits and the results have disappointed the expectations of those who saw in this a means of increasing the prosperity of the farmers. The agrarian population merely reacted to this soil improvement by an increase which at best left every one's share in the augmented product what it was before. At best, for the more intensive utilisation of the soil also showed such evil consequences as exhaustion, reduction of the average yield, increase of pests and failure of crops. It is not surprising that the population reacted in this way to the improvement of the soil, considering that no sacrifice or effort of those concerned was required and that the gift, consisting in improvement of the conditions of production, was not limited to the best and most energetic farmers, but benefited without distinction all landowners in the irrigated region. Owing to this reaction of the beneficiaries the irrigation policy could only in a limited degree fulfill the second requirement, that of enlarging the monetary revenue of the population.

To be placed on a par with irrigation is the promotion of the cultivation of secondary crops and of cultivation of the homestead with the aid of technical advice, the providing of better seed for sowing, the introduction of new varieties etc. The end in view is here also expansion of the production and increase of the productivity of agricultural labour. But it may be doubted whether these measures will really raise the level of prosperity of the native "tani" or farmer. With all due admiration for the energetic, unremitting and expert work done by the Agricultural Advisory Service one should not shut one's eyes to the sober fact that all its efforts can contribute little towards a solution of the population problem.

In this series of measures the promotion of the use of artificial manure has a special place. In this case the farmer who has to buy the manure must make a financial sacrifice. So this is limited to the more enterprising farmers and there is a chance that by this means he will be able to attain greater prosperity. This method however also has its drawbacks. So long as artificial manure is only applied to market-crops, a monetary return is obtained which may make good the financial outlay for the production. But if it is applied in the cultivation of alimentary crops such as rice, maize or cassave, intended for home consumption, the farmer will be compelled to sell part of this product in order to defray his expenses, and so willy-nilly he is driven to the market and drawn into a money-economy, with the risk that his product will not fetch a satisfactory price on the weak home-market. That this danger is far from imaginary is demonstrated in Japan where the rural population is crushed by an irredeemable burden of debt, incurred by accumulated credits for procuring artificial manure.

Another way of assisting the farmer in his struggle for existence is the promotion of the cultivation of commercial crops. Since the cultivation of rice on Java as far as productivity is concerned, is long past its upper limit, only the extension of the cultivation of market crops may help the Javanese

farmer to his desirable and necessary monetary revenue. It is however not
to be expected that the results of these efforts will be very considerable.
The extent to which the soil has been cut up requires above all intensity of
labour for any new culture that is undertaken, which limits the possibilities.
Furthermore, a market for the product must be found. It is not likely that
this will be a home market, since buying-power and demand are both
lacking. Export therefore; but this means competition, fluctuating prices,
import-barriers etc. So, what with one thing and another, the small farmer
is exposed to risks which he cannot bear. Even in the Outer Islands,
though extensive export crops may be undertaken there under much more
favourable conditions, a tendency of the farmers is noticeable to revert to
their own familiar alimentary crops. The difficulties of transportation from
the producer to the market are also numerous. The piece-meal production
for a distant market necessitates a chain of middlemen and the percentage
of the price that sticks to these intermediaries is astounding. The technical
difficulties caused by the fact that most crops are sensitive to the influence
of soil and climate are self-evident.

Of an entirely different character is the method of industrialisation which
is expected to raise the Javanese from his primitive farmer's existence and
to modernise native society. It should however be realised that the idea of
industrialisation here appears with an entirely new mission. In the outline
of development in our own country, sketched at the outset, industrialisation
was a late phase in a process of evolution, an actual fact, and the fruit of an
ever growing and ramifying society contributing in its turn to a richer growth.
In the East Indies on the other hand industrialisation is an import product,
organically without roots in native society, a means to an end but not a
result, an aspiration but not a fact. The problem is tackled from the other
end with the hope of forcing by this means a development that will not come
about by itself. But that creates insuperable difficulties. All this imposes
strict limits on every policy of industrialisation and reduces its significance
for the population problem.

Finally there remains one more method for combatting Java's surplus
population, that is, colonisation, regarded as the most important by the
Dutch East Indian authorities.

In connection with the population problem colonisation means no more than that the acreage needed for the static expansion, now wanting on Java, is made available in the Outer Islands. It is an extension of the Javanese environment to the other islands of the Archipelago. Put in this way, this method of colonisation at once shows its weak side. It is not a solution of the problem but merely a territorial transference and extension of it. In the colonisation territories the colonists find an existence not essentially different from that which they quitted on Java. Since a supranormal increase of population may be expected from these colonists who are young married couples, physically selected, and placed under a careful hygienic and medical supervision, in a few generations the same symptoms of overpopulation as now on Java will show themselves among them.

It may however be asked if there is not a reasonable expectation that the colonists will utilise the greater scope which they will enjoy at first, to raise their level of prosperity and that thus they will acquire the economic appreciation of a better standard of living leading to a rational moderation of the birthrate. This might be so, if the government could limit their choice to the most enterprising and energetic Javanese, But this is impossible. As a policy for combatting overpopulation the colonisation has to be on a large scale. One or two thousand model colonists *per annum* are not enough. At least one hundred thousand are necessary, be they of an average kind. They can not be pioneers of new native-grown crops but they remain riceplanters in the old style; nor can they obtain a larger acreage in tenure, for that would make the costs too high. Their livelihood must again be based on selfsupport, on a modest cultivation of alimentary crops, independent from the exchange of goods, but with a minimum monetary revenue.

If however one abandons these gloomy prognostications, if the policy of colonisation is not tested so severely on its efficacy as a means for solving the population problem, and if one is prepared to judge it on its momentary merits, then the present colonisation policy should rouse the warmest enthusiasm. Here in fact great things are being done. In a few years an organisation has been created capable of handling migrations of fifty thousand souls or more *per annum* and surrounding the colonists with the most attentive care which does not overlook the minutest details. There is a spirit of enterprise, of courage and of thoroughness in these Government measures worthy of the highest admiration.

CHAPTER 13

Welfare Policy

MATERIAL WELFARE — NATIVE AGRICULTURE

More than seventy percent of the population find their living in native agriculture. It not only nourishes, almost entirely, the seventy million souls inhabiting the Indies, but also supplies an export surplus of millions of florins. This surplus amounts to more than one quarter of the total export of the Archipelago and forms an important contribution to the worldmarket of tropical products.

In the unfavourable year 1938 native agriculture supplied 48 % of the rubber export, 95, 58, 83 and 99 of that of cocos, coffee, kapok and pepper, for a value of respectively 64, 42, 7, 6 and 9 million florins. In that year the value of the exported part of the native products was 173 million florins, which amount used to be considerably higher in the years before the depression. The value of products that are not exported but find their destination within the country, is many times greater.

Even in the populous islands of Java and Bali where the land held *per capita* is very little, native agriculture is still able to feed the natives almost entirely and, moreover, to supply a good many export products and a large part of the materials for native industry.

It is therefore no exaggeration to say that the importance of native agriculture is extraordinarily great.

Now the farmer in the East Indies cannot, like his brother farmer in western Europe, within the limits of the law dispose freely of his land, his labour and his capital, but in many parts of the Archipelago he is bound to the rules of customary law current in his community, be it tribe, family or village. The religious ideas demand that the community maintain a magic harmony or good relations with the spirits within its territory. Agriculture greatly affects that harmony and those relations, since it has constantly to do with the magically powerful soil, and encroaches upon the abode of the spirits. Hence the community is obliged carefully to watch this activity. It must constantly demand sacrifices and prohibit certain activities at certain times held to be particularly critical. The search for virgin land, sowing, planting and harvesting, are all matters that concern the entire community.

Such ideas, quite strong in some parts of the Archipelago, are on the wane elsewhere, so that one finds very different forms of society, and the degree to which the farmer is free or dependent on the community also varies a great deal. Among the Dayak tribes for example the community manages everything, while among the Hulu-Sungei in south-east Borneo the individual element is quite pronounced, so that every farmer can, to a large extent, freely dispose of his land, his labour, his stores etc.

In many old-fashioned desas of Java this dependence on the community also exists, so that the community is concerned in the use of all property and controls the division of land, water, labour etc. In such a system the influence of tradition is naturally far greater than where the individual has more freedom of action.

In most European countries there is a differentiation in small-scale, middle-sized and large-scale agricultural units. In the Indies nearly everywhere there is far less differentiation. Especially on Java there are very many dwarf units that do not afford the farmer and his family sufficient scope for profitable labour so that subsidiary activity in trade, transportation, home-industry etc. is necessary. Fortunately larger-scale agriculture is not entirely lacking, so for example in South-Djombang and Malang on Java.

In the Outer Islands ordinary farming, in which the farmer and his household can nearly always find work enough, predominates. In some regions there are enterprises of greater scope, that generally, as in the rubber districts, have to employ wage-labour.

The farmer's use of the soil depends on circumstances. On the one hand it is conditioned by natural factors, such as climate, altitude, type of soil, lie of the land. On the other by economic factors, such as relative position with regard to the market, density of population etc.

A sketch is given here of the principal ways in which the soil is utilized.

In the rainy tropical zone primeval forest is the natural vegetation. If the population is sparse and its technical development in a primitive stage, agriculture generally consists of cutting the undergrowth in the forest and planting easily growing tuberous plants under the remaining trees. The next step is that the high wood is also removed and burnt and that, without tilling, something is sown or planted on the free space. If the wild shoots of the stumps and the weeds are not too noxious, after the harvest this planting may be repeated once more and after that another part of the forest is chosen for this kind of cultivation. In a few years, unless conditions are specially adverse, the deserted plot becomes forest again. This type of agriculture is called forest-ladang-agriculture.

The result of the recovery of the forest is that, after a few years, owing to the formation of humus, the soil may again be used for agriculture. The forest is then no longer primeval but secondary forest, *belukar*, so that one speaks of *belukar-ladang*-agriculture. Both types of ladang agriculture are predatory: they leave the recovery of the soil entirely to nature. They are very common in remote parts of the Outer Islands.

As the density of the population increases the land space *per capita* becomes less, so that the same plot must be used more often and nature is not given the necessary time for the recovery of the soil because the forest does not get a chance to grow sufficiently. At most some low shrubs and grasses will shoot up in the fallow period. As a rule the farmer will assist nature by planting something that grows easily and promotes the recovery of the soil. Sometimes this kind of crop at the same time has some utility as a foodstuff, but in any case this is secondary. This type of cultivation is called artificial *belukar-ladang*-agriculture.

With further relative increase in the population this type also will not be sufficient to nourish it. By returning too often to the same plot the harvest will deteriorate and require more labour. The fallow period will become ever shorter and instead of young forest or shrubs there will appear a grass wilderness. Deeper tillage and more labour on the crop will become necessary and often manure will be indispensable. This form of agriculture is called grasswilderness-*ladang* agriculture, and if grass entirely predominates grass-*ladang* agriculture. With this latter system one generally sees a regular

rotation of cattle-breeding and agriculture. These forms are still found in
certain parts of Flores and on the mountain slopes of Bali.

If the fallow period is dispensed with altogether, so that the soil is permanently cultivated, it will recover only by great care for proper terracing,
tillage, rotation of crops and manure or, instead of this, irrigation with
water that is rich in silt. According to the natural conditions this will lead
to permanent agriculture either on dry fields, the so-called *tegallan* agriculture, or on wet fields, the *sawah* agriculture. Both forms are found in all
densely populated parts of the Archipelago and are most common on Java.

If water is plentiful and easily obtainable, sawah cultivation may develop
early and several phases on the road to more intensive forms of agriculture
may be skipped. Sawah cultivation creates the conditions for high and regular production on a small area, favouring great increase in population.

In several parts of the Indies, for example on Bali and in the Toradja
districts on Celebes there are true masters in the laying out of sawahs.

Forest and *belukar-ladangs* in the Outer Territories have, in the last decades, been converted into plantations of superannual crops. When copra
came into demand, coconut trees were planted on the ladangs no longer
used for alimentary crops. This was done chiefly in districts, such as the
residency Menado on Celebes and parts of the Moluccas, where the rainfall
is plentiful the year round, and the coconut tree thrives easily. When afterwards the demand for rubber became great, in other regions, especially on
Borneo and Sumatra, hevea was planted in the ladang which, after a few
years, could be tapped. Coconut trees and hevea, once having the start of the
forest growth will, as a rule, hold their own. When the time has come for
picking or tapping the undergrowth is cut away and one can go ahead.
That is to say, if there are the necessary workers, for this kind of plantation
has become too large for one family and creates a demand for labour.

If such cultivation for export pays well food may be imported from elsewhere. In times of low prices however the ordinary cultivation of alimentary
crops is again favoured.

In the dry belts of the tropics forest growth is less dense and, after having
been cut, the forest does not recover so rapidly. While in the regions of the
real tropical primeval forest cattle breeding is out of the question, since
there is neither place nor fodder nor work for cattle, here it may thrive

freely. On the abandoned ladang it soon finds various grasses. The grazing of the cattle however retards the recovery of the forest. All wild shoots are constantly eaten or trodden under foot. In such regions there will, as a rule, first be ladang agriculture alternating with cattle-raising and, after a while, the forest will have no chance of recovery, so that large grassy plains appear. These plains can only be used for alimentary crops by the use of more intensive agricultural methods which frequently are applied in the vicinity of the villages, while the cattle feeds on the large plains.

Hunting also promotes the formation of such plains. Burnt off ground attracts game by the salty ashes and the young grass blades that will shoot up after the fire. This burning for the sake of hunting prevents recovery of the forest and automatically leads to the necessity of tilling the fields more thoroughly because the forest area becomes limited.

Cattle breeding is not very profitable, since dairy products are only used in some rare parts of the Archipelago and people on the whole eat little meat. Cattle serve almost entirely as draught-animals and for supplying meat to the large population centres; hence only in exceptional cases can it fetch high prices; in other words cattle-breeding as principal business only pays if cattle can be kept very cheaply. Such is the case if the ground has little value and is not covered with forest, as in the thinly populated regions in the south-east of the Archipelago, provided enough drinking water for the cattle is available. There, for example on Sumbawa and Sumba, one finds a half-wild kind of cattle. Young male animals unfit for breeding and old females that can no longer be bred, are sold and shipped over very long distances to the centres of demand.

If the area available for cattle shrinks because increase in population demands the use of more fields for alimentary crops, cattle-breeding must adapt itself, change its character and become subordinate to agriculture. Therefore, as a rule, the live stock in the very populous parts of the Indies decreases as the population increases. In such regions, as in the greater part of Java, cattle-breeding as an occupation is secondary to agriculture to which it is subservient by supplying animal labour for ploughing and transportation.

Apart from the arable land proper and the grazing grounds the farmer has the space round his homestead. The need of herbs and medicinal plants, of fruit and other vegetable foodstuffs caused him to plant that space. In many regions of Java and elsewhere this is done in a very intensive and varied way, often in stories one above the other. There are coconut and other fruit trees, lower down there is pisang (banana), lower again arrowroot, cassave, maize, edible canna's and all kinds of herbs for relishes and medicine. This kind of homestead cultivation often yields a large part of the products sold and sometimes constitutes the main source of monetary revenue for the family. Because the planting is so varied and includes products that may be harvested regularly this revenue is also very regular. Every market day there are coconuts and such like fruit ready to be taken to the market. This is a great advantage in a family with regularly recurring small money-needs and no balance in the bank.

The different ways of using the soil here briefly discussed are often coexistent. A farmer on Java may cultivate his own place, the tegal and the sawah; one in the Outer Islands his own place, the ladang and the sawah. The ladang is then mostly restricted to the unsuitable slopes where the steep incline would make the laying out of sawahs too troublesome. The sawahs are then in the river valleys or in the plains adjoining the hills.

The principal alimentary crop is rice, cultivated on dry and wet fields. The great variety in the manner of its cultivation clearly illustrates how well agriculture in the Indies adapts itself to circumstances and locality.

In dry regions, here and there in the hills, maize is the principal alimentary crop, replacing or supplementing rice. Elsewhere this is done by the sweet potato. In certain parts of the Moluccas wild or cultivated sago forms the staple diet and in other parts the banana, generally planted underneath coconut trees, plays that part.

After rice, in densely populated regions, if conditions permit, secondary crops are grown that are often intended for sale. The chief of these is maize; soya beans and arachis are also important, and in some privileged regions one sees the profitable onions or tobacco; elsewhere sweet potatoes.

The remuneration in kind or money earned by the native farmer is very modest. Especially in populous regions, where the farms are mostly small, the proceeds are scanty. In such regions it is essential to find and promote methods for augmenting the annual proceeds of labour without demanding much outlay of capital or encroaching upon the productivity of the soil.

River at sun

In less populous regions ways should be discovered and promoted enabling the farmer to adapt himself to changes in the economic conditions. Road construction may bring him closer to the market, reservation of forests or assignment of ground to western plantations may decrease his acreage and compel him to intensify his methods of tilling before he is properly familiar with them. Increase of needs as a result of education, communications, missionwork etc. also conduces to the same course.

The Work of the Agricultural Advisory Service

There were some early attempts by Daendels and other Governors-General to introduce improvements into native agriculture. From the seventies on these attempts became more and more numerous, though the work done often had an amateurish character. In 1903 an agricultural school was founded at Buitenzorg for the training of native scientific assistants, and agricultural advisers were appointed. From 1905 on the Department of Agriculture took the matter in hand; it was put in charge of the Botanical Gardens with its experimental institutes.

In 1910 an energetic chief became head of the Department to whom the credit is due of having really created the Advisory Service. At first the agricultural training was perhaps too theoretical, overrating the ability of the native farmer to put general principles into practice, but gradually such errors were avoided and the agricultural education, both in schools and by direct advice, became simpler and more practical. Especially during the last twenty years very good results were achieved in this way.

There is a large staff of advisers, men with full academic training, each of whom, with his assistants, constantly studies the natural, economic and social conditions of agriculture in his district. Sometimes years of research will be necessary on such problems as selection of varieties, manure, rotation of crops, selection of crops, tillage, use of water etc., as well as a careful study of economic and social conditions, before he will be able to point the way to better results. In another district, on the other hand, a brief examination will be sufficient for him to indicate methods of improvement. The problems are generally so numerous that he must make a judicious choice and first tackle the more urgent ones in each district. If there is repeated failure of a crop through inundations he will, for example, not waste his time in a

Mission 13

study of manure problems, but will consult the irrigation bureau, or try to think of varieties, better able to stand the effect of floods. The Central Experiment Station at Buitenzorg will assist him in all technical questions requiring laboratory research.

It has been shown that on the whole native agriculture is well adapted to natural and economic conditions. This does not mean however that further advice is superfluous. On the contrary; the collective scientific experience of workers in the entire world is far greater than that of an individual farmer and may render him invaluable service. Left to his own devices he would perhaps in the long run work out the solution which now he may get almost at once.

The difficulty of the adviser often does not consist in pointing out improvements that are technically possible, but rather in indicating such improvements as may fit into the scope of the native farmer's agriculture that is generally on a very small scale and lacking in capital. For a farmer who calculates in cents and only sells the surplus of the rice needed by himself, an outlay of ten florins for artificial manure is an enormous sum, even though he may be almost certain that those ten florins will yield twenty florins worth more produce from his field.

Now, if the adviser has found some practical methods of improvement, how does he set about having these accepted?

It may be done through lectures, short courses, meetings, demonstrations, films, exhibitions. He also may influence the farmer through personal conversations, longer courses and teaching at schools. At agricultural schools the pupils perform all the necessary operations themselves and learn to understand their value for the success of the crop. Schoolteachers are also specially trained in methods of agricultural amelioration. Competitions are organised with awards for those who have best put into practice what they have learnt.

This advisory work leads to questions of better seed and plant material of the most satisfactory varieties of rice, maize, cassave, green manure, shade-trees etc. The adviser needs nursery-beds for raising that seed and plant material under his supervision. A large number of such nursery-beds have indeed been established on Java by the Central Experiment Station and the same thing is being done in the Outer Islands.

The Service is also concerned with questions of the supply of manure, ploughs and other implements such as patjuls, weeding-hooks, cane-mills, rubber-mangles etc. The supply of these things often presents a major problem for the agricultural adviser and his staff, since generally the quantities involved are minute and the customer moreover can only buy on credit. The adviser tries to get commercial firms interested in furnishing these supplies so that he can limit himself to giving advice and exercising a certain amount of supervision. Frequently the People's Credit Bank undertakes the delivery so that the adviser merely advises the Bank about deliveries and loans.

An important part of his task is also to advise the Civil Servants in all agricultural matters. He is a member of various boards and so constantly advocates the interests of agriculture whenever projects are under discussion for concessions for sugarcane or long lease, or whenever a Forest Inspector proposes the reservation of certain forests. No irrigation work is undertaken without his advice and, when such a work is completed, it is he who has to show people, unfamiliar with water, how to use it in the most economical way. He also keeps an eye on plant diseases and combats these in collaboration with the Institute of Plant Diseases which is a section of the Central Experiment Station. He watches the economic situation, especially with regard to the supply of food, the condition of the crop and the harvest forecast. As a rule he also is a member of the board of a People's Bank. No colonisation or emigration is organised without his aid and advice. In short, his work is as varied as it is interesting.

There is also a Veterinary Service, organised in 1901. Much is being done to combat cattle diseases and improve the stock. Gelding of inferior males, selection and cross-breeding are all advocated, Government breeding-farms have been established; exhibitions and competitions are organised. The export or killing of female cattle still fit for breeding is prohibited.

Veterinary surgeon and agricultural adviser often have to collaborate, especially in those regions where, as is the case in most districts of the Archipelago, cattle is subordinate to the interests of agriculture.

The results of all this advisory work are not easily expressed in figures. Nevertheless they are considerable. Many good varieties of rice, arachis, soya beans, cassave and other plants were spread over wide regions. Ex-

periments that bring out an improved quality nearly always lead to the
bringing into practice of the new variety. After a few years the good variety
frequently takes up a larger area than the adviser is aware of, because the
size of his district prevents him from visiting regularly all the fields. If a
productive variety is not accepted by the farmer, one may be sure that something is wanting either in taste, sturdiness or some other quality. Good
material of well-known varieties is also supplied in fairly large quantities.

Green manure, that is plants cultivated because of their fertilising value,
have been eagerly accepted in many places. This is of fundamental importance because they improve the soil and offset the damage done by the
washing of heavy rains.

The binding of slopes by means of stones or vegetation to prevent washing
has also been advocated with considerable success.

All these improvements generally are well received by most farmers. If
this is not the case it is almost sure that there is a flaw somewhere and the
adviser had better revise his work with a critical eye.

Other improvements do not find such easy acceptance because they are
more expensive, and the native farmer generally has no money to spare.
Nevertheless the use of artificial manure, good ploughs and other implements
has become popular in many regions, especially where profitable crops are
cultivated such as sugarcane, tobacco, pepper, onions and rubber.

In one region of Celebes where the cultivation of the homestead was unknown, this practice was successfully introduced. A good demonstration,
followed up by competitions was the method of propaganda in this case.
Revolutionary changes of this kind may of course easily meet with resistance.
Though in combatting blights and diseases there has sometimes been
rather bad luck, there are some outstanding examples of great success. In
South Celebes the cultivation of coconut trees was saved by the extermination of a beetle-pest.

All this may be sufficient to show that the Agricultural Advisory Service,
in spite of shortage of personnel, has already done great things and shows
good promise of ever greater results in future.

INDUSTRY

In the last few years before the war a great deal of interest, both officially and privately, has been evinced in industry in the Dutch East Indies. This interest is not new. As early as 1905, when the economic condition of the Indies was far from rosy, increase of the national income was sought in the extension of native industry. The wish for more independence of foreign countries also entered in; especially during the world war of 1914 to 1918, when foreign import was difficult, projects for industrialisation were realised, but of the industries started in those years, only those that had sufficient reason for existence in normal times were able to maintain themselves.

In the boom years till 1929 the monetary revenue of the population increased as a result of the enormous increase in export. In the years of crisis after 1929 however the general drop in prices on the world market, especially of agricultural products, and the restrictions imposed upon the western cultivation of the major products, resulted in an appreciable decline of the national income, both by the decrease in the receipts for the population's own products and by the restriction of the opportunity to earn a living on the plantations.

Other factors also caused anxiety: in the years after the war free trade was more and more hampered; every country strove as much as possible for economic autarchy or purchased wanted products in countries of racial affinity or those to which it was bound by a commercial treaty. Moreover synthetic products, especially in countries lacking certain natural products, began to gain ground. Such tendencies were bound to affect unfavourably a country like the Dutch East Indies dependent on export.

A growing population in a country where the national income is largely dependent on export, the expectation that export of agricultural products would for the time being not increase: such considerations were conducive to serious efforts, privately and officially, to extend production for domestic use.

The rapid growth of Java's population is responsible for the interest of recent years in the problem how to bolster up the national income.

Industry was regarded as one of the means by which the purchasing power of the population might be increased. Let us see how far the interest centred on it was justified.

The East Indies are first and foremost an agricultural country, and, as far as one can see, they will remain so. Densely populated as it is, Java is for the greater part of its area taken up by alimentary crops for domestic use. Agricultural products also constitute two thirds of the total export value, mining products nearly one third, and only a few percent of the total amount remains for other products, chiefly timber and other forest crops and skins; industrial articles play no part in these figures.

The significance of industry therefore does not lie in its value for export but in its value for the home market.

In 1937 some general principles for the promotion of industry were formulated by the Government. At first ideas were rather vague but gradually the conviction grew that a rapid industrialisation of Java would be neither to the purpose nor desirable.

Not to the purpose, because mechanised industry employs so few hands. As a rule factories on Java employ no more than a few hundred workmen; very few have more than a thousand. In comparison with the numbers employed on plantations or in mining, — the tin mines alone give work to 30.000 men, — these figures are paltry.

A few years ago the number of people engaged in small-scale industry was estimated at 1.600.000, while only 120.000 people were employed in mechanical industry.

Though a factory industry may have its own importance for the country, it has little significance for creating employment; a few factories can certainly not contribute much to the solution of the problem created by an annual population increase of more than half a million. From the point of view of employment of the many who have but a meagre subsistence the smale-scale industry, ordinary handicraft, offers better possibilities.

Nor was industrialisation deemed desirable, because it would not be a normal growth but a forced development. Considerable increase of production for domestic consumption might easily upset the balance of trade. A country like the Dutch East Indies whose very existence is dependent on export should be more than ever careful of its markets in a period of autarchy and universal protection. If it should manufacture on a large scale articles hitherto purchased in a country that was at the same time a market for its products, that market would be jeopardised. This danger is the more acute in the case of factory industries since these are able, in a short time, to throw much larger quantities of mass-production articles on the market than handicraft ever could.

It has also been argued that mechanical large-scale industry is not suited to native society and that by its competition it would oust native industry. It is very difficult to prophesy in such a matter. There are, curiously enough, several examples of the coexistence in the Indies of western and native industries in the same field. There are also examples of factories not able to cope with the competition of primitive native industries because these can produce cheaper, though inferior, articles.

It has been doubted whether promotion of native industry can contribute toward increase of the national income and raising of the purchasing power of the population. The returns earned by the manufacture of articles for the home market, requiring a good deal of labour and sold at an extremely low price, are generally too small to provide a livelihood. It may be said that, owing to the very fact that the purchasing power of the population is small, expansion of its industry can only augment that purchasing power by very little; however, even that small increase is important.

A special feature of native industry is the fact that a great many people only devote part of their time to a handicraft: leisure hours remaining after the daily work on the field or in the household; sometimes a few weeks when there is not enough work in the fields and therefore the earnings are insufficient to live on. The woman will batik, weave or make pottery; the man in his spare time will make baskets or straw cigarettes or, in the quiet season, he will hire himself out in some manufactory. The manufacture of such secondary industrial articles is therefore very variable and is dependent on the results of the harvest.

Starting as this kind of secondary occupation industry sometimes became a chief occupation, practised either as simple home industry or as factory industry. Its forms are generally well adapted to the sphere of an oriental community. Five principal forms may be distinguished.

1. Home industry, working exclusively for the benefit of the family; the products are not for sale. Examples are batiking and weaving.

2. Handicraft, in which the artisan works independently for the environment and sells his goods directly to the customer. Example: furniture making.

3. Home industry, manufacturing articles sold on the pasar or to a whole-sale dealer. Examples: straw braiding, making of pottery, making of straw cigarettes, weaving, batiking, leatherwork.

4. Workshops where people work in common in a subordinate position under a boss and where articles are delivered from stock. Examples: weaving, stamp-batiking, making of straw-cigarettes.

5. Factories where in a mechanised plant mass products are manufac-tured. A few simple native factories like oil-presses and rice hulling mills belong to this category; as a rule however such factories are larger and are in European hands.

The typical native industry, especially in the three firstnamed forms, has its own marked characteristics. It is absolutely uneconomical. No effort is made to produce as cheaply as possible, no account is taken of the time spent in it, little heed is paid to the wishes of the customer, and reactions to price variations are slow. There is a strong tendency to demand perma-nent credit for the supply of materials and manufacturing tools; it will not occur to the artisan that from his profits, small though they be, he may save a modest sum that can be used for that purpose; the idea of building up a working-capital even in the simplest form is foreign to him. Often he will borrow money from the same Chinese who afterwards will buy his articles so that he is bound to him in two ways. He prefers to leave the marketing of his goods to others, and therefore the part played by the Chinese dealer is very important and provides ample opportunity for abuses.

Rarely has the native craftsman a sense of organisation. The larger work-shops that employ a number of workers and where there is an organised division of labour are generally managed by Chinese or Arabs.

Competition is generally absent, rather the reverse is the case: there is a feeling of solidarity between the artisans of one desa practising the same industry in which they specialise collectively, not individually.

In the manufacture of native industrial articles there often is a lack of precision and care. A careful finish of the very cheap articles destined for the native market can hardly be expected. If however delivery fails to come up to a certain standard or sample or if the quality is not uniform western customers will not be satisfied.

Naturally the Government should first of all try to remedy the shortcomings of native industry. Leaving alone that kind of home industry that only works for family use, it should promote those industries that supply the market and particularly those that manufacture articles of mass production belonging to the vital necessities of the population.

The Industrial Bureau, which comes under the Department of Economic Affairs, has attempted to improve the organisation for the buying of materials and the sale of goods by introducing something like cooperative organisations in a few centres of the weaving and pottery industry. It is still too early to say whether this attempt will be a success.

At the end of 1936 a "Fund for the Small Industry" was established for the purpose of advancing money to new small industries in order to stimulate enterprise and prevent undesirable dependence on money-lending wholesale dealers. This "Fund" has been largely drawn upon. This "Fund" also finances the recently founded Central Organisations of Industry whose purpose is to buy materials on behalf of all craftsmen united in them, to check the quality of their products and advertise their articles. They keep stores, make price lists and take care of the filling of orders. Sometimes these central organisations have a factory under their own management for finishing off the half finished articles of the artisans. There is for example a small factory where spoons, forks and suchlike metal ware are polished, another one where unfinished household pottery is glazed. On delivery of their half finished product the artisans at once receive their money and the central organisation sells the finished article.

Important advice is also given about simple technical improvements benefiting both production and product. For some branches of industry special organisations have been founded that do extremely useful work, like the Textile Bureau at Bandung, the Keramic Laboratory and the Leather Laboratory.

Although the industrial policy of recent years did not aim at the promotion of factory industry, in some cases such industries have been protected, on the ground that the factory represented a national interest. The motive was then the desire for economic self-sufficiency.

Naturally native industry has always manufactured articles of mass production for the daily needs of the population, such as clothing and articles of domestic utility.

One of the oldest and chief branches of native industry is that of batiking.

It provides a large part of the population with clothing, batiked kains and sarongs, worn both by men and women and headcloths. This is a typical example of a handicraft to which most workers devote only part of their time. When the domestic duties are over women at home earn a trifle by batiking. It is impossible to tell how many people are engaged in this work, but they amount certainly to several hundred thousand. This small home industry still exists as it did in former years, but there are also workshops employing 500 to 600 men.

Batiking, in all stages, is done by hand. The only mechanical process that has been introduced into the work and that debases it to a mass product is, that nowadays the tracing of the pattern freehand with the aid of a stilus has largely been replaced by stamping it on to make the so-called chopbatik. Such stamping is always done by men, the hand-batik always by women.

The great importance of batik industry is evidenced by the fact that in recent years about seventy million batik sarongs were made with a production value of 41 million florins. It is true that a large amount of this figure is spent on imported material, but at least 7 million benefits the population in the form of wages.

By far the largest part of this batiked cloth finds its way on Java; about one fourth is shipped to the Outer Islands and an insignificant portion is shipped abroad as fancy article.

The second branch of industry that provides clothing for the population is weaving. Its principal product, the woven sarong, is also worn by all classes of the people. While batiking is entirely handwork, in weaving one finds various stages of mechanisation. There still is the old and primitive home industry, but there also are workshops equipped partly with hand-looms and partly with mechanical looms and there are some European mechanised weavingmills.

The Textile Bureau at Bandung has done extraordinarily useful work in the last decades by making experiments and giving advice. Originally the people used very primitive weaving looms on which work was slow. In 1926 the Bureau launched an improved loom capable of weaving ten times as much per day, and the population eagerly welcomed this great improvement. The weavers soon learnt to copy the standard model in djatiwood and in 1939 not less than 30.000 of these looms were in operation. There are now at least five thousand mechanical looms on Java mostly manufactured in Japan.

The principal article of the weavingmills is still the many-coloured sarong of cotton or cotton mixed with artificial silk, of which annually more than 7 million are woven. There is now also a special factory for weaving bleached cotton used in large quantities for batiking; the yarn required is now also spun in a spinning-mill, the first of its kind in the East Indies.

From 1931 on the weaving industry expanded enormously; in a few years the import of yarn was quintupled. It is true that during that period some large factories were established operating with hundreds of mechanical looms and producing annually millions of meters of sarongs and other goods. But a large proportion of the increase of textiles is due to the small weaving industry that, with the aid of the Textile Bureau, developed rapidly in the years of crisis when the people's sources of revenue were diminishing. In West Java there are entire desas living on weaving.

If the weaving industry imports much of its materials this is not the case with that of pottery. Of old, wherever suitable clay is found, red clay domestic utensils, bricks and tiles were made. Especially on Java there are numerous more or less primitive pottery works employing at least 60.000 people.

Bricks are used for European houses and for native ones if bamboo or wood are not easily obtainable. Cobbles are used in cities but nowadays most hard roads are made of asphalt or concrete. More important than bricks are roof tiles, because in the last decades these are also used as roofing for native houses. The Plague Prevention Service strongly recommends their use, since it was shown that the roofs of native houses made of atap (leaves of the sago or nipah palm) are favourite nesting places for rats and so increase the danger of plague transmission. When the improvement of houses began, in a short time tens of millions of roof tiles were ordered. So, while this simple industry was brought to the fore for hygienic motives, its expansion greatly benefited prosperity in certain regions. With the cooperation of the Keramic Laboratory the quality of the products, often poor, was also improved.

Still there is a difference between native bricks and tiles and those from the modern brick-factories now existing on Java. These also manufacture other articles such as culverts and tiles, much in demand in the Indies. Fireproof material for lining ovens, boilers etc., that previously all had to be imported, is now also manufactured on Java. New is also the manufacture of white earthenware, for which, after many experiments, the proper raw material has been discovered. It is hoped that this will replace part of the enormous import from Japan.

Another branch of industry using almost exclusively raw material from the country itself is the cigarette and cigar industry that has naturally developed in a country that raises much tobacco. Annually about 20.000 tons of native-grown tobacco is used in that industry. The natives are inordinately fond of smoking, especially of straw cigarettes, made of native tobacco mixed with ground cloves and wrapped round with a leaf of the corn cob. The clove lends it a peculiar flavour and crackles when the cigarette is smoked, which seems to heighten the pleasure. Cloves from the Moluccas seem to be less suitable for this purpose; hence they are imported from Zanzibar.

The straw cigarette industry has grown rapidly. There is still the old-fashioned, scattered home-manufacture but there are also large workshops, manufacturing up to 50 million straw cigarettes per year. They are sold in small packages costing only a few cents but there is a turnover of millions. The importance of the straw cigarette industry is shown by the value in the retail trade amounting to 18 million florins annually; less the import value of the cloves and the tobacco-tax, this amount comes entirely into the hands of the population.

Ordinary cheap cigarettes are also manufactured by hand. In the last few years this industry had to compete sharply with European mechanised cigarette factories, of which the first was founded in 1925. Their production increased very rapidly; in 1938 it had a sales value of 25 million florins. The cheapest kinds of cigarettes were manufactured as well as better brands for Europeans. Mass production made it possible to lower the prices to such an extent that the hand-made cigarette was threatened with extinction and the Government had to impose price-regulations.

The factories use native and foreign tobacco; latterly the population has been growing Virginia tobacco in order to replace the imported tobacco.

The soap industry is important for the population whose millions need a great deal of washing soap. Its principal ingredient, coconut oils, is plentiful and the manufacture is comparatively simple. There are a great number of small soap factories mostly managed by Chinese, producing annually

30.000 tons. Some larger factories manufacture the finer kinds of toilet soap.

There are several more native industries for which cheap raw material abounds, like that for the braiding of roofcovering, mats, baskets, hats, which latter article is exported by the million. The manufacture of sacks should not be forgotten either. Millions of sacks used to be imported from India for the packing of export products. Now however sacks are manufactured from the fibre of rosella, not unlike that of jute, and it is expected that this will shortly replace most of the import of this article.

The economic progress of the country since the development of western agricultural and mining enterprise greatly stimulated factory industry. The oldest and most important factory industry is the metal- and machine-industry. When shipping expanded docks were constructed for repairs even of large ships; later new ships, both wooden and steel, could be built there. Railways necessitated workshops for repair and construction; so did the large agricultural estates. The workshops developed into complete engineering works, capable of building machines or sheet-iron factory plants or bridges or steamrollers or almost anything.

An important modern concern is also the Portland Cement Company near Padang. Concrete required for the building of factories, offices, sheds etc. used to be imported, at first from Europe, later from Japan. When the necessary raw material was discovered in the neighboorhood of Padang this factory was established there in 1912.

A motorcar assembling plant of General Motors exists at Tandjung Priok and a rubber tire factory of the Goodyear Concern was started at Buitenzorg in 1935. It is an interesting experience that native workmen very soon adapt themselves to work on the assembly line.

The spiritual awakening of the Indies, creating a need for books, periodicals and newspapers, set the printingpresses going. There are now well over two hundred printing-houses. It also started the paper industry. Native rice-straw is used for making printing and writing paper, but paper for newspapers and packing paper is still imported.

There are of course a great number of smaller factories for such products as alcohol, beer and arak, margarine and vegetable oil, canned goods, biscuits, candy, paint. There are large projects for an aluminium factory, a glass factory, a factory for ammonia and sulphuric acid etc.

All this may be sufficient to show that industry in the East Indies is certainly not a negligible factor. Its significance lies in manufacturing articles for the domestic market. The promotion of industry in a few years resulted in an increase of production worth many millions of florins.

The outbreak of war and the subsequent interruption of communications with Europe compelled the Indies to supply more than ever before their own needs. Moneys have been appropriated for the building of factories for which in normal times there was no urgent need. In the last world war there was a similar development but many of the factories then founded were but shortlived. Now however there is much more conscious planning and it may be confidently expected that the results will be more lasting.

PHYSICAL WELFARE — HYGIENE AND NUTRITION

It is a general and striking observation that the countries in temperate zones show a much higher level of mental and physical development than those in the tropical and subtropical parts of the world. The degree of prosperity appears to have kept step with this development. The conclusion seems obvious that climate and race are responsible for this.

History however shows us a different picture. Great civilisations like those of the Hindus, the Kmers in Further India, the Arabs and Egyptians all developed in tropical and subtropical zones. Even the two great civilisations of Europe, those of the Greeks and Romans, were located in the extreme southern part of our continent. And if we pause to think of Palestine, from where the Christian faith spread over the earth, we perceive that nearly all great religions had their cradles in southern countries. It is often alleged that wars and mutual strife ruined and atrophied these civilisations. But is this easy explanation true? A close study of the history of Hellas and Rome rather leads to the conclusion that their downfall should, to a very large extent, be ascribed to epidemics, especially malaria. This is also true of Mohammedan and particularly of Hindu civilisation, and there are many indications showing that Kmer culture was ruined by the same cause.

These object-lessons from history clearly demonstrate the important part played by sickness in retarding the development of civilisation in many countries of the tropical and subtropical zones. This also was, and partly still is, the case with the East Indies. Only with this in mind can one properly understand the significance of hygiene in that country and the great possibilities for the future that proper medical care may open up.

When the first Dutch ships visited the Indies medical care was confined to the crew and the Company's staff on shore. Natives coming in daily contact with the Dutch would occasionally have the benefit of medical treatment. Up to the 19th century no more was done. It must be admitted that with the then existing state of medical science it would have been difficult to do much more. Army doctors were the first to apply the results of modern medical science by inoculating against smallpox.

It was the development of the theory of infectious diseases, the new sciences of bacteriology, parasitology and nutrition that opened unlimited possibilities to medical men in the Indies. For human life in the tropics was found to be much more menaced by infectious diseases than by the climate. When this view had been attained the gigantic work began that today has already achieved great results and is still opening up great perspectives for this part of the globe. The Dutch realised this at an early date and more quickly, more fully and more thoroughly than any other colonising people they placed this new medical science at the service of general hygiene. At first they did so in selfprotection, but before long from altruistic motives they extended their activities to the native population. From 1893 on the missions also undertook medical work.

In a later stage, about the beginning of our century, enlightened self-interest prompted them to enlarge these activities still further. It was realised that only healthy people are capable of efficient work. The plantations, especially those on the east coast of Sumatra, were the first to prove beyond cavil that proper medical care of the workers was neither altruism nor luxury, but that no part of the territory could ever be well and profitably brought under cultivation unless at the same time a sound system of hygiene were organised. The Government soon followed this lead and it was gradually realised that an all-embracing medical care was a prerequisite for creating a healthy and prosperous land. So the last stage was reached: no longer was the organisation of medical care prompted solely by self-interest, but it was much more firmly based on a purely humanitarian ideal. Though there remained many who would or could not understand that this was the only possible way to give the Indies a great and beautiful future, nevertheless this new policy was rapidly triumphant.

Some of the activities and results of this medical service may here be summarised.

Smallpox used to exact a very heavy annual toll of human lives. Today smallpox has practically disappeared. At first vaccine was supplied by Europe, but today the Pasteur Institute at Bandung (Java) is able to supply excellent vaccine for the 65 million inhabitants of the Indies. This Institute, originally founded for the treatment of rabies, now combats all kinds of epidemics with its arsenal of preventive vaccines and serums.

An efficient quarantine system, modern sanitation and aqueducts were all established to this same end. The terrific scourge of cholera has disappeared; typhoid fever and dyssentery are becoming rarer; the hard struggle against the plague has been taken up and, with great perseverance and ingenuity, successfully carried to a point where it can be controlled.

There are however two widely prevalent and often fatal diseases that, particularly on account of their sapping the energy of the people, have for years claimed the special attention of authorities and doctors. These are the hookworm disease and malaria. What used to be called tropical anaemia is now ascribed to these diseases that, by sapping people's strength, chronically affect prosperity. It is now known how hookworm can be combatted and this is being done with the utmost zeal. In the last 30 years the Rockefeller Foundation has undertaken a wide campaign against this disease in nearly all tropical and Asiatic countries and it was astonished and disappointed when the Dutch replied to their offer of aid that they were perfectly capable of solving this problem themselves. Later an agreement was reached whereby the Rockefeller Foundation's assistance toward defraying costs of propaganda was accepted.

The hardest problem however is that of malaria. Great sanitary engineering works have been carried out. Walch's ingenious biological purification of water has been successfully applied in many places and slowly but surely one victory after another has been scored in this hard struggle.

Other problems such as those of framboesia, leprosy and tuberculosis have also been tackled. Hospitals have been founded or subsidised by Govern-

Fishing prahu's in Sunda Stra

ment, province, municipalities or mission organisations. For these a large
staff of nurses, both men and women, and midwives had to be found and
trained. A medical school at Batavia, started as early as 1851, was reorganised into a full-fledged medical college, fully on a par with the best institutions of the kind in other Asiatic countries and certainly superior to the
medical colleges in Japan. In 1913 a second medical school was founded at
Surabaya. Both schools are centres of scientific research of a high order.
The Indies were always well represented at all international scientific con-
gresses and when in 1937 the League of Nations organised a general conference of all East-asiatic countries for the study of important health-pro-
blems, Java was selected as host so as to give the Conference an opportunity
to study at first hand what has been achieved there.

Schools for midwives have been founded with numerous policlinics in the
kampongs. The missions have also done pioneer work here. Children's hospitals, infants. clinics, sanatoria for tubercular patients, a cancer institute
have been opened· Innumerable hospitals have been established by the
plantations and the splendid work done there for the physical wellbeing of
their workers has had a far reaching influence.

It may be asked: how did the native react to this flood of sanitary measures? It is often suggested that the population received this shower of benefits to health passively and even somewhat negatively. A few examples then
serve to support this superficial contention, too readily accepted by outsiders
in Holland. Considering in how short a time all these revolutionary measures
were introduced in the Indies, it is absurd to expect that adaptation should
have kept pace. Compared with the way in which hygienic reforms were
received in many countries of Europe, even in the Netherlands, one must
admit that the native population has frequently been more progressive and
understanding than the European. They certainly never show the positive
negativism so common in Europe when sanitary measures have to be carried
out in quick succession. Close observation shows that in spite of certain
difficulties their degree of adaptation has been remarkable. Active propaganda by means of films, demonstrations, practical advice and exhibitions
does a great deal to smoothe the way, and to instruct the people in the first
principles of hygienics.

Thus in every way that science can devise diseases in the Indies are

Mission 14

fought and, if possible, exterminated. The high death-rate of former years is steadily declining and the tropics have lost their terror. It is now possible to live there under hygienic conditions permitting a healthy life.

For a healthy and vigorous people however more is needed than mere protection against the baleful external influences of pathogenic organisms. It is equally necessary to raise the power of resistance of each individual so as better to equip him in his fight against many of these diseases and in his struggle in society. For a people to attain prosperity it is further necessary that, irrespective of sickness, health and vigour find favourable conditions in which to develop so that the standard of achievement is raised. This is largely a dietary problem.

The natural composition of the native diet in the Dutch East Indies proved for the first time that the old theory of dietetics with its calories, carbo-hydrates, fats and albumens did not work. In all Asiatic countries beri-beri raged among workmen, prisoners, soldiers, in many places also among the free population, sent thousands to their graves and made other thousands invalids for life. Our countrymen Eyckman and Gryns had the good fortune to shed the first light on the origin of this disease. At Batavia they made their admirable experiments whereby they were able not only to discover the cause of beri-beri, thus saving thousands of human lives in all oriental countries, but they opened up an entirely new approach for the study of dietetics. Both in a scientific and in a practical respect the results of this work were considerable, for from it originated the now so popular theory of vitamins. In this case the Indies provided the incentive leading to a complete revolution of ideas. The dietary problem in tropical countries always was a fascinating one. The deeper one penetrated into it, the greater its significance was seen to be, not only for human pathology but also for a vigorous development of the entire people.

The dietary problem on the one hand is dependent on economic conditions, while, on the other, better dietary conditions lead to greater economic possibilities. The rapid increase of the population, stimulated by improved medical care, makes the problem of how to feed all these people and feed them in accordance with our present knowledge of dietetics, constantly more pressing. This urgency, also existing in other tropical and subtropical lands, was realised in the Dutch East Indies at an early date. Fortunately modern medicine and also the progress of agriculture and dairy-farming have opened up wide possibilities. A study of the problem undertaken on different sides soon revealed that fragmentary work could not lead to lasting results and coordination was imperative. This was achieved by the foundation of a special institute for the study of dietary problems where there is close collaboration between medical men, chemists, agriculturalists, veterinary surgeons, engineers, social-economists and statisticians. Nearly all Indian foodstuffs have been carefully analysed. In towns as well as in the country the daily diet has been carefully studied, its costs have been calculated and possibilities of modifying and improving it have been examined.

In a short time a wealth of data has been collected. Much that seemed incongruous and strange in the food and habits of the natives proved to be of much more real value than had been supposed. The variety in the diet also was shown to be greater.

Experiments were also made with western vegetables and fruit. The cultivation of potatoes was extended and provision was made for the supply of meat, milk and butter. It is now possible to keep to a normal western diet in the Indies.

For raising the general standard of people's physical fitness improvement of the people's diet is essential. Without economic prosperity this is impossible, — on the other hand economic prosperity is impossible without proper nutrition and hygiene. The problem therefore should be tackled from both angles at the same time. This is what the Dutch have attempted to do in the last 25 years. Time will show how important their work has been.

SPIRITUAL WELFARE

The idea that Holland has a moral responsiblity for the spiritual development of the peoples of the Archipelago has taken centuries to mature.

The conception was not entirely lacking in the days of the East India Company. True, this was a mercantile body first and foremost and it preferred to avoid too close a contact with the peoples with whom it dealt. Nevertheless it was animated by a strong conviction that it had a missionary

calling which prompted it to establish schools. These were regarded as
"true seedbeds" of the Christian religion; they were closely connected with
the Church and were only established there where the Church sought an
entrance among the native population.

The situation became different when the Company was abolished and
the Indies came under the Government's direct administration. The Government realised that first of all the schools founded under the Company should
be preserved, but that it also should start schools in the non-Christian parts
of the Archipelago. Daendels, Governor-General from 1808 to 1811, gave
instructions for founding schools "for the instructing of youth in the manners, customs, laws and religious ideas of the Javanese". Later van der
Capellen, who became Governor-General after the restoration of Dutch
independence, advocated making use of the native religious schools as an
instrument of popular education. This idea was afterwards abandoned as
the conviction gained ground that school teaching should be a distribution
of the riches of western knowledge.

It is not surprising that it was many years before any large number of
schools were established. The budget did not permit any indulging of idea-
listic tendencies, nor was the population greatly interested. The Government's
attitude towards education was, as a Frenchman once characterised it, one of
"prudence" and "conscience". There was prudence, the fear of dangerous
experiments, and there was conscience, the sentiment of duty. In the long
history of education sometimes the one, then the other feeling predominated.

The need of good schools for future native officials was first felt. In 1892
a fundamental distinction was introduced between "class A" schools, intended for children of native chiefs and other notables, and "class B" schools
for the mass of native children. The standard of teaching at schools of the
former type could be considerably higher than at those of the latter. They
were only primary schools of course, but they laid the foundation for the
education of young men who became native officials or employees in western
concerns. The teaching of the Dutch language was more and more emphasised at these schools. When from the turn of the century on the native population awoke to the need of western learning, they were invaded by grea-
numbers of youths aspiring for a good place in society. Thanks to the fact
that many great concerns could employ educated natives in increasing num-

bers, the schools became very popular. In 1911 they were reformed into so-called Dutch-Native schools with practically the same program as the Dutch primary school. Dutch-Chinese schools of this type had been started in 1908.

The popularity of this kind of education should, doubtless, be partly ascribed to the desire of many to obtain better paid and more or less leading positions in society which could only be reached by way of the Dutch-Native school. At the same time this interest is a symptom of the awakening of the Indies. This awakening was characterised by a strong desire to be equipped with the advantages of western learning in order to shed the bonds of tutelage and to attain an honoured place in the Far Eastern world. Many consciously turned away from their own culture and welcomed the new thought. Thus the Indies responded to the call of the times.

In the long run these Dutch-Native schools gave rise to many problems. When the number of pupils began greatly to exceed the normal need for western-trained young men, the question arose what to do with graduates of these schools who would be unable to find employment either with the Government or with a private concern. They would be thrown back into their old environment and the danger was not imaginary that they would develop into a large group of malcontents. Another difficulty was of pedagogical order. Was it wise to bring children, at an age when they barely know their own language, into contact with a foreign language of an entirely different structure? Would this not result in the children neither knowing their own nor the foreign tongue? Was the Dutch-Native school not vitiated at the very root by the fact that it was too western, that it lost all contact with the culture of the people itself and that it therefore dislocated the youth? Meanwhile, though the Government was not blind to the difficulties, more schools of a western type were organised for natives. Secondary schools, formerly only open to western children, were reorganised and opened to native children as well. A kind of high school was also established, differentiated into three types: one with mathematics and science as main subjects, one with modern languages and Latin and the third with modern and oriental languages. The graduating certificate of this high school gives admittance to Dutch universities.

Higher education was also introduced into the Indies. A Technical College for the training of engineers was founded at Bandung in 1920; in 1924

a Law College and in 1927 a Medical College, both at Batavia. A Faculty
of Letters and Philosophy has recently been added to these so that there is
an almost complete university. The Indies are now able partly to provide
for their own need of engineers, doctors and lawyers.

The "class B" schools mentioned before have a history of their own. Their
character was far less western than that of the other type. Their teaching
was not done in Dutch, but in the native language of the country, — that is
to say, teaching is now done in more than thirty different native languages.
Nevertheless these schools could not simply go on in the old traditional way.
Daendels' idea that the school should serve "for the instructing of youth in
the manners, customs, laws and religious ideas of the Javanese" proved im-
practicable. Though the native language was used, the school building
countrified and homely, the teaching-matter was bound to be somewhat
western. Reading, writing and arithmetic were the three principal subjects.
None of these was taught in connection with religion or the ancestral ideas
and customs; they were, on the contrary, presented as purely social accom-
plishments of a secular character.

Originally projected as a three grade school, it gradually expanded to
four or five grades. Then it was discovered that it would be far too expensive
to provide the Indies with a sufficient number of schools of this type. It
would run into hundreds of millions of florins annually. The Government
was confronted with the alternative either of abandoning its ideal of school
education for all or of launching a new and cheaper type of school.

Governor-General van Heutsz cut this Gordian knot. He found the solution by making the desas responsible, at least in part, for these schools.
This had the double advantage of making the desa more interested in its
own school and, because of the economy of large sums of money, enabling
the Government to make this education much more general. From 1907
on this policy was followed. The desa schools, subsidised by the Government, were very simple and cheap. Their number has increased enormously.
In 1908 there were not quite 400, in 1918 nearly 6000, in 1928 about 12.000
and in 1938 nearly 15.000. Though the natives were not everywhere equally
enthusiastic about these schools, on the whole they understand more and
more the significance of school education. As the number of literates increases
illiteracy is regarded as a sign of backwardness.

But is such a primitive three grade school sufficient for attaining the avowed aim, the extermination of illiteracy? And is after all the abolition of illiteracy such a desirable end in itself that it is worth the effort? It has been observed that abolition of illiteracy would not bring us a step further; what is needed first of all are the building up of character, the formation of habits of cooperation, interest in the improvement of village conditions. The Government has not remained deaf to the criticisms voiced from many quarters and it is constantly trying to make the simple village school into a true means of popular education.

A great variety of technical schools was also established: agricultural, commercial, professional for boys; for girls schools for domestic science. No pains are spared to find the right type of school adapted to the different needs of the population.

A survey of the entire educational system in the Dutch East Indies leaves one, nevertheless, with a feeling of disappointment. The original ideal of connecting school teaching up with the native world view has not been realised. One may incorporate into our teaching various fragments from native cultural life, but that does not transform that system into a plant naturally growing from the soul of the people. The school may teach native arts and crafts, woodcarving, brasswork, native songs, etc., but all these efforts do not alter the character of the teaching. In other words: it has been found impossible to build up an educational system on the basis of that magicomystical philosophy that was so characteristic of native thought. The "sacred tradition", "the heritage of the ancestors" could not be respected and could not be made the starting point of all educational enterprises. This means that the system of education, developed by us in the Indies, bears of necessity a revolutionary character; it overthrows old values and opens the gates to a new world.

It would be unfair to hold this up as a reproach to the Government. This is a universal phenomenon, equally found in China and Japan and all other oriental countries. It is but a small part of the gigantic clash of the two worlds of East and West going on in our time. The remarkable thing is that the oriental peoples themselves, with undiminished ardour, demand western education in order to secure for themselves full recognition in the family of nations. The school system as it was built up in the Indies is merely a symptom of this grave world crisis.

Among the leaders of the national movement in the Indies there are some who strongly criticise the western character of school education. The founder of the Taman-Siswo schools, Ki Hadjar Déwantoro, especially represents this view. In his schools the Javanese traditional relationship between *guru* (teacher) and *siswo* (pupil) is maintained. That is, the guru is at the same time the spiritual father of his pupils, he is their counsellor and helper in all difficulties. Many Taman-Siswo schools are residential; the resident master is as it were the family head of the pupil-boarders. Though these schools could not avoid the necessity of gratefully accepting western learning, yet they follow somewhat different lines of teaching than the government schools. In order to safeguard their independence they never applied for a government grant. In a short time they have attained a remarkable popularity, which shows that their founder has rightly interpreted the sentiments of many Indonesians. In 1938 there were 225 primary schools of this type, totalling 17.000 pupils and some secondary and normal schools.

Aware of the difficulties of the educational problem the Government has acted with the same prudence and conscience cited before. Requests for monetary aid by organisations or corporations centring around a religious idea or promoting the safeguarding of ancestral culture always found a willing ear. Neither Protestant nor Roman-Catholic Missions nor Mohammedan societies ever applied in vain for assistance.

Attempts to create a new literature are also encouraged by the Government. The old mystical books are no longer read by the younger generation. What is needed are books with educational value that at the same time are attractive to young people. Awards are given for the best literary productions of this kind.

At some secondary schools the teaching is done in one of the native languages. These experiments are very valuable. The native languages have to adapt themselves to new needs and express scientific concepts. If they stand this very severe test of their elasticity and flexibility they may become vehicles of scholarship.

In the native world there are now young people with a good modern education themselves and keenly interested in the numerous pedagogical problems of the schools. Their devotion will go far to help in solving them. And, taking all in all, there is ample reason to admire the educational results already achieved in the Indies.

CHAPTER 14

How the Dutch East Indies are governed

In order to form a picture of the way in which the Dutch East Indies are governed one has to bear in mind the wide variety of peoples inhabiting the extensive archipelago, all at very different stages of development. At the turn of this century not one of these peoples evinced any desire for emancipation so that the Government's task was limited and its interference in native society but slight.

It should also be remembered that the Dutch had gone to the Indies in order to trade and not to found an empire. Compelled by circumstances to exercise actual rule from the first they adopted the principle to leave the inhabitants as much as possible under their own rulers. This meant that in many regions they actually remained under their own princes while in regions placed under direct Dutch rule native chieftains were used wherever possible. According to the same principle for Chinese and Arabs "officers" of these respective nationalities were appointed.

In a society of this type a centralised government was indicated. It was exercised to the remotest corners by civil servants appointed as his representatives by the Governor-General and responsible to him. These civil servants thus acquired such intimate knowledge of the indigenous population as no one else could attain. The Civil Service decreed what was good or ill for the population, what it needed or what it could do without, what burdens could be laid upon its shoulders. The Civil Service did not only exercise complete rule over the population, but it also was its daily judge, it watched over the health of men and beasts, it looked after the interests of agriculture and cattle-breeding. There was no government concern that was not either entirely in the hands of the Civil Service or greatly influenced by it.

Various circumstances brought about a gradual change of this simple structure. At the beginning of the XXth century the Netherlands came to realise their moral duty with regard to the Indies and the Indonesians. The direct result was a considerable extension and intensification of the government's activities in the interest of the population. It was a fortunate circumstance that increasing revenues were able to meet the increase of expenditure entailed by this extension; also that the Awakening of the East penetrated into the archipelago thus creating for the measures taken the possibility to come to fruition. As a rule the initiative to ever greater activity on new fields of Governmental interest was taken by the Civil Service. As these interests gradually developed, special services with expers were created with a strictly centralised organisation.

The history of the East Indian governmental system in the last forty years is dominated by the question how to find the most efficient forms for carrying out a governing task so greatly changed in character. Expanding beyond all expectation it overburdened the central government so that a partial transfer of responsibilities was necessary. This might have been brought about by granting lower officials a greater measure of independence in carrying out certain policies but, as it happened, the course of events was different.

The centripetal tendencies of the special services had awakened a desire in local residents to have a say in matters affecting their town or region. The idea of local councils began to take shape.

So, from 1905 on, a number of municipalities were organised. This was followed in 1918 by the creation of a central representative body, called the Volksraad (People's Council), at first with an advisory character only but from 1927 on invested with co-legislative powers. Finally, from 1925 on, the territory was divided into provinces and "governments".

No attempt will here be made to give a chronological account of this development. It will be clearer to present a brief sketch of how the East Indies were governed just before the outbreak of the war.

According to the Netherlands' constitution the supreme authority over the Indies was vested in the Queen. Considerable influence however was exercised by Parliament. Not only did its colegislative powers extend to legislation pertaining to the Indies but the Minister of Colonies (the colonial secretary of state) appointed by the Queen was responsible to it. He was able to bear this responsibility because the Governor-General, also appointed by the Queen in whose name he exercised the general government of the East Indies, for all his actions was responsible to the Minister of Colonies. This implied that the Governor-General had to heed all rulings of the Minister of Colonies in matters of government and legislation. The seemingly wellnigh dictatorial power of the Governor-General was therefore narrowly limited by the effective interference of the Minister of Colonies and by the democratic governmental system of the mother country.

The Governor-General was assisted by a Council of the Netherlands East Indies whose advice in all important matters it was mandatory for him to seek and in certain specific cases he could only act in full agreement with that Council.

Legislation of the East Indies relative to internal affairs was effected by the Governor-General in agreement with the central representative body, the Volksraad. The budget, in so far as agreement had been reached between the Governor-General and the Volksraad was provisionally fixed by the Governor-General, subject to definitive approval by Parliament in Holland. Lacking the required agreement in legislative matters even after repeated debate in the Volksraad, the Governor-General could request the Minister of Colonies to promulgate the disputed ordinance or, in case of urgency, do so himself. Such cases, though comparatively rare, always attracted an inordinate amount of attention whenever they occurred.

The Volksraad met in two sessions with a combined duration of four months. The briefness of these sessions had the advantage that members were able to keep on in their normal functions and thus did not lose contact with social life. Since on the other hand a co-legislative body cannot be spared during eight months of the year, a Committee of Delegates was instituted, consisting of one fourth of the total membership and chosen by the Volksraad itself. This Committee, with the sole exception of the discussion of the budget, enjoyed the same powers as the council-in-pleno. Mutual friction between the two bodies was prevented by certain measures found quite satisfactory in practice.

In composing the membership of the Council consisting of 61 members care was taken that the diversity of population groups was reflected as much as possible. About one half of the total number of seats was allotted to Dutchmen, and there was a fixed allocation of some seats to Chinese and Arabs. A division of the native population into a number of electoral districts took care of the interests of the different nationalities according to their relative importance. Since half the members (Dutch, native or Chinese) were elected and the other half directly nominated by the Governor-General, it was possible to meet widely diverging desires and needs.

It may be said that a considerable part of the Government's responsibility was, in this way, transferred from the Hague to Batavia. This does not mean that the relationship between Holland and the East Indies was settled to everybody's satisfaction. In practice there still remained moot points requiring further attention. The Indies insisted especially that internal affairs should indeed be left to the East Indian Government bodies and that the East Indian budget, discussed in the Volksraad with minute and expert care, be fixed directly in the East Indies in so far as agreement between Governor-General and Volksraad had been reached. Thus would be reserved for discussion by the States-General at The Hague those parts of the budget and those East Indian ordinances about which no such agreement had been reached, as well as bills of law touching the joint interests of Holland and the East Indies or those of the Kingdom of the Netherlands as such. In the last few years before the world war proposals for such alterations were repeatedly placed before the public attention and the question was raised whether the time had not yet come to create in Holland an imperial body composed by representatives of the four parts of the Kingdom, that is to say Holland, the Dutch East Indies, Suriname and the Antilles, for dealing with general interests of the Kingdom, now still treated by Dutch governmental bodies alone. This multiplex problem of alteration of the structure of the Kingdom has far-reaching and unpredictable consequences; it would involve a transfer of the responsibilities of the different bodies not rashly to be undertaken. There was far from unanimity about the way in which improvements might be introduced; a time in which all attention had to be centred on the internal political construction of the East Indies and on the economic problems was judged by many inopportune for taking further steps in the political development.

The public debate in the Volksraad took up much time and laid a heavy burden on the Government bureaux. Hundreds of questions asked during the debate on the budget necessitated inquiries and further information. All this was coupled with an undiminished volume of home correspondence. At the same time the position of chiefs of departments, though more difficult, also became stronger and was brought into greater relief. True, they did not speak in defense of a policy as Ministers of the Crown with a responsibility of their own, they always had to keep in touch with the Governor-General in all important matters, nevertheless they were much more independent, since the Government was not bound to any majority party. It was inevitable that the Governor-General should leave all technical matters (and where did these cease to be technical?) to the chief of a department appointed because of his special knowledge of the concerns of that department. The latter in turn would be compelled by sheer weight of work to entrust greater responsibilities to his subordinates. Thus reality mocked all theory: an all-inclusive central control is only possible so long as the business of government is simple. In a more complicated organisation control should be limited to matters of major importance. Human weakness however demands supervision also in matters of minor importance left to lower officials. So long as this could not be entrusted to lower autonomous bodies the Volksraad had to exercise this control and so the chiefs of departments were again involved in all these matters. This made it the more urgent to relieve the central Government from part of its burden.

Thus on the one hand the authorities' wish for greater efficiency, on the other that of the inhabitants to collaborate in the government from 1925 on led to the so-called Administrative Reform, that is to say the organisation of provinces and "governments". This Reform worked out quite differently on Java and on the Outer Islands.

On Java 3 provinces were organised, subdivided into about 70 regencies and a few score of municipalities. These provinces, as regards their relationship to the central government and the regencies and municipalities under them, were copied on the model of the Dutch provinces. These however had a historic growth; those in Java were artificially created and, moreover, each comprised an area larger than the whole of the Netherlands and numbered respectively 12,12 and 16 million inhabitants! The chances of vitality

were made as favourable as possible. West-Java with its Sundanese population formed an ethnic unity, but the boundaries between Central and East-
Java were arbitrarily fixed mainly because the territory would otherwise
have been too unwieldy for one province. To these provinces a large task
was immediately assigned and later this task was even still more enlarged.
They were also equipped with adequate personnel and never were seriously
harassed by financial troubles.

To the political collaboration of the inhabitants was given due scope by
the organisation of Provincial Councils of more than 50 members, in which
a certain number of seats were allotted to each of the three groups of Dutchmen, Indonesians and Chinese. Each of these groups was represented also in
the Executive Board. It can hardly be said that the population showed much
enthusiasm over these councils; they were entirely beyond the sphere of
interest of the ordinary folk. Of the more educated people, some were indifferent; others recognised the utility of these councils.

It is a different matter with the autonomous regencies. This reform was
much more hazardous. With a few exceptions the Regencies were historical
territorial units and the population was fully conscious of belonging to a
certain Regency. This however does not mean that they had any idea of
the Regency as an autonomous organisation.

It was by no means certain that the Regent would be equal to his new
task. After 1912 some responsibilities of Dutch officials had gradually been
shifted to native Regents in order to "de-guardianise" him, as it was called.
Now by the Administrative Reform Law all of a sudden this emancipation
was applied to all Regents to whom, at the same time, was given the difficult
task of presiding over the newly created Regency-Councils. It was also a
risky experiment not to make the Regent, enjoying so much traditional
respect, the actual head of the Regency. The Council was made the actual
head, the Regent being merely the executor of the Council's decisions.
There was no lack of gloomy forebodings but so far these were not fulfilled.
On the contrary, the position of the Regent seemed rather to have gained
in authority resulting in increased prestige of the native civil service. Granted
that among the Regents it was not all gold that glittered and that a good
deal of criticism might be lavished on the activities of many Regencies,
taken all in all there was reason for great satisfaction. Many Regents acquit-

ted themselves well of their new task, some did exceedingly well, and so they contributed not a little toward the success of the newly created autonomous Regency.

Though the task of Provinces and Regencies did not yet by any means come to its fullest expansion, it may already be said that the administrative reform on Java actually did bring relief to the central Government and the central services. In each province provincial services were organised with their own staff of experts to take over the task of the central departments. In education, irrigation, building and repair of roads, agricultural advice, forestry etc. a large part of the work was transferred to the provincial services. The central services however retained the supervision of the general interests for the whole of the East Indies and the decisions entailing questions of principle.

This devolution was not only applied to the provincial services, but as much as possible local interests were transferred to the Regencies under the supervision of the provincial government. The Regencies in turn organised separate services. In this way measures formerly decreed from one central point were adapted as much as possible to local needs.

In an even greater measure transfer of responsibility took place in the case of the municipalities organised from 1905 on. In their organisation they entirely copied the Dutch municipal law. The responsibilities entrusted to them at first were slight; only slowly did they succeed in gaining more say in administrative affairs. The civil servants and the special services, conscious of a good record, were not in a hurry to shed some of their responsibilities to greenhorns. They rather regarded municipalities as "western enclaves in an oriental country" and did not permit them to have anything to do with the affairs of natives living within the municipality. These remained under their own chiefs or under the Civil Service. The larger part of the municipal area, the native kampongs, thus fell outside the scope of municipal activity. It took far too long before this theoretical question was solved in favour of the municipalities. It cannot be denied that the kampong population was greatly benefited by the work of the municipality, though the problem of kampong improvement that would devour millions of florins was not yet solved.

The administrative reform of the Outer Islands had quite a different character. The diversity of peoples, differing in customs, standard of education and political habits, made it impossible to copy there the reform introduced on Java. Opinions differed and are still differing on the manner of reform. Meanwhile the first steps were taken in 1938 by the organisation of three "governments": Sumatra, Borneo and "the Great East" being the eastern part of the Archipelago, each under a governor. Autonomous group-communes were to be established under these governments, not, like those on Java, all of a pattern, but area and responsibility for each one was to be fixed separately. Within a few years these governments were to be transformed into provinces, that is to say councils were to be adjoined to the governors and their responsibilities were to be fixed separately. The tendency towards uniformity here remained a menace to the best intentions.

On the whole the form of government-by-discussion, embodied in the councils, was found satisfactory. The councils, whether of province, regency or municipality, always had the decisive vote. The governor, regent or burgomaster could only suspend a decision and refer it to a higher authority for annulment.

The manner of representation was different for the different councils and groups of the population. The principle followed was not that every adult had the right to cast his vote for a representative, but that the best possible representation should be found for the heterogeneous East Indian society. The electoral systems were changed repeatedly as circumstances demanded. Moreover it was felt that elections alone did not give sufficient guarantee for the best representation. Party system was still little developed and it was obvious that many suitable persons would not be willing to stand for election so that certain groups might not be represented at all. This difficulty was solved by direct nomination of about one third of the total membership. Though it would be an overstatement to say that these nominations were always universally applauded, there never was serious dissatisfaction. The principal grievances were concerned with the nominations in Regency Councils, since the members of those councils (and of the Municipal Councils) were electors of the Provincial Councils and the Volksraad. Thus the direct nomination of electors met with more opposition than that of representatives! When some years ago it was proposed by the electoral reform committee to introduce this system of partial nomination also for the Municipal Councils, this proposal was supported by the Volksraad.

Bay of Labuan-Bajo (Island of Flores) with a pearl-fisher in the background

The political division of the Dutch East Indies is not so simple that a subdivision of the entire territory into 6 provinces (3 on Java and in future 3 on the Outer Islands) and of these in turn into regencies and municipalities (or group-communes and municipalities on the Outer Islands) should suffice. On the contrary: such a division leaves out a very large part of the territory, that is to say the autonomous native states. On Java there are four autonomous states, the chief of which are Jocjakarta and Surakarta, numbering 1½ and 2½ million inhabitants. On the Outer Islands their area comprises more than half the territory. They vary in importance and size from a village to a minor Dutch province and the level of their civilisation varies greatly. When our administration in the Outer Islands was intensified, it was impossible to leave these states alone. Not all their princes and rulers however were able to direct the necessary development and there was little hope that education could soon make them equal to that task. In the last decades before the war the constant urge to stimulate the development of native society often led to more interference with the internal affairs of the native states than was originally intended. This was made possible by the terms of the treaties concluded with the native princes. For practical reasons some of the native states were even abolished: in 1914 there were 340, in 1930 only 273. From that date on there was a reaction in the policy of the Government aiming at greater development of the autonomous administration, and even leading to the restoration of some abolished states. In this new policy they were regarded as free forms of decentralisation also fit to take over their share of the Central Government's task. The measure in which the native population might be given a voice depended on the existing political structure and the possibility of democratising it, perhaps in an Indonesian democratic spirit.

As stated at the outset the Civil Services, both Dutch and Native, played an extraordinarily important part in the development of the East Indies. The task of the civil servants changing in character as society developed both services passed through a period of great vicissitudes. This was due to a variety of causes. Each special service that was organised lopped off some part of the original task of the civil servants. Still the native population having a natural confidence in its chiefs, in the first place the heads of desa's and through them in the civil servants, the latter were eminently fit to keep in touch with the population and to give advice about the speed and manner of execution of some proposed measure. So it was often necessary to maintain the civil service as a connecting link between a special service and the population.

The organisation of autonomous regions also greatly influenced the position of the civil servants. Beside their position as servants of the Central Government the Governor and the Regent acquired a leading function as chairman of the Provincial and Regency Council. Since the Provincial Board of Deputies had the task of superintending the government bodies of Regencies and Municipalities, the Governor, beside his important central government work, directed the provincial administration and supervised the actions of the administration of Regencies and Municipalities. After what was said above there is no need to expatiate further on the difficult position in which the Regent found himself by the administrative reform. The transfer of responsibilities was felt down to the lower positions both of the European and the Native Civil Service.

Finally the mutual relationship of the two services was altered as a result of the improved training and better education of the native civil servants in the general policy of assigning to natives a more important part in government functions. It was especially intended to lend more colour to the office of the newly emancipated Regent by a rigid selection and, if possible, the application of the hereditary principle. The decentralising legislation as well as the process of specialisation not being so far advanced on the Outer Islands, where moreover the idea of "de-guardianisation" had been entirely absent, the position of the Civil Service there remained practically unchanged. To a far greater extent than on Java the work of the Dutch Civil Service there retained the character of auto-activity.

A retrospective view over the development of the Civil Service in the last forty years shows a radical encroachment on the patriarchal rule. By democratisation, though on a limited scale and with due regard for the activity of the executive power, by specialisation and, on Java, by a transfer of responsibility from the Dutch to the Native Civil Service, the Service had been adapted to altered political views and the rapid development of land and people of the Indies.

CHAPTER 15

The Dutch East Indies as Purveyor and Customer on the World Market

The purveying by the Indies of products to the world market does not date from the advent of the Europeans. From the end of the 14th century on trade with Europe had increased considerably, stimulated by the opening of a new trade route that from Malacca, passing by Ceylon, went to Alexandria. Remarkable economic transformations in the Indies were the result: at the coast of Java, in Malacca and Atchin, more or less independent of the feudal Javanese rulers, Islamic coastal states were founded, economically based on trade. In the Moluccas the growing of cloves and nutmeg became the paramount interest; here, as well as in Bantam exporting a considerable quantity of pepper, rice had to be imported.

This capitalistic development was interrupted by the arrival of the Dutch. The sole end of the Company at first was trade; on the Moluccas and on Java it first secured rights of preemption, then gradually complete monopoly. In the Moluccas cloves and nutmeg were raised by Europeans with the aid of Chinese and slaves and sold to the Company at fixed prices. On Java the rulers of the trader-states in the long run became vassals of the Company. From a commercial body this developed more and more into a sovereign power and it procured its products partly by a system of compulsory deliveries and quota imposed on the native princes. This destroyed the independent Javanese trade; the desa had not only to produce for its own needs and for those of the ruler and his vassals but also for the Company. It may therefore be said that the economic system of the Company consisted in a combination of commercial capitalism and feudalism firmly upheld and even strengthened on Java.

The deliveries to the Company were only partly export articles. On Java pepper was the most important of these, then in the 17th century came sugar (on West Java) and in the beginning of the 18th century coffee. The volume was not large; one reads of sugar deliveries of 12.000 piculs in 1653 and coffee deliveries of 21.740 piculs in 1739. The sugar production is curious, because capitalistic elements entered there, the handling of sugar-cane being entrusted to Chinese millers who made use of slaves or even paid labour. On the Moluccas as well as on Java clove- and coffee-bushes were alternately exterminated and planted by compulsion in large numbers. Sugar mills were also alternately restricted and multiplied.

Apart from spice, coffee and sugar the Company traded in tea, timber, forest products, opium, cottons, silk, tin, gold, silver and other articles. By no means all these articles were produced in the Indies: tea was imported from China and sold to Europe, opium came from Bengal and the Near East and was sold to China and India; cottons were bought in India and sold to Europe and the Indies; gold was partly mined in the Indies, partly supplied by China and Japan; silk came from China, Persia and Bengal and was sold to Japan and Europe. The Company therefore was first and foremost a commercial body and was a producer only as an alternative. As for the Moluccan spices, the Company for a long time held a world monopoly.

Towards the end of the Company's rule and especially after its failure this and the industrial development of Europe gave rise to new ideas about the economic policy to be followed in the Indies. It was advocated to replace the monopolistic commercial policy by a system of greater liberty, restriction of feudal privileges, abolition of compulsory deliveries and their conversion into monetary taxes. During the British interregnum these reforms were indeed carried out in part; more especially a landrent was introduced that was to be paid individually in money. It was assumed that this would sti-mulate the population to a free production for the world market, that money economy would penetrate deeper into the desa and that Java would become a greater market for European industrial articles.

These reforms, only very partially effected by Raffles, were advocated in a famous memorandum, dated 1817. Great things were expected from free-dom of production and trade for the population, and the objection that the Javanese was too indolent was eloquently refuted. The alternative policy, viz. to promote production by means of European capital and native wage-labour, was also discussed. It was argued that the European employer will always strive to get the maximum amount of labour for the minimum pay; therefore only uncultivated and uninhabited land that was no one's property should be allotted for that purpose. The system of colonisation, as the allotting of land to European planters was then called, on the other hand found a warm advocate in Commissary-General Du Bus de Gisignies in a report of May 1st 1827. From such a policy only did he expect a rapid expansion of export, and he was convinced that the Javanese, left to himself, would plant rice, not crops for export, and with a free, independent production would fall into the hands of moneylenders. He proposed therefore to allot land to Europeans in the proximity of densely populated regions but without any manorial rights with regard to the residents. Then "the capital, invested in Java's soil by the European planter, would produce other capital that partly would be used for new plantations, but partly would be invested in other industrial enterprises of all kinds".

These two reports, supplementing and correcting each other, foreshadowed the entire colonial policy and economic history of the next hundred years. They were far ahead of their time. The then prevailing economic conditions were not ripe for these modern capitalistic ideas. All applications for allotment of land to private individuals requested at the same time the right to dispose freely of the labour of the natives. This would have meant an allotment of land of the sort as had been practised by the Company, by Daendels and by Raffles, that is to say, a combination of capitalistic and feudal methods. The ideas of Du Bus were not carried out until after 1860; those of Muntinghe, the author of the first-named report, in the 20th century, chiefly in the Outer Islands.

"The period of doubt" as the time between 1795 to 1830 has been characterised, came to an end in 1830 with the introduction of an economic system that was to last for forty years. This was van den Bosch's "culture-system". The primary motive for its introduction was the sore financial plight of the home country, necessitating at short notice an increase in Java's export trade. Van den Bosch was also of the opinion that European planters in the Indies, employing free labourers, would be unable to compete with planters in the West Indies, employing slaves. Thus a system was adopted that greatly resembled that of the Company, with this difference that the State took the place of the Company. The population was to surrender one fifth of its land for the raising of export crops and to be exempted from landrent. The Government was to take over the produce and, if the estimated value should be higher than the landrent, the difference was to be credited to the population. The native was to work under the direction of his own chiefs who were to obtain so-called "cultivation percentages", hereditary office and permission to hold land. The desa and its ablebodied men were regarded as a unit for purposes of the compulsory cultivation. The products were consigned to the Netherlands' Trading Company that obtained a practical monopoly, later officially so recognised, and made Amsterdam once more the emporium for colonial products.

This was a reversal to the combination of feudalism and commercial capitalism of the Company. The power of the native chiefs, with whom the delivery contracts were made, was enhanced. The pressure on the population soon became heavy, partly because, contrary to the original scheme, many other personal services continued to be required. The peasants, in order to reduce the burden of service on public works, which custom confined to land-holders, more and more preferred communal possession of land, which was also encouraged by officials so as to facilitate the allocation of large areas for sugar plantations. This had the tendency to obliterate hereditary social distinctions, and cut at the root of the traditional social order.

The entire system was founded on coercion and primitive methods; it led to waste and uneconomic administration since the compulsory labour was supposed "to cost nothing". Of the various crops that were thus cultivated only sugar and coffee yielded large profits.

It is true that during the "culture-system" Java's export increased rapidly and considerably. While Du Bus de Gisignies had estimated the export-value at no more than 7 million florins annually, in 1835 it amounted to 28, in 1845 to 56, in 1855 to 70 and in 1865 to 89 million florins. In this export coffee and sugar constituted by far the major portion and 80 to 90 % of it went to the Netherlands.

The treasury greatly profited: from 1831 to 1866 672 million and from 1867 to 1877 another 151 million florins were remitted home.

While the "culture-system" was a consequence of the impoverished condition in which the Netherlands found themselves, these large sums flowing into the country, as a result of this system, created the very conditions needed for a more modern economic policy in the Indies. With the strengthening of industrial and commercial capital in Holland after 1850 "free labour" found more and more advocates. From 1860 on the compulsory cultivation was gradually reduced or abolished; the Government no longer supported the sugar industry by advancing moneys; several agricultural banks were established and even the Netherlands' Trading Company assumed the character of an agricultural bank. This development was brought to a head by the Agrarian Law of 1870, laying down the rules subject to which Western planters may acquire rights on the land in the Indies, and by the Sugar Law, regulating the substitution of cultivation by the Government for that by private persons. In 1872 a Tariff Law was passed ending all preferential tariffs in the Indies for the mother country. Since then the Government's policy has aimed at directing private investments, whether Dutch or foreign, to the Indies.

The results of this policy have been remarkable. An almost uninterrupted flow of investments, chiefly Dutch, but also foreign, poured into the Indies between 1870 and 1930. In the course of a few decades large agrarian and mining enterprises were developed, producing and exporting in rapidly growing quantities foodstuffs, raw materials and minerals. The export of the Dutch East Indies rose to 175 million florins in 1880, 257 million in 1900, 2275 million in 1920 and 1443 million in 1929.

At the same time the population continued to grow their traditional foodcrops, being even able to extend this cultivation considerably with the aid of the Government's welfare policy of irrigation works and agricultural advice. By supplying labour and leasing out land they were interested in the Western enterprises and in this way a money economy became more widespread.

The plantations of the Dutch East Indies have as principal crops: sugar, rubber, tea, coffee, cinchona bark, vegetable fibres, tobacco, tapioca and palmoil. They were developed after 1870, but especially from 1900 onward, in certain parts of the Outer Islands such as the east coast of Sumatra. Mining has its principal sites also on the Outer Islands and includes gold, tin and petroleum products, the crude oil being refined in the Indies.

While Du Bus' prophecy, quoted above, has in this way been brilliantly fulfilled, the ideas of Muntinghe have later also been realised.

On Java, but even more on the Outer Islands, especially in the 20th century an important production by the population of crops for export was developed. This includes chiefly tea, tobacco, tapioca, kapok on Java, and rubber, coffee, copra and pepper on the Outer Islands. In 1929 on Java 18 % and on the Outer Islands 59 % of the principal export crops were native-grown.

The mass production of the large-scale agriculture as well as the native-grown crops must be sold almost entirely abroad. For a few articles like sugar and coffee the domestic market is of some, though minor, importance. Being thus dependent on the world market the Indies are very sensitive to price-fluctuations. The small mother country could never guarantee a market for these enormous exports. The economic relationship between the Netherlands and the Indies could therefore not develop as a more or less self-contained unit.

The figures are illuminating. In 1929 the export of the Indies amounted to 1443 million florins, having been octupled since 1875. While in that year 64 % of the total export was shipped to the Netherlands, in 1929 it was only 16 % or 231 million florins. Out of this amount one half was destined for consumption within the country, the rest for re-sale. This limited importance of the home country as customer and the limited possibility of sale in the Indies themselves, rendered the economic position of Western producers insecure. There was no harm in this lack of security as long as the world market was mostly free. In the past it was offset by the strenuous efforts of the Western plantations to reach technical perfection and keep the costprice low, by the fact that their costs partly are on the level of native society and by the endeavours of the Government to keep the costs of production low. Hence at the beginning of this period preferential tariffs were abolished.

It is clear that serious economic difficulties were to be expected, as soon as the free world market, one of the main pillars of the East-Indian economy, should drop out. This is precisely what happened after 1929 and caused an economic landslide that cannot be further discussed within the scope of this chapter. One should however remember that 1929 marks the end of the economic epoch for the Indies that began in 1870.

The Dutch East Indies are to a great extent self-contained as far as the principal foodstuffs are concerned. For Java the import of rice compared to its production of nearly 4 million tons always was small and lately has become quite insignificant; the Outer Islands, especially those regions where there are important Western enterprises, import quantities of rice that, though considerable, are decreasing. Since there are export surplusses of maize and cassave the import of the Dutch East Indies largely consists of more or less factory-made foodstuffs and luxuries and manufactured articles that may be distinguished as articles of consumption and means of production. Among the former textiles take a foremost place; in the last years before 1930 they comprised 25 to 30 % of the total import value and before 1870 this even was as high as 50 %.

As was explained at the outset of this chapter the Company in origin was a commercial body aiming at trade from port to port. Just as tea was shipped from China to the Indies and from there on to Europe, the Company traded in cottons, plain and decorated, chiefly bought in India and sold from there to Europe or the Indies. Systematic efforts to create an export trade from the Netherlands to the Dutch East Indies were never made. In the Indies there existed a hand textile industry; among the quota fixed by the Company cotton yarns are mentioned.

In the beginning of the 19th century in all Western Europe, but principally in England, an important textile industry was developed that sought an outlet on Oriental markets. Raffles' agrarian reforms aimed at promoting this export. British industry being far ahead in technical development, export from the Netherlands had no chance in competing with that from Great Britain. In order to stimulate it a preferential import tariff was fixed after 1816: import from the Netherlands (then including Belgium) was to be free from duty, but a duty of 25 % was to be raised from all countries west of the Cape (which, of course, included Great Britain). In 1824 however a treaty with Great Britain was concluded limiting this preferential position. With the aid of the newly founded Netherlands' Trading Company the Government continued to stimulate the export of textiles to the Indies, and it is certainly owing to its various protectionist measures that the textile industry of Twente developed and the decline of home industry, so rapid in British India, was retarded in the East Indies.

The introduction of the "culture-system" on Java drove the import figures up, though they did not increase as much as the export. Du Bus in his report of 1827 had estimated Java's annual import at 5 to 6 million florins; in 1835 this figure had mounted to 11,4 million and in 1855 to 29 million; the share of the Netherlands rose from from 27 % in 1825 to 50 % in 1855 and 58,5 % in 1870.

The new economic course from 1870 on abandoned preferential tariffs, maintained a low rate of import duties, stimulated the import of consumption articles by extending money economy and caused considerable import of capital-goods by Western companies and the Government. All this resulted in a very considerable increase of import: from 112 million florins in 1875 it mounted to 1088 million in 1929; for both import and expoit the increase after 1900 was much greater than before that date. The share of the Nether lands during this period fell from 47 % in 1875 to 19,6 % in 1929. The absolute value of imports from the Netherlands however was quadrupled between 1875 and 1929, so that from every point of view a favourable solution seemed to have been found.

This phenomenal rise may be further analysed. It was, in the first place, strongly influenced by the import of capital-goods: in 1929 this amounted to more than 300 million florins, that is to say 27 % of the total imports. In the second place a considerable rise in the price level should be taken into account; from 1913 to 1929 the East Indian price level for consumption articles rose as much as 66 % and in the years of and immediately after the first world war this percentage was even higher.

By deducting from the total import of Java during this period that of rice, of capital-goods and the export to the Outer Islands and by fuither reducing the remaining volume to the price level of 1913, one finds that the import of consumption articles per head during this period of unprecedented prosperity scarcely increased. By applying this same calculation to the Outer Islands however one finds an increase of import per capita of as much as 30 %. This demonstrates on the one hand the tension of Javanese economic life and, on the other, the far reaching results of the adoption of large-scale cultivation of export crops.

Under these conditions the Dutch East Indies have become, though not *the* most important, at least one of the most important countries for Dutch export. In 1929 they held the fourth place; 8,66 % of Dutch export was destined for the Dutch East Indies. In looking at this figure one should bear in mind that only a very small fraction of the vast agrarian export of the Netherlands can go to the East Indies. The economic systems of both parts of the Netherlands' empire, in import as well as in export, supplement each other only in part. Nevertheless for certain Dutch industries as textiles and machines the East Indian market is very important.

In the years before 1929 the Netherlands normally were the greatest importers into the Dutch East Indies; Great Britain, Germany, the United States and Japan came next. After 1929 import from Japan rose sharply and that from the Netherlands fell proportionally. Owing to measures of a protective character in the years before 1940 the Netherlands had again attained the first place among the importing countries.

Apart from the factories connected with the great plantations and mining, working for export, the industrial development of the Indies up to about 1930 was comparatively slight. Mention has already been made of a fairly extensive hand-weaving industry; the batik industry was also important. Gradually other industries of a simple kind developed; agricultural industries such as ricehulling factories and oil-mills pressing copra into coco-oil, cigar and cigarette factories, a paper factory using rice straw, plants for machine-repair etc. From 1930 on there was a considerable industrial expansion, more particularly in the manufacture of textiles, for which the yarns were at first imported from Japan and China. Later a cotton-mill was established. In this industrial development one should distinguish between large-scale industrial enterprises using Western capital and Western technique and small-scale Oriental enterprises which, however, are not always in the hands of the population. An important factor in this development was the fact that from 1930 on, for fiscal reasons, import duties were much raised. Thus, since 1830, there was a curious circular economic movement: a century ago high preferential tariffs brought into existence the Dutch textile-export to the Indies; high duties and fixed quota after 1930 again stimulated the East Indian textile industry.

In the sphere of native agrarian production for export a tendency towards industrialisation is also noticeable. There are not only oil-mills, but native-grown rubber that originally was shipped to Singapore as a raw and wet product is now more and more worked in the Indies.

A large part of the import trade is controlled by a small number of powerful concerns with their ramifications all over the Archipelago buying in Europe as well as in America, Australia and Japan. The so-called intermediate trade and a large part of the retail trade is in the hands of Chinese firms, forming an indispendable link between whole-sale trade and consumer. To a limited extent there are also Oriental elements in whole-sale business.

After 1930 there were far-reaching modifications in the economic structure of the Dutch East Indies, strongly influencing both import and export. Within the scope of this chapter they can only be briefly indicated.

From 1929 on prices of Indian export crops fell heavily; in some cases, especially that of sugar, impoitant markets dropped out partly or wholly. Under these circumstances the export values from the Dutch East Indies between 1929 to 1935 decreased by two thirds. The first consequences were that the Western enterprises began to retrench drastically, to lower wages, to send colonists working in the Outer Islands back to Java and to replace human labour by machines. For a number of impoitant export products, such as sugar, rubber, tea, quinine, tobacco and tin restrictions on output were fixed, partly by international agreement. The flow of capital investments that between 1870 to 1930 had poured uninterruptedly into the Indies dried up completely. The import curve was bound to follow that of export; from 1929 to 1935 the value of Indian import decreased by three quarters, though even during the depression the active credit balance remained unimpaired. This was made possible not only by a drop in the volume of imported goods but also by a great drop in the prices of the imported articles, coinciding with a shift in the lands of origin: the Netherlands as first purveyor were replaced by Japan. The land that became available because of the sugar restriction on Java was partly used for the planting of food crops so that Java, during these last years, normally had no longer a rice impoit balance .The Government of the East Indies proceeded to carry out an active welfare policy that included stimulating industrial development. The tariff of import duties, as stated before, contributed to this development and furthermore a system of fixed quotas was introduced which improved the position of the Netherlands as importing country. The tendency towards industrialisation was not only influenced by the desire to make the Indies less sensitive to the fluctuations of the world market, but also by the strong increase in Java's population for which other remedies, like colonisation in the Outer Islands, have also been sought. With regard to the export of native grown crops the Government likewise took an ordering hand by establishing central organisations for export.

As a result of all this the economic structure of the Dutch East Indies was greatly modified during the last ten years. The year 1930 will prove to have been as much a turning-point as were 1830, 1870 and, in a sense, 1900.

CHAPTER 16

The Dutch East Indies in Statistics

THE ECONOMIC STRUCTURE OF THE DUTCH EAST INDIES

Previous chapters described from many angles the development of the Indies since their first contact with the Dutch. This chapter intends to give a picture of the present economic structure of the Dutch East Indies by listing a number of the principal statistics. These figures represent, as it were, a momentary phase in the development; they make us pause on the threshold between past and future.

In describing the economic structure of any country attention should be paid to:

a. factors of production, — labour, soil and capital;

b. the goods produced and

c. the returns resulting for each of the factors of production.

In discussing these three points a distinction should be made between that part of economic activities that is under Western control and the native economy proper. Further the great difference in economic structure, between, on the one hand, Java and Madura, and, on the other, the Outer Territories, necessitates a distinction between these two.

Occupational Analysis of the Dutch East Indies

An answer to the question, who work in the Dutch East Indies, is given by the census held in 1930. The following figures list the total population according to the four principal racial divisions, and the numbers of those engaged in some trade or profession.

For a proper understanding these figures should be further subdivided into classes of trade. To the "production of raw material" are reckoned agriculture (both large-scale and native), mining and oil-exploitation. The

TABLE 1. NUMBER OF INHABITANTS AND NUMBER OF THOSE ENGAGED
IN TRADE OR PROFESSION

Racial Group	Population	Engaged in Trade or Profession
Europeans	240 000	85 000
Chinese	1 233 000	470 000
Other Foreign Asiatics	116 000	36 000
Indonesians.	59 138 000	20 280 000
Total	60 727 000	20 871 000

TABLE 2.   ANALYSIS BY CLASSES OF TRADE

Racial Group	Raw Material Production	Industry	Trade and Commerce	Government Service	Remainder	Total
Europeans . .	18 800	4 676	22 400	20 731	18 714	85 321
Chinese. . . .	144 888	93 988	184 733	3 039	43 287	469 935
Foreign Asiatics	7 000	5 058	20 766	495	2 833	36 152
Natives	14 193 158	2 105 129	1 381 608	491 911	2 107 836	20 279 642
Total.	14 363 846	2 208 851	1 609 507	516 176	2 172 670	20 871 050

TABLE 3.   ANALYSIS BY CLASSES OF TRADE FOR JAVA WITH
MADURA AND THE OUTER TERRITORIES

Branch of Trade	Europeans		Chinese		Foreign Asiatics		Natives	
	Java and Madura	Outer Territories	Java and Madura	Outer Territories	Java and Madura	Outer Territories	Java and Madura	Outer Territories
Raw Material Production . .	11 758	7 042	16 662	128 226	381	6 619	9 428 000	4 765 000
Industry	3 897	779	38 063	55 925	1 473	3 585	1 655 000	450 000
Trade and Commerce . .	18 874	3 526	110 623	74 110	10 555	10 211	1 116 000	265 000
Government Service. . . .	16 584	4 147	1 004	2 035	124	371	377 000	115 000
Remainder . . .	15 630	3 084	16 532	26 755	1 313	1 520	1 862 000	246 000
Total	66 743	18 578	182 884	287 051	13 846	22 306	14 438 000	5 841 000

agrarian character of Indian economy is clearly shown by the figures: nearly
70 % of the native population are engaged in agriculture. Europeans are
naturally very numerous in Government service, in trade and commerce
(including Post, Telegraph and Telephone Service and Railways) and in
the large-scale agriculture.

This is made clearer by a further distinction between Java and the Outer Territories, showing some interesting differences. Chinese on Java for example are most numerous in trade, those on the Outer Islands as coolies in mining or on plantations.

The figures of the census are unfortunately somewhat out of date. An important structural shift since 1930 consists in the strong expansion of native industry on Java, by which the number of native hands employed in industry increased by some hundreds of thousands. Among the European population there were considerable fluctuations. The economic depression made it necessary to economise as much as possible on expensive European personnel both in private and public service. In lower positions Europeans were replaced gradually by cheaper native personnel.

Foreign Investments in the Dutch East Indies

It is characteristic of a colonial country like the Dutch East Indies to be

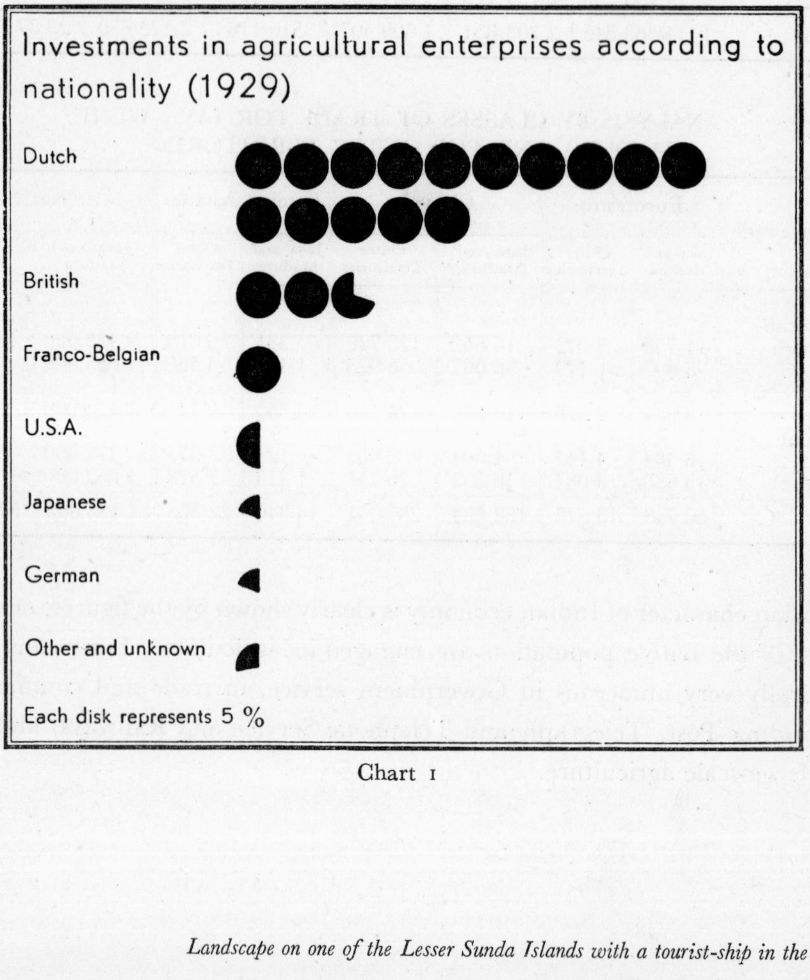

Investments in agricultural enterprises according to nationality (1929)

Dutch
British
Franco-Belgian
U.S.A.
Japanese
German
Other and unknown

Each disk represents 5 %

Chart I

Landscape on one of the Lesser Sunda Islands with a tourist-ship in the background

TABLE 4.   AREA OF ARABLE LAND OF THE POPULATION ON JAVA AND
           MADURA (in thousands of hectares)

Year	Sawahs	Dry fields and homestead lots	Total
1921	3136	3793	6929
1925	3200	3955	7155
1929	3268	4335	7602
1930	3274	4372	7646
1931	3288	4370	7658
1932	3291	4394	7685
1933	3299	4404	7703
1934	3301	4425	7726
1935	3311	4441	7752
1936	3334	4463	7797
1937	3362	4486	7848
1938	3372	4501	7873

poor in capital. All the capital needed for its economic development has to
be found abroad. The Open Door Policy offered equal opportunity to all.
Consequently, along with Dutch capital, a great deal of foreign capital has
been invested in the Dutch East Indies. The total amount is not precisely
known.

It is estimated that the Dutch investments in the Indies amount to 4 billion florins, the total national wealth of the Netherlands being computed

TABLE 5.   FIELDS LEASED TO OR AVAILABLE FOR LARGE-SCALE
           AGRICULTURAL PLANTATIONS (in thousands of hectares)

	Year	Longlease	Agricultural Concession	Private Lands	Free lease from the Population	Leaselands (Principalities)	Government Plantations	Total[1])
Dutch East Indies	1925	1525	1231	609	196,4	85,2	x	3647
,, ,, ,,	1930	1758	1251	505	204,9	70,1	x	3789
,, ,, ,,	1931	1661	1246	492	201,5	69,8	x	3671
,, ,, ,,	1932	1562	1196	492	167,9	69,2	40,2	3527
,, ,, ,,	1933	1492	1146	491	98,1	66,7	40,7	3336
,, ,, ,,	1934	1385	1125	491	57,9	56,7	34,2	3150
,, ,, ,,	1935	1355	1125	492	52,4	51,5	31,6	3108
,, ,, ,,	1936	1285	1099	492	58,5	56,9	30,9	3022
,, ,, ,,	1937	1215	1064	492	94,3	60,4	31,2	2956
,, ,, ,,	1938	1193	1059	492	101,8	61,3	31,2	2938
Java and Madura.	1938	611	—	489	101,4	61,3	20,5	1284
Outer Territories .	1938	582	1059	3	0,4	—	10,7	1654

× = Unknown
[1]) For 1925, 1930, 1931 exlusive of Government Plantations.

Mission 16

at 20—25 billions. This figure includes all investments, also those in Netherlands Indian Government bonds.

The distribution of foreign investments over the different agricultural enterprises is very uneven. In the sugar industry nearly 100 % of the investments are Dutch, but in rubber not more than about half.

Some Data About the Use of the Soil

Here follow some of the most important data about the area of arable land on Java and Madura. As a result of the increase in population this area is steadily enlarged.

The area of the fields leased to or available for the large-scale agricultural plantations naturally follows the fluctuations of the world market. Table 5 gives some important figures.

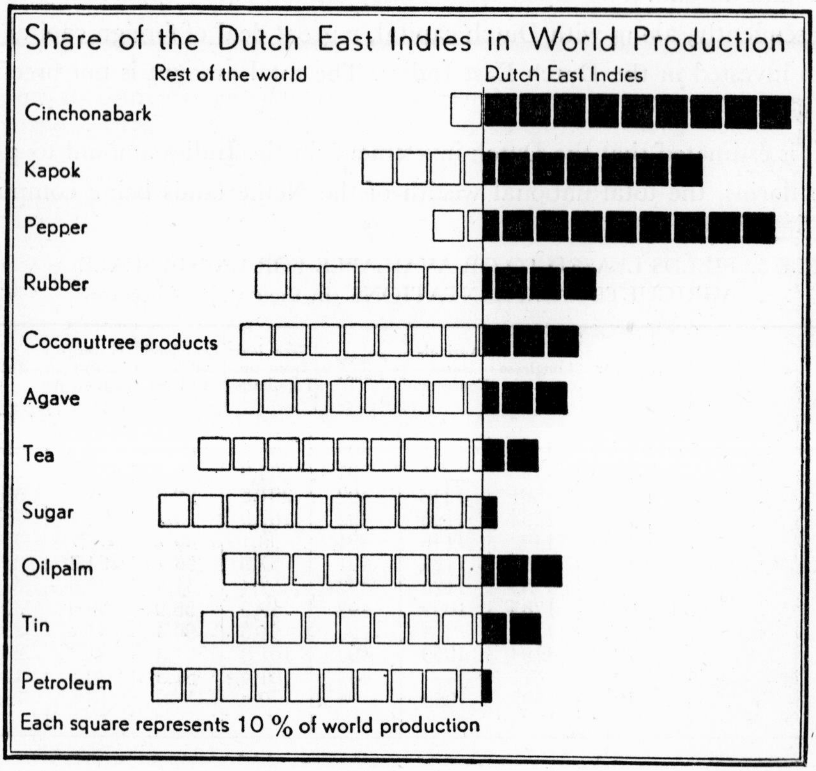

Chart 2

The Products of the Dutch East Indies

The Dutch East Indies are one of the most important areas of the world for the production of raw material. Chart 2 shows their share in the world production of some of the principal raw materials. In studying these data one should bear in mind that there are cases, like that of sugar, where the share in world production is comparatively small, but the importance for East Indian economy is nevertheless considerable. On the other hand for some products the share of the Indies in world export is large, while the product is only of secondary importance.

A distinction should further be made between large-scale agriculture and native grown products. Chart 3 illustrates the relative importance of these two groups.

The great difference in economic structure between Java and the Outer Islands is again demonstrated. While on Java the population chiefly practises agriculture for the supply of its own needs, the production for the world market is preponderant in the thinly populated Outer Territories.

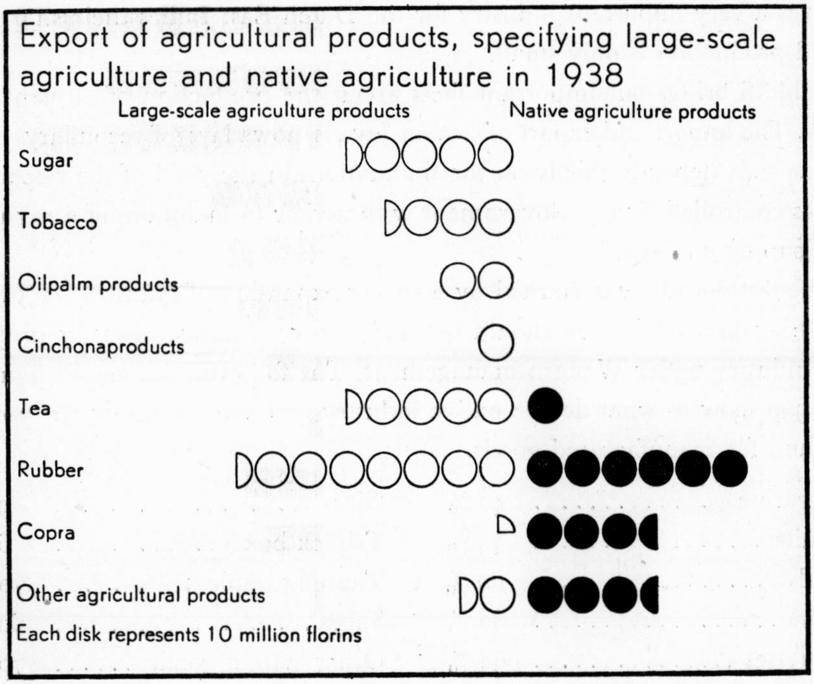

Export of agricultural products, specifying large-scale agriculture and native agriculture in 1938

Each disk represents 10 million florins

Chart 3

TABLE 6. ESTIMATED VALUE OF THE PRINCIPAL NATIVE ALIMENTARY
CROPS ON JAVA AND MADURA (in millions of florins)

Products	1928	1930	1932	1934	1936	1938
Sawahpadi	434	431	189	156	171	247
Padigogo	34	35	16	10	12	15
Maize.	121	120	52	47	57	67
Cassave	97	110	34	46	65	79
Sweet Potatoes	18	23	7	9	12	12
Potatoes.	10	7	6	3	2	3
Peanuts	28	27	14	10	11	17
Kedelee.	17	16	10	10	13	19
Total Value	759	769	328	291	343	459

There are also marked differences in large-scale agriculture. The sugar
industry requiring many hands is found exclusively on Java with its dense
population. Thinly populated areas on the Outer Islands are, on the contrary, well suited for several other agricultural enterprises. The necessary
labour has then to be imported from Java or elsewhere.

Apart from agricultural products the Dutch East Indies also supply important minerals, chiefly tin and petroleum. Though the pumping of petroleum is a very important industry for the Dutch East Indies their share in
world production is only small.

Table 6 brings out important facts about the production of alimentary
crops. The import and export of rice on Java is nowadays of secondary importance. It depends chiefly on the fluctuations in the yield of the ricecrop
and is controlled by the Government with a view to maintaining a regular
food supply on Java.

The last decade was marked by a strong expansion of industry on Java,
where again a distinction should be made between native industry proper
and industry under Western management. The following estimated figures
for 1939 show to what degree native industry was able to supply the home
demand for manufactured goods.

Margarine	40 %	Glass	9 %
Biscuits	45 %	Triplex boxes	6 %
Candy	60 %	Tanning implements	70 %
Cigars	80 %	Shoes	60 %
Cigarettes	92 %	Other leather goods	70 %
Sterilised cottonwool	30 %	Pajongs . (native umbrellas)	38 %

Refined sulphur	20 %	Processed paper	27 %
Copperas	80 %	Castiron pans	90 %
Paint	75 %	Bicyles	35 %
Soap	72 %	Flashlights	40 %
Asbestos-cement sheets	16 %	Cigar-lighters	80 %
		Textiles	6 %

The National Revenue of the Dutch East Indies

A large part of the national income of the Dutch East Indies benefits the native population. This is true first of all for that part of native agriculture that serves their own alimentary needs. For a not inconsiderable part this is an economy in kind in which money plays no part. In so far as the population is engaged in the cultivation of crops for export, a very considerable part of the export returns is put to their credit. The returns of special export duties are generally set aside by the Government for the benefit of the region concerned, as for building roads, schools etc. Moreover the native population receives important revenues in the form of wages and other payments from the western plantations. Though available data are incomplete, in Table 7 are listed the wages paid by the sugar industry.

Furthermore the wages earned in Government service, trade and commerce form an important source of the national income, to which in the last few years industry is rapidly adding.

A very considerable portion of the returns of the export products of the large plantations is paid and spent in the Dutch East Indies. This is not only

TABLE 7. REVENUES OF THE NATIVE POPULATION FROM THE SUGAR INDUSTRY (1929—1938) (in millions of florins)

Year	Wages	Landlease	Compensations Deliveries etc.
1929	101,8	23,9	3,9
1930	97,9	25,0	2,9
1931	84,0	25,0	2,1
1932	53,1	21,7	0,8
1933	21,9	11,9	0,3
1934	9,7	6,5	0,2
1935	7,3	4,0	0,2
1936	7,5	3,2	0,2
1937	15,3	5,5	0,5
1938	16,5	5,6	0,4

TABLE 8. SOME ITEMS FROM THE BALANCE SHEET OF THE DUTCH EAST
INDIES (in millions of florins)

	Payments abroad		Of which to the Netherlands	
	1937	1938	1937	1938
Interests	68	53	52	39
Dividends and profits	89	167	62	117
Remittances to relatives etc.	19	19	6	5
Costs of management, incl. bonuses	20	27	14	19
Pensions, leave-salaries, life insurance. . . .	53	54	45	48
Total	249	320	179	228

true of the wages paid to native labour, but also of the salaries of European
employees, taxes paid in the Indies etc.

Table 8 shows a list of the amounts that go out of the country in the form
of interest, dividends and other payments, together with the estimated part
of it that goes to the credit of the Netherlands.

This shows that in the last years before the war the Netherlands annually
received about 200 million florins from the Indies. Apart from this there
are the profits from shipping to and from the Indies, (about 70 million
florins gross), the export of manufactured goods (about 100 million florins)
and several other profits, for example from the international trade in colonial products at Amsterdam.

A further view of the national income is obtained by studying the statistics for the income-tax. Table 9 shows some figures for the number of assessed
taxpayers and the amounts of their income for 1936.

In these figures only annual incomes of more than 900 florins are listed.
The Table clearly shows how small a section of all those engaged in trade
or a profession has a higher income. Consequently the "income-pyramid"
has a very curious shape: a very broad base, chiefly formed by the millions

TABLE 9

	Number of Assessed	Total Income
Europeans	65 000	266 mill. fl.
Indonesians	27 000	50 ,, ,,
Chinese.	37 000	82 ,, ,,
Other Foreign Asiatics	3 000	9 ,, ,,
Total.	132 000	407 mill. fl.

of the native population, on which a narrow and tall steeple, representing chiefly the European population.

Economic Fluctuations in the Dutch East Indies.

The development of the economic structure described in these paragraphs was not an even one. As in all other countries there is a fluctuating curve showing a rise and decline in prosperity. In Tables 10—12 a number of facts have been collected for the period 1920—1938 that give a rough picture of this development in the Indies. As every country that produces raw material the Indies are keenly sensitive to this kind of fluctuation, since the prices of raw material are the most affected. Especially the great crisis of 1929 and after had severe repercussions and caused a grave shrinkage of economic life. The country has far smaller reserves than the Netherlands and therefore had to adapt itself much more to the conditions of a diminished world market. In principle the difficulty was the same here as elsewhere: first the prices of export products fell; the prices of import products and those of the domestic market could not keep pace with this rapid fall and economic life was caught between these pincers. The difficulties were aggravated by the devaluation of the pound, the dollar and other monetary units, which seriously impaired the competetive power both of the Netherlands and Netherlands India. Only when in 1936 the florin was devaluated economic life in the florin countries got a new start.

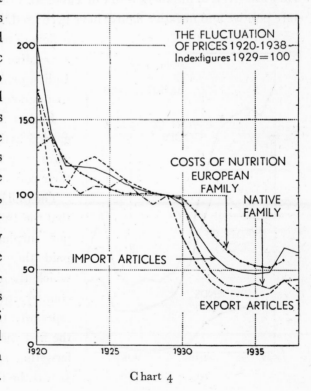

Chart 4

The first crisis in this period, from 1921 to 1922, was also very grave as far as the fall of prices is concerned, but it was not prolonged by these monetary complications. Recovery was rather rapid partly owing to increasing American demand in 1922. The loss of markets was, in general, not so great either as in the years after 1930, when the protection of national markets became a general policy for combatting the depression.

After the devaluation of 1936 the Indies only shared for a brief period in the revival of the world market: as early as 1937 the turning point on the markets of raw material was reached. The depression that followed was however short-lived; partly as a result of increasing war preparation increased demand soon set in.

The Balance Sheet of Payments

An excellent insight into these price fluctuation problems in the Dutch East Indies is gained by a mere glance at the figures of the Balance Sheet. They are given in numbers 1—11 of Table 10. Contrary to the usual procedure positive and negative figures have been used. A positive figure indicates a flow of money towards the Indies; a negative figure a payment by the Indies, or, in other words, a flow of money directed away from the Indies.

Import and export are to be regarded as the principal item. Chart 5 gives a graphic representation of their course.

The well known fact is here reflected that the Indies always have an export surplus. From this surplus are paid the dividends and interests which the country, being a debtor country, owes to other countries, especially the Netherlands. In 1925, the first year to which the graph refers, that surplus was considerable. It was the time of high rubber prices.

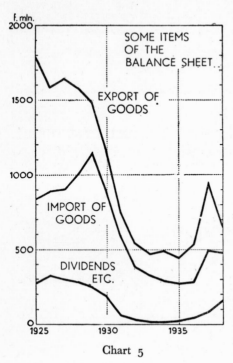

Chart 5

Between 1925 and 1929 there was some decline in the value of export, partly because rubber piices fell steeply after the boom of 1925—1926; nevertheless the export value was maintained at a high level. The value of import still went on rising considerably; the import of means of production increased, on account of the more favourable world conjuncture, stimulating confidence and investments. In 1929 the depression set in; then the downward curve both of export and import began, that of export however falling first and more steeply, so that the export balance shrank. Consequently payments of dividends fell to one tenth of what they had been. A noticeable recovery only began in 1937 reaching a peak at once; in 1938 there was again a considerable decline in export. An important figure is also that about shoit term loans, showing that in the very good year 1925 a considerably amount greater was refunded than was borrowed, while on the contrary in 1929 a great deal more was borrowed. Especially in 1937 a large amount was again refunded.

Export Figures

The export figures of a number of the chief products are mentioned under numbers 14—25 of Table 10. The fluctuations of these figures are irregular, because the vicissitudes of the different markets were varied and highly dramatic. Here follow some general explanatory remarks.

For petroleum products it is striking that the general rising tendency was so strong that only during one year, that of 1930—1931, the volume fell. The prices however strongly felt the effect of the depression so that only after 1937 the value showed an appreciable increase.

Even stronger was the rising tendency for palmoil, the exported volume of which did not fall at all and in 1938 was four or five times that of 1930. During the depression years however the prices were badly mauled.

Sugar, rubber, tin and tea were subject to the international restriction of output in order to bolster up prices. (Compare Table 11). This restriction was the most radical for sugar, previously the most important product. The Indies, more especially Java, became the victim of the closing of important markets for this good and cheap product. The Table shows that the volume was reduced to about half of what it had been, while moreover rigorous price concessions had to be made. The exported volume for the depression years is of course inclusive of sold stocks. The actual restriction of output therefore was considerably greater. The allotment of output to the different factories was one of the most difficult problems of organisation to be solved.

TABLE 10.   BALANCE SHEET, IMPORT AND EXPORT

No.	Designation	Unit	1925	'26	'29	'30	'33	'34	'35	'36	'37	'38
	Principal Items Balance Sheet (Credit+)											
1	Export of goods	mill. fl.	1805	1590	1483	1162	471	490	449	540	953	660
2	Export duty	„ „	13	15	13	9	2	15	26	57	38	29
3	Receipts of the Netherl. Gov. in div., interest etc.	„ „	12	11	13	11	6	7	6	9	11	19
4	New capital investments	„ „	82	48	59	180	117	151	8	12	25	12
5	Increase floating debt of the Gov. in the Netherl.	„ „	—	—	—	—	12	−115	8	−52	−44	17
6	Short term loans	„ „	−451	−55	227	60	−9	−50	−19	−47	−164	122
7	Debt amortization	„ „	−42	−40	−55	−43	−58	−45	−33	−34	−26	−39
8	Div. large-scale plantation Companies	„ „	−279	−329	−250	−189	−21	−20	−28	−49	−89	−167
9	Interest	„ „	−92	−90	−79	−81	−89	−90	−80	−76	−68	−53
10	Import of goods	„ „	−841	−895	−1152	−890	−330	−291	−277	−287	−499	−486
11	Total		0	0	0	0	0	0	0	0	0	0
	Quantitative indices											
12	Import	1913=100	101	116	156	132	85	79	79	79	108	108
13	Export	„	181	171	177	197	168	184	165	192	262	225
	Export separate products											
14	Petroleum Products	mill. kg.			3831	4197	4400	4912	5139	5355	5972	6067
	„ „	„ fl.				184	104	99	86	97	165	162
15	Hevea rubber	„ kg.				279	340	385	287	315	439	303
	„ „ (from 1934 export duty inclusive)	„ fl.				171	37	101	94	141	321	156
16	Tea	„ kg.			72,5	72,0	71,9	64,2	65,6	69,6	66,7	71,9
	„ „	„ fl.				69,5	26,4	44,9	36,7	42,9	49,1	56,2
17	Factory sugar	„ kg.				2222	1152	1089	1029	880	1129	1071
	„ „	„ fl.				244	61	45	35	34	50	44
18	Leaf tobacco	„ kg.				77,7	48,7	43,7	48,7	47,8	47,8	48,0
	„ „	„ fl.				57,8	31,8	36,6	29,1	37,6	40,8	38,5
19	Copra	„ kg.			457	376	488	417	485	508	498	556
	„ „	„ fl.				73,8	38,5	16,9	26,0	41,5	62,6	38,3
20	Tin and tin ore	„ kg.				41,9	17,0	23,5	28,0	39,5	50,9	26,5
	„ „ „ „	„ fl.				57,9	22,5	32,9	36,1	46,1	84,1	33,5
21	Palmoil	„ kg.				48	116	121	143	172	197	221
	„ „	„ fl.				13,6	10,7	8,7	13,6	21,4	26,1	16,5
22	Hulled coffee	„ kg.			82	61	71	82	82	95	99	69
	„ „	„ fl.				35,3	25,6	22,5	18,6	15,8	26,0	13,7
23	Hard ropefibre	„ kg.				65,7	94,9	69,7	92,3	76,6	85,2	88,4
	„ „	„ fl.				22,9	8,6	5,8	7,3	8,9	14,9	9,1
24	Tapioca products	„ kg.				130	172	145	157	285	417	247
	„ „	„ fl.				13,8	8,6	7,1	6,9	11,7	18,0	9,0
25	Pepper	„ kg.				32,4	44,0	48,2	58,5	78,1	31,0	54,5
	„ „	„ fl.				39,9	13,3	15,3	11,7	10,7	7,0	8,5
26	Native-grown rubber in % of total rubber export	%			41	37	40	48	50	48	48	48

In a sense it was convenient that the production of sugar is confined to Western factories. For the restriction of rubber production a difficulty of an entirely different kind was encountered: about half of it was produced in native gardens existing in great numbers and up to that time free from all supervision. In order to make an immediate restriction possible as a temporary measure an export duty on rubber was introduced. The revenue of this duty was used as much as possible for local purposes of public utility. By means of this temporary measure the output of native rubber was kept

TABLE 11.   MOVEMENT OF PRICES

No.	Designation	1920	'25	'29	'33	'34	'35	'36	'37	'38
	Indexfigures 1913 = 100									
	Wholesale Prices:									
31	Imp. art., Textiles	348	208	172	77	77	74	76	97	94
32	,, ,, Foodstuffs	300	161	149	85	77	77	81	92	91
33	,, ,, Metals	303	160	142	66	64	61	67	130	115
34	,, ,, Chemicals and paints	270	150	143	69	61	58	58	80	76
35	Total import art.	303	172	151	78	74	72	74	98	94
36	,, export art.	214	146	123	43	42	41	43	54	44
37	,, import and export art. .	279	166	145	71	67	65	67	89	83
	Retail trade prices:									
38	Art. of consumption: Native .	250	169	162	93	85	83	79	84	87
39	,, ,, ,, Foreign.	237	152	145	105	95	91	90	95	97
40	,, ,, ,, Food . .	249	159	151	94	85	81	78	84	
41	,, ,, ,, Total. .	244	160	153	99	90	87	84	90	92
	Foodcost:									
42	Native population (12 art.) .	270	165	157	62	61	64	60	68	69
43	European family (24 art.) . .	219	172	166	105	93	88	87	94	
	Indices on basis 1929 = 100:									
35'	Import articles.	201	114	100	52	49	48	49	65	62
36'	Export articles	174	119	100	35	34	33	35	44	36
	Foodcost:									
42'	Native population	172	105	100	40	39	41	38	43	44
43'	European family	132	104	100	63	56	53	52	57	
	Separate prices									
51	Rubber	1,05	1,74	0,54	0,11	0,20	0,19	0,27	0,37	0,27
52	Sugar at Surabaya exclusive excise.	76,18	18,62	13,66	4,88	3,67	3,88	4,04	5,99	5,84
53	Tea	0,415	0,785	0,57	0,26	0,335	0,26	0,315	0,435	0,395
54	Tin.	303,22	303,88	243,40	157,76	164,98	154,96	150,55	207,56	162,06
	Wages in cents/day									
	Average day wages: Factory coolies sugar industry.									
61	Java: Men	—	46	47	31	27	25	23	24	25
62	Women	—	36	38	25	22	21	21	21	
	Income workmen plantations									
63	Sumatra's East coast: Men. .	54	52	58,50	48	48	49,13	49,89	51,56	
64	Women	42	42	44,50	32	30	29,65	28,57	28,98	

under control. This was no easy matter and the restriction was only satisfactory when, beginning in 1937, individual restriction on the basis of a complete registration of all gardens could be introduced. From the moment the international restriction convention was concluded prices picked up considerably so that the restriction unquestionably attained its end of bolstering up the market. The Table also shows that the share in export of native grown rubber after 1934 was fixed at a level previously not attained.

The restrictions placed on the production of tea and tin also had a salutary effect. In general restriction schemes were most successful for products produced in a relatively small number of countries. For tin the exported volume could already be increased in 1934 and in the good year 1937 very considerable quantities were exported. For tea the volume was not so variable, but a comparison of the years 1930, 1933 and 1938 with almost equal volumes shows how badly prices in 1933 had fallen and how in 1938 they had recovered.

Import

As a result of the strong decrease of export value the level of prosperity of the population sank rapidly. Consequently there was a marked decline in the demand for imported goods. At the same time Japan strove to raise her export in view of her need of foreign exchange. Partly because of the depreciation of the yen, Japanese prices were much lower than those of countries that supply the Indies with industrial products, among which, for textiles especially, were the Netherlands and Great Britain. The Government found itself in a quandary: it was in the interest of the native population that cheap Japanese products should remain available, while the interest of the Dutch textile industry lay in a restriction of Japanese competition. The interests of trade and the newly developed industry also demanded restriction of import. The solution was sought in subjecting part of the import to the so-called country of origin quota-system and another part to the so-called free quota-system. With the country of origin quota-system rise of prices is to be expected; with the free quota-system the choice of the country of origin is free so that the cheapest goods offered can be imported. The latter was applied to the cheapest qualities of textiles in which groups of the population with the lowest incomes are interested; the former was applied to products of better quality.

The import of means of production fell automatically as is the case in every depression.

In spite of the heavy fall of import the export surplus decreased very considerably and dividends practically ceased.

Incomes

As stated before, incomes, closely connected with export, showed a catastrophic decline. This is shown by the totals of the taxation statistics as well as by the figures for the separate occupations. Between 1930 and 1934 the total taxable income fell from 1,9 billion to 1,0 billion florins. The sugar industry, of great importance for native incomes both on account of the landrent paid to landowners and on account of the wages paid, showed a very dark picture. The difficulties were the more grave, because the native population needs to have part of their income in money for buying indispensable articles not manufactured by themselves, and for paying taxes. Partly as a result of the successful restriction schemes, but for the greater part as a result of the devaluation of the florin and the revival of the world market in which the Indies then could take part, there was a marked improvement in 1937, continuing, with a brief interruption in 1938, till the outbreak of war.

Financial Data

The data of the Java Bank listed in Table 12 reflect again the economic conjuncture. In the years of very high prices about 1920 and 1925 the circulation of banknotes and the stock of precious metal are both very large; in the depression period after 1929 the process of deflation was so violent that both, like the current-account balances, decreased considerably. After 1936 there was a change.

The national finances were strongly affected by the economic ups and downs. In the depression years, 1920, 1921 and 1929—1935, there were considerable deficits; especially in the years of the rubberboom 1924—1926 there was a credit balance. A comparison of the figures of the top years shows that expenditure generally presents a declining curve (1920: 1060; 1929: 905; 1938: 682 million florins), largely due to the falling price-level, for, as everywhere else, Government activities had multiplied. This is also illustrated by the figures of the total Government debt showing a rising curve. In the depression years the increase is particularly strong, and, though in and after the good years debts are paid off at a considerable rate, this is not sufficient to prevent the general rising tendency.

TABLE 12.   FINANCIAL DATA
                                   (in millions of florins)

No.	Designation	1920	'21	'26	'29	'33	'34	'35	'37	'37	'38
	Java Bank										
71	Banknotes in circulation on March 31st	321	329	336	311	217	199	180	162	197	195
72	Current account balances.		159	52	53	33	29	33	25	31	79
73	Stock of precious metal (gold and silver) on March 31st	189	237	242	186	159	145	145	106	105	136
	National finances										
	Entire service:										
74	Expenditure	1060	1056	751	905	554	509	480	508	567	682
75	Receipts	756	792	808	849	461	455	467	537	572	579
76	Balance (credit = +)	-304	-264	+57	-56	-93	-54	-13	+29	+5	-104
77	Regular service:										
	Balance (credit = +)	-166	-75	+100	+8	-122	-84	-33	-16	+27	-29
78	Extraordinary service:										
	Balance (credit = +)	-138	-189	-43	-64	+28	+30	+20	+45	-22	-75
79	Floating debt	473	592	3	43	261	139	132	84	34	70
80	Permanent debt	412	530	1082	984	1261	1369	1364	1343	1324	1288
81	Total debt	885	1121	1085	1027	1522	1509	1496	1427	1358	1358